Llewellyn's

SUN SIGN
BOOK

Forecasts by
Terry Lamb

Book Editing and Design: K. M. Brielmaier
Cover Design: Kevin R. Brown

Copyright 2004
Llewellyn Publications
A Division of Llewellyn Worldwide, Ltd.
P.O. Box 64383 Dept. 0-7387-0137-8 St. Paul, MN 55164-0383

2004

	JANUARY								FEBRUARY								MARCH								APRIL				
S	M	T	W	T	F	S		S	M	T	W	T	F	S		S	M	T	W	T	F	S		S	M	T	W	T	F	S

JANUARY	FEBRUARY	MARCH	APRIL
S M T W T F S	S M T W T F S	S M T W T F S	S M T W T F S
. . . . 1 2 3	1 2 3 4 5 6 7	. 1 2 3 4 5 6	. . . . 1 2 3
4 5 6 7 8 9 10	8 9 10 11 12 13 14	7 8 9 10 11 12 13	4 5 6 7 8 9 10
11 12 13 14 15 16 17	15 16 17 18 19 20 21	14 15 16 17 18 19 20	11 12 13 14 15 16 17
18 19 20 21 22 23 24	22 23 24 25 26 27 28	21 22 23 24 25 26 27	18 19 20 21 22 23 24
25 26 27 28 29 30 31	29	28 29 30 31	25 26 27 28 29 30

MAY	JUNE	JULY	AUGUST
S M T W T F S	S M T W T F S	S M T W T F S	S M T W T F S
. 1	. 1 2 3 4 5	. . . . 1 2 3	1 2 3 4 5 6 7
2 3 4 5 6 7 8	6 7 8 9 10 11 12	4 5 6 7 8 9 10	8 9 10 11 12 13 14
9 10 11 12 13 14 15	13 14 15 16 17 18 19	11 12 13 14 15 16 17	15 16 17 18 19 20 21
16 17 18 19 20 21 22	20 21 22 23 24 25 26	18 19 20 21 22 23 24	22 23 24 25 26 27 28
23 24 25 26 27 28 29	27 28 29 30	25 26 27 28 29 30 31	29 30 31
30 31			

SEPTEMBER	OCTOBER	NOVEMBER	DECEMBER
S M T W T F S	S M T W T F S	S M T W T F S	S M T W T F S
. . . 1 2 3 4	. . . . . 1 2	. 1 2 3 4 5 6	. . . 1 2 3 4
5 6 7 8 9 10 11	3 4 5 6 7 8 9	7 8 9 10 11 12 13	5 6 7 8 9 10 11
12 13 14 15 16 17 18	10 11 12 13 14 15 16	14 15 16 17 18 19 20	12 13 14 15 16 17 18
19 20 21 22 23 24 25	17 18 19 20 21 22 23	21 22 23 24 25 26 27	19 20 21 22 23 24 25
26 27 28 29 30	24 25 26 27 28 29 30	28 29 30	26 27 28 29 30 31
	31		

2005

JANUARY	FEBRUARY	MARCH	APRIL
S M T W T F S	S M T W T F S	S M T W T F S	S M T W T F S
. 1	. . 1 2 3 4 5	. . 1 2 3 4 5	. . . . . 1 2
2 3 4 5 6 7 8	6 7 8 9 10 11 12	6 7 8 9 10 11 12	3 4 5 6 7 8 9
9 10 11 12 13 14 15	13 14 15 16 17 18 19	13 14 15 16 17 18 19	10 11 12 13 14 15 16
16 17 18 19 20 21 22	20 21 22 23 24 25 26	20 21 22 23 24 25 26	17 18 19 20 21 22 23
23 24 25 26 27 28 29	27 28	27 28 29 30 31	24 25 26 27 28 29 30
30 31			

MAY	JUNE	JULY	AUGUST
S M T W T F S	S M T W T F S	S M T W T F S	S M T W T F S
1 2 3 4 5 6 7	. . . 1 2 3 4	. . . . . 1 2	1 2 3 4 5 6
8 9 10 11 12 13 14	5 6 7 8 9 10 11	3 4 5 6 7 8 9	7 8 9 10 11 12 13
15 16 17 18 19 20 21	12 13 14 15 16 17 18	10 11 12 13 14 15 16	14 15 16 17 18 19 20
22 23 24 25 26 27 28	19 20 21 22 23 24 25	17 18 19 20 21 22 23	21 22 23 24 25 26 27
29 30 31	26 27 28 29 30	24 25 26 27 28 29 30	28 29 30 31
		31	

SEPTEMBER	OCTOBER	NOVEMBER	DECEMBER
S M T W T F S	S M T W T F S	S M T W T F S	S M T W T F S
. . . . 1 2 3	 1	. . 1 2 3 4 5	. . . . 1 2 3
4 5 6 7 8 9 10	2 3 4 5 6 7 8	6 7 8 9 10 11 12	4 5 6 7 8 9 10
11 12 13 14 15 16 17	9 10 11 12 13 14 15	13 14 15 16 17 18 19	11 12 13 14 15 16 17
18 19 20 21 22 23 24	16 17 18 19 20 21 22	20 21 22 23 24 25 26	18 19 20 21 22 23 24
25 26 27 28 29 30	23 24 25 26 27 28 29	27 28 29 30	25 26 27 28 29 30 31
	30 31		

2006

JANUARY	FEBRUARY	MARCH	APRIL
S M T W T F S	S M T W T F S	S M T W T F S	S M T W T F S
1 2 3 4 5 6 7	. . . 1 2 3 4	. . . 1 2 3 4	 1
8 9 10 11 12 13 14	5 6 7 8 9 10 11	5 6 7 8 9 10 11	2 3 4 5 6 7 8
15 16 17 18 19 20 21	12 13 14 15 16 17 18	12 13 14 15 16 17 18	9 10 11 12 13 14 15
22 23 24 25 26 27 28	19 20 21 22 23 24 25	19 20 21 22 23 24 25	16 17 18 19 20 21 22
29 30 31	26 27 28	26 27 28 29 30 31	23 24 25 26 27 28 29
			30

MAY	JUNE	JULY	AUGUST
S M T W T F S	S M T W T F S	S M T W T F S	S M T W T F S
. 1 2 3 4 5 6	. . . . 1 2 3	 1	. . 1 2 3 4 5
7 8 9 10 11 12 13	4 5 6 7 8 9 10	2 3 4 5 6 7 8	6 7 8 9 10 11 12
14 15 16 17 18 19 20	11 12 13 14 15 16 17	9 10 11 12 13 14 15	13 14 15 16 17 18 19
21 22 23 24 25 26 27	18 19 20 21 22 23 24	16 17 18 19 20 21 22	20 21 22 23 24 25 26
28 29 30 31	25 26 27 28 29 30	23 24 25 26 27 28 29	27 28 29 30 31
		30 31	

SEPTEMBER	OCTOBER	NOVEMBER	DECEMBER
S M T W T F S	S M T W T F S	S M T W T F S	S M T W T F S
. . . . . 1 2	1 2 3 4 5 6 7	. . . 1 2 3 4	. . . . . 1 2
3 4 5 6 7 8 9	8 9 10 11 12 13 14	5 6 7 8 9 10 11	3 4 5 6 7 8 9
10 11 12 13 14 15 16	15 16 17 18 19 20 21	12 13 14 15 16 17 18	10 11 12 13 14 15 16
17 18 19 20 21 22 23	22 23 24 25 26 27 28	19 20 21 22 23 24 25	17 18 19 20 21 22 23
24 25 26 27 28 29 30	29 30 31	26 27 28 29 30	24 25 26 27 28 29 30
			31

Table of Contents

Meet Terry Lamb 5

New Concepts for Signs of the Zodiac 6

Understanding the Basics of Astrology..............................8

Signs of the Zodiac..9

The Planets 10

Using this Book 11

2005 at a Glance 12

Ascendant Table 14

Astrological Glossary...16

Meanings of the Planets...22

2005 Sun Sign Forecasts

Aries 28

Taurus..51

Gemini...74

Cancer 97

Leo 120

Virgo...143

Libra 166

Scorpio 189

Sagittarius 212

Capricorn 235

Aquarius 258

Pisces..281

2005 Sun Sign Articles

Around the Chart: Your Personal Sun
  by Sasha Fenton 306

Breaking It Down: Sun Sign Decans
  by Stephanie Clement 314

Sun Sign Finance
  by Bruce Scofield 326

Handling Those Difficult Signs
  by Nina Lee Braden 338

Romancing the Signs
  by Rowena Wall 347

Feng Shui Astrology
  by Alice DeVille 355

Grassroots and Groundswells: World Predictions for 2005
  by Leeda Alleyn Pacotti 364

About the Authors 374

Meet Terry Lamb

All horoscopes and sign descriptions for this book were written by Terry Lamb. A counselor, instructor, and healer using a spiritually oriented approach to astrology and healing, Terry specializes in electional astrology (choosing the right day for an event according to planetary influences), as well as family and relationship matters. She is the author of *Born To Be Together: Love Relationships, Astrology, and the Soul*,

and is a contributing author to Llewellyn's *Moon Sign Book. The Beginning Math Workbook* was released by the National Council for Geocosmic Research in 2003, and she has also been published in *Cosmos*, the *NCGR Journal*, and the *Mountain Astrologer*, and has written a monograph on her research into planetary cycles and childhood called *The Cycles of Childhood*. In addition, her publications have appeared on various websites, including StarIQ.com, and her own site, www.terrylamb.net.

Terry is also director of the Astrological Certification Program, a two-year online and home study course, which may be used to gain certification and success in an astrological career. Fourth-level certified by the National Council for Geocosmic Research (NCGR), she is an instructor in the NCGR Online College, and serves on their Board of Examiners. She is also NCGR's executive director, the president of the San Diego chapter of NCGR, and a past board member of the San Diego Astrological Society. Terry is a faculty member of the United Astrology Congress and is a featured speaker at the State of the Art Astrology Conference and NCGR Education conferences, and regional conferences and seminars. She currently resides in Spring Valley, California.

New Concepts for Signs of the Zodiac

The signs of the zodiac represent characteristics and traits that indicate how energy operates within our lives. The signs tell the story of human evolution and development, and all are necessary to form the continuum of whole life experience. In fact, all twelve signs are represented within your astrological chart.

Although the traditional metaphors for the twelve signs (such as Aries, the Ram) are always functional, these alternative concepts for each of the twelve signs also describe the gradual unfolding of the human spirit.

Aries: The Initiator is the first sign of the zodiac and encompasses the primary concept of getting things started. This fiery ignition and bright beginning can prove to be the thrust necessary for new life, but the Initiator also can appear before a situation is ready for change and create disruption.

Taurus: The Maintainer sustains what Aries has begun and brings stability and focus into the picture, yet there also can be a tendency to try to maintain something in its current state without allowing for new growth.

Gemini: The Questioner seeks to determine whether alternatives are possible and offers diversity to the processes Taurus has brought into stability. Yet questioning can also lead to distraction, subsequently scattering energy and diffusing focus.

Cancer: The Nurturer provides the qualities necessary for growth and security, and encourages a deepening awareness of emotional needs. Yet this same nurturing can stifle individuation if it becomes too smothering.

Leo: The Loyalist directs and centralizes the experiences Cancer feeds. This quality is powerfully targeted toward self-awareness, but can be shortsighted. Hence, the Loyalist can hold steadfastly to viewpoints or feelings that inhibit new experiences.

Virgo: The Modifier analyzes the situations Leo brings to light and determines possibilities for change. Even though this change may be in the name of improvement, it can lead to dissatisfaction with the self if not directed in harmony with higher needs.

Libra: The Judge is constantly comparing everything to be sure that a certain level of rightness and perfection is presented. However, the Judge can also present possibilities that are harsh and seem to be cold or without feeling.

Scorpio: The Catalyst steps into the play of life to provide the quality of alchemical transformation. The Catalyst can stir the brew just enough to create a healing potion, or may get things going to such a powerful extent that they boil out of control.

Sagittarius: The Adventurer moves away from Scorpio's dimension to seek what lies beyond the horizon. The Adventurer continually looks for possibilities that answer the ultimate questions, but may forget the pathway back home.

Capricorn: The Pragmatist attempts to put everything into its rightful place and find ways to make life work out right. The Pragmatist can teach lessons of practicality and determination, but can become highly self-righteous when shortsighted.

Aquarius: The Reformer looks for ways to take what Capricorn has built and bring it up to date. Yet there is also a tendency to scrap the original in favor of a new plan that may not have the stable foundation necessary to operate effectively.

Pisces: The Visionary brings mysticism and imagination, and challenges the soul to move beyond the physical plane, into the realm of what might be. The Visionary can pierce the veil, returning enlightened to the physical world. The challenge is to avoid getting lost within the illusion of an alternate reality.

Understanding the Basics of Astrology

Astrology is an ancient and continually evolving system used to clarify your identity and your needs. An astrological chart—which is calculated using the date, time, and place of birth—contains many factors which symbolically represent the needs, expressions, and experiences that make up the whole person. A professional astrologer interprets this symbolic picture, offering you an accurate portrait of your personality.

The chart itself—the horoscope—is a portrait of an individual. Generally, a natal (or birth) horoscope is drawn on a circular wheel. The wheel is divided into twelve segments, called houses. Each of the twelve houses represents a different aspect of the individual, much like the facets of a brilliantly cut stone. The houses depict different environments, such as home, school, and work. The houses also represent roles and relationships: parents, friends, lovers, children, partners. In each environment, individuals show a different side of their personality. At home, you may represent yourself quite differently than you do on the job. Additionally, in each relationship you will project a different image of yourself. Your parents rarely see the side you show to intimate friends.

Symbols for the planets, the Sun, and the Moon are drawn inside the houses. Each planet represents a separate kind of energy. You experience and express that energy in specific ways. (For a complete list, refer to the table on the next page.) The way you use each of these energies is up to you. The planets in your chart do not make you do anything!

The twelve signs of the zodiac indicate characteristics and traits that further define your personality. Each sign can be expressed in positive and negative ways. (The basic meaning of each of the signs is explained in the corresponding sections ahead.) What's more, you have all twelve signs somewhere in your chart. Signs that are strongly emphasized by the planets have greater force. The Sun, Moon, and planets are placed on the chart according to their position at the time of birth. The qualities of a sign, combined with the

Signs of the Zodiac

Aries	♈	The Initiator
Taurus	♉	The Maintainer
Gemini	♊	The Questioner
Cancer	♋	The Nurturer
Leo	♌	The Loyalist
Virgo	♍	The Modifier
Libra	♎	The Judge
Scorpio	♏	The Catalyst
Sagittarius	♐	The Adventurer
Capricorn	♑	The Pragmatist
Aquarius	♒	The Reformer
Pisces	♓	The Visionary

energy of a planet, indicate how you might be most likely to use that energy and the best ways to develop that energy. The signs add color, emphasis, and dimension to the personality.

Signs are also placed at the cusps, or dividing lines, of each of the houses. The influence of the signs on the houses is much the same as their influence on the Sun, Moon, and planets. Each house is shaped by the sign on its cusp.

When you view a horoscope, you will notice that there appear to be four distinctive angles dividing the wheel of the chart. The line that divides the chart into a top and bottom half represents the horizon. In most cases, the left side of the horizon is called the Ascendant. The zodiac sign on the Ascendant is your rising sign. The Ascendant indicates the way others are likely to view you.

The Sun, Moon, or planet can be compared to an actor in a play. The sign shows how the energy works, like the role the actor plays in a drama. The house indicates where the energy operates, like the setting of a play. On a psychological level, the Sun represents who

The Planets

Sun	☉	The ego, self, willpower
Moon	☽	The subconscious self, habits
Mercury	☿	Communication, the intellect
Venus	♀	Emotional expression, love, appreciation, artistry
Mars	♂	Physical drive, assertiveness, anger
Jupiter	♃	Philosophy, ethics, generosity
Saturn	♄	Discipline, focus, responsibility
Uranus	♅	Individuality, rebelliousness
Neptune	♆	Imagination, sensitivity, compassion
Pluto	♇	Transformation, healing, regeneration

you think you are. The Ascendant describes who others think you are, and the Moon reflects your inner self.

Astrologers also study the geometric relationships between the Sun, Moon, and planets. These geometric angles are called aspects. Aspects further define the strengths, weaknesses, and challenges within your physical, mental, emotional, and spiritual self. Sometimes, patterns also appear in an astrological chart. These patterns have meaning.

To understand cycles for any given point in time, astrologers study several factors. Many use transits, which refer to the movement and positions of the planets. When astrologers compare those positions to the birth horoscope, the transits indicate activity in particular areas of the chart. The *Sun Sign Book* uses transits.

As you can see, your Sun sign is just one of many factors that describes who you are—but it is a powerful one! As the symbol of the ego, the Sun in your chart reflects your drive to be noticed. Most people can easily relate to the concepts associated with their Sun sign, since it is tied to their sense of personal identity.

Using this Book

This book contains what is called "Sun sign astrology," that is, astrology based on the sign that your Sun was in at the time of your birth. The technique has its foundation in ancient Greek astrology, in which the Sun was one of five points in the chart that was used as a focal point for delineation.

The most effective way to use astrology, however, is through one-on-one work with a professional astrologer, who can integrate the eight or so other astrological bodies into his or her interpretation to provide you with guidance. There are factors related to the year and time of day you were born that are highly significant in the way you approach life and vital to making wise choices. In addition, there are ways of using astrology that aren't addressed here, such as compatibility between two specific individuals, discovering family patterns, or picking a day for a wedding or grand opening.

To best use the information in the monthly forecasts, you'll want to determine your Ascendant, or rising sign. If you don't know your Ascendant, the tables following this description will help you determine your rising sign. They are most accurate for those born in the continental United States. They're only an approximation, but they can be used as a good rule of thumb. Your exact Ascendant may vary from the tables according to your time and place of birth. Once you've approximated your ascending sign using the tables or determined your Ascendant by having your chart calculated, you'll know two significant factors in your chart. Read the monthly forecast sections for both your Sun and Ascendant to gain the most useful information. In addition, you can read the section about the sign your Moon is in. The Sun is the true, inner you; the Ascendant is your shell or appearance and the person you are becoming; the Moon is the person you were—or still are based on habits and memories.

I've also included information about the planets' retrogrades this year. Most people have heard of "Mercury retrograde." In fact, all the planets except the Sun and Moon appear to travel backward (retrograde) in their path periodically. This only appears to happen because we on the Earth are not seeing the other planets from the middle of the solar system. Rather, we are watching them from our own moving object. We are like a train that moves past cars on the freeway that are going at a slower speed. To us on the train, the cars look like they're going backward. Mercury turns retrograde about every four months for three weeks; Venus every eighteen months for six weeks; Mars every two years for two to three months. The rest of the planets each retrograde once a year for four to five months. During each retrograde, we have the opportunity to try something new, something we conceived of at the beginning of the planet's yearly cycle. The times when the planets change direction are significant, as are the beginning and midpoint (peak or culmination) of each cycle. These are noted in your forecast each month.

Your "Rewarding and Challenging Days" sections indicate times when you'll feel either more centered or more out of balance. The rewarding days are not the only times you can perform well, but the times you're likely to feel better integrated! During challenging days, take extra time to center yourself by meditating or using other techniques that help you feel more objective.

The Action Table found at the end of each sign's section offers general guidelines for the best time to take a particular action. Please note, however, that your whole chart will provide more accurate guidelines for the best time to do something. Therefore, use this table with a grain of salt, and never let it stop you from taking an action you feel compelled to take.

You can use this information for an objective awareness about the way the current cycles are affecting you. Realize that the power of astrology is even more useful when you have a complete chart and professional guidance.

2005 at a Glance

We'll be treading exciting new paths as three planets—Jupiter, Saturn, and Chiron—change signs in 2005. Together they create a dynamic pattern in the heavens that will energize us and challenge us to makes changes in our lives. They triangulate with each other all year, even when they are not in exact aspect.

Jupiter is in Libra for most of the year, moving into Scorpio on October 25. While it sojourns in Libra we'll feel its expansiveness through lessons of balance, justice, and harmony. It will also invite us to develop our sense of artistry and beauty, especially because of its harmonious trine to Neptune. We can expect some positive changes in world affairs, as well as a more robust international economy, due to a resonant sextile with Pluto. Once it enters Scorpio we will observe an expansion in interest in matters of the occult, as well as other mysteries of life. Since this ingress coincides with Halloween, we are likely to be greeted by a particularly large and lucrative set of horror films, some of which will introduce innovations into the entertainment industry.

Saturn, after more than two years in Cancer, has taught us as much as it can about our human emotions. Before it moves into Leo on July 16 we can look forward to finalizing those lessons in our lives. This is also the energy under which "homeland (in)security" became an issue, and the problems of personal safety in a free society need to be resolved. Saturn in Leo presents us with a new lesson, one we visited thirty years ago, about the nature of happiness. It teaches us how to find fulfillment by following our own path.

Chiron enters Aquarius on February 21, shifting the focus of our healing energies to issues of equality, group consciousness, and the role of the individual in the group. Issues of personal freedom and expression are likely to receive focus in public policy during the coming six years that Chiron is in this sign.

From the beginning of the year, Jupiter, Saturn, and Chiron are in contact with each other in an abrasive T-square pattern that moves from cardinal to fixed signs as these planets make their ingresses. This situation invites us to face the cardinal dilemma of self-definition, which shifts to the fixed issue of self-value. On the world scene cardinal patterns tend to play out as aggressive tendencies, while fixed patterns lead us to confront problems that resist resolution.

Significant harmonies can be found, however, between Jupiter and Uranus, as well as Saturn and Pluto. Each of these blends presages progress and innovation. Jupiter–Uranus suggests growth in overcoming social problems as well as scientific and technological advances. Saturn–Pluto brings progress in public policy related to political and legal dilemmas that arose in 2000 and 2001. This brings hope that the rifts that lead some to engage in terrorism and unrest may be truly uprooted.

Ascendant Table

Your Sun Sign	Your Time of Birth					
	6–8 am	8–10 am	10 am–Noon	Noon–2 pm	2–4 pm	4–6 pm
Aries	Taurus	Gemini	Cancer	Leo	Virgo	Libra
Taurus	Gemini	Cancer	Leo	Virgo	Libra	Scorpio
Gemini	Cancer	Leo	Virgo	Libra	Scorpio	Sagittarius
Cancer	Leo	Virgo	Libra	Scorpio	Sagittarius	Capricorn
Leo	Virgo	Libra	Scorpio	Sagittarius	Capricorn	Aquarius
Virgo	Libra	Scorpio	Sagittarius	Capricorn	Aquarius	Pisces
Libra	Scorpio	Sagittarius	Capricorn	Aquarius	Pisces	Aries
Scorpio	Sagittarius	Capricorn	Aquarius	Pisces	Aries	Taurus
Sagittarius	Capricorn	Aquarius	Pisces	Aries	Taurus	Gemini
Capricorn	Aquarius	Pisces	Aries	Taurus	Gemini	Cancer
Aquarius	Pisces	Aries	Taurus	Gemini	Cancer	Leo
Pisces	Aries	Taurus	Gemini	Cancer	Leo	Virgo

Your Time of Birth

Your Sun Sign	6–8 pm	8–10 pm	10 pm–Midnight	Midnight–2 am	2–4 am	4–6 am
Aries	Scorpio	Sagittarius	Capricorn	Aquarius	Pisces	Aries
Taurus	Sagittarius	Capricorn	Aquarius	Pisces	Aries	Taurus
Gemini	Capricorn	Aquarius	Pisces	Aries	Taurus	Gemini
Cancer	Aquarius	Pisces	Aries	Taurus	Gemini	Cancer
Leo	Pisces	Aries	Taurus	Gemini	Cancer	Leo
Virgo	Aries	Taurus	Gemini	Cancer	Leo	Virgo
Libra	Taurus	Gemini	Cancer	Leo	Virgo	Libra
Scorpio	Gemini	Cancer	Leo	Virgo	Libra	Scorpio
Sagittarius	Cancer	Leo	Virgo	Libra	Scorpio	Sagittarius
Capricorn	Leo	Virgo	Libra	Scorpio	Sagittarius	Capricorn
Aquarius	Virgo	Libra	Scorpio	Sagittarius	Capricorn	Aquarius
Pisces	Libra	Scorpio	Sagittarius	Capricorn	Aquarius	Pisces

How to use this table: 1. Find your Sun sign in the left column.
2. Find your approximate birth time in a vertical column.
3. Line up your Sun sign and birth time to find your Ascendant.

This table will give you an approximation of your Ascendant. If you feel that the sign listed as your Ascendant is incorrect, try the one either before or after the listed sign. It is difficult to determine your exact Ascendant without a complete natal chart.

Astrological Glossary

Air: One of the four basic elements. The air signs are Gemini, Libra, and Aquarius.

Angles: The four points of the chart that divide it into quadrants. The angles are sensitive areas that lend emphasis to planets located near them. These points are located on the cusps of the First, Fourth, Seventh, and Tenth Houses in a chart.

Ascendant: Rising sign. The degree of the zodiac on the eastern horizon at the time and place for which the horoscope is calculated. It can indicate the image or physical appearance you project to the world. The cusp of the First House.

Aspect: The angular relationship between planets, sensitive points, or house cusps in a horoscope. Lines drawn between the two points and the center of the chart, representing the Earth, form the angle of the aspect. Astrological aspects include conjunction (two points that are 0 degrees apart), opposition (two points, 180 degrees apart), square (two points, 90 degrees apart), sextile (two points, 60 degrees apart), and trine (two points, 120 degrees apart). Aspects can indicate harmony or challenge.

Cardinal Sign: One of the three qualities, or categories, that describe how a sign expresses itself. Aries, Cancer, Libra, and Capricorn are the cardinal signs, believed to initiate activity.

Chiron: Chiron is a comet traveling in orbit between Saturn and Uranus. Although research on its effect on natal charts is not yet complete, it is believed to represent a key or doorway, healing, ecology, and a bridge between traditional and modern methods.

Conjunction: An aspect or angle between two points in a chart where the two points are close enough so that the energies join. Can be considered either harmonious or challenging, depending on the planets involved and their placement.

Cusp: A dividing line between signs or houses in a chart.

Degree: Degree of arc. One of 360 divisions of a circle. The circle of the zodiac is divided into twelve astrological signs of 30 degrees each. Each degree is made up of 60 minutes, and each minute is made up of 60 seconds of zodiacal longitude.

Earth: One of the four basic elements. The earth signs are Taurus, Virgo, and Capricorn.

Eclipse: A solar eclipse is the full or partial covering of the Sun by the Moon (as viewed from Earth), and a lunar eclipse is the full or partial covering of the Moon by the Earth's own shadow.

Ecliptic: The Sun's apparent path around the Earth, which is actually the plane of the Earth's orbit extended out into space. The ecliptic forms the center of the zodiac.

Electional Astrology: A branch of astrology concerned with choosing the best time to initiate an activity.

Elements: The signs of the zodiac are divided into four groups of three zodiacal signs, each symbolized by one of the four elements of the ancients: fire, earth, air, and water. The element of a sign is said to express its essential nature.

Ephemeris: A listing of the Sun, Moon, and planets' positions and related information for astrological purposes.

Equinox: Equal night. The point in the Earth's orbit around the Sun at which the day and night are equal in length.

Feminine Signs: Each zodiac sign is either masculine or feminine. Earth signs (Taurus, Virgo, and Capricorn) and water signs (Cancer, Scorpio, and Pisces) are feminine.

Fire: One of the four basic elements. The fire signs are Aries, Leo, and Sagittarius.

Fixed Signs: Fixed is one of the three qualities, or categories, that describe how a sign expresses itself. The fixed signs are Taurus, Leo, Scorpio, and Aquarius. Fixed signs are said to be predisposed to existing patterns and somewhat resistant to change.

Hard Aspects: Hard aspects are those aspects in a chart that astrologers believe to represent difficulty or challenges. Among the hard aspects are the square, the opposition, and the conjunction (depending on which planets are conjunct).

Horizon: The word "horizon" is used in astrology in a manner similar to its common usage, except that only the eastern and western horizons are considered useful. The eastern horizon at the point of birth is the Ascendant, or First House cusp, of a natal chart, and the western horizon at the point of birth is the Descendant, or Seventh House cusp.

Houses: Division of the horoscope into twelve segments, beginning with the Ascendant. The dividing line between the houses are called house cusps. Each house corresponds to certain aspects of daily living, and is ruled by the astrological sign that governs the cusp, or dividing line between the house and the one previous.

Ingress: The point of entry of a planet into a sign.

Lagna: A term used in Hindu or Vedic astrology for Ascendant, the degree of the zodiac on the eastern horizon at the time of birth.

Masculine Signs: Each of the twelve signs of the zodiac is either "masculine" or "feminine." The fire signs (Aries, Leo, and Sagittarius) and the air signs (Gemini, Libra, and Aquarius) are masculine.

Midheaven: The highest point on the ecliptic, where it intersects the meridian that passes directly above the place for which the horoscope is cast; the southern point of the horoscope.

Midpoint: A point equally distant to two planets or house cusps. Midpoints are considered by some astrologers to be sensitive points in a person's chart.

Mundane Astrology: Mundane astrology is the branch of astrology generally concerned with political and economic events, and the nations involved in these events.

Mutable Signs: Mutable is one of the three qualities, or categories, that describe how a sign expresses itself. Mutable signs are Gemini, Virgo, Sagittarius, and Pisces. Mutable signs are said to be very adaptable and sometimes changeable.

Natal Chart: A person's birth chart. A natal chart is essentially a "snapshot" showing the placement of each of the planets at the exact time of a person's birth.

Node: The point where the planets cross the ecliptic, or the Earth's apparent path around the Sun. The North Node is the point where a planet moves northward, from the Earth's perspective, as it crosses the ecliptic; the South Node is where it moves south.

Opposition: Two points in a chart that are 180 degrees apart.

Orb: A small degree of margin used when calculating aspects in a chart. For example, although 180 degrees form an exact opposition, an astrologer might consider an aspect within 3 or 4 degrees on either side of 180 degrees to be an opposition, as the impact of the aspect can still be felt within this range. The less orb on an aspect, the stronger the aspect. Astrologers' opinions vary on how many degrees of orb to allow for each aspect.

Outer Planets: Uranus, Neptune, and Pluto are known as the outer planets. Because of their distance from the Sun, they take a long time to complete a single rotation. Everyone born within a few years on either side of a given date will have similar placements of these planets.

Planets: The planets used in astrology are Mercury, Venus, Mars, Jupiter, Saturn, Uranus, Neptune, and Pluto. For astrological purposes, the Sun and Moon are also considered planets. A natal or birth chart lists planetary placement at the moment of birth.

Planetary Rulership: The sign in which a planet is most harmoniously placed. Examples are the Sun in Leo, Jupiter in Sagittarius, and the Moon in Cancer.

Precession of Equinoxes: The gradual movement of the point of the Spring Equinox, located at 0 degrees Aries. This point marks the beginning of the tropical zodiac. The point moves slowly backward through the constellations of the zodiac, so that about every 2,000 years the equinox begins in an earlier constellation.

Qualities: In addition to categorizing the signs by element, astrologers place the twelve signs of the zodiac into three additional categories, or qualities: cardinal, mutable, or fixed. Each sign is considered to be a combination of its element and quality. Where the element of a sign describes its basic nature, the quality describes its mode of expression.

Retrograde Motion: Apparent backward motion of a planet. This is an illusion caused by the relative motion of the Earth and other planets in their elliptical orbits.

Sextile: Two points in a chart that are 60 degrees apart.

Sidereal Zodiac: Generally used by Hindu or Vedic astrologers. The sidereal zodiac is located where the constellations are actually positioned in the sky.

Soft Aspects: Soft aspects indicate good fortune or an easy relationship in the chart. Among the soft aspects are the trine, the sextile, and the conjunction (depending on which planets are conjunct each other).

Square: Two points in a chart that are 90 degrees apart.

Sun Sign: The sign of the zodiac in which the Sun is located at any given time.

Synodic Cycle: The time between conjunctions of two planets.

Trine: Two points in a chart that are 120 degrees apart.

Tropical Zodiac: The tropical zodiac begins at 0 degrees Aries, where the Sun is located during the Spring Equinox. This system is used by most Western astrologers and throughout this book.

Void-of-Course: A planet is void-of-course after it has made its last aspect within a sign, but before it has entered a new sign.

Water: One of the four basic elements. Water signs are Cancer, Scorpio, and Pisces.

Meanings of the Planets

The Sun

The Sun indicates the psychological bias that will dominate your actions. What you see, and why, is told in the reading for your Sun. The Sun also shows the basic energy patterns of your body and psyche. In many ways, the Sun is the dominant force in your horoscope and your life. Other influences, especially that of the Moon, may modify the Sun's influence, but nothing will cause you to depart very far from the basic solar pattern. Always keep in mind the basic influence of the Sun and remember all other influences must be interpreted in terms of it, especially insofar as they play a visible role in your life. You may think, dream, imagine, and hope a thousand things, according to your Moon and your other planets, but the Sun is what you are. To be your best self in terms of your Sun is to cause your energies to work along the path in which they will have maximum help from planetary vibrations.

The Moon

The Moon tells the desire of your life. When you know what you mean but can't verbalize it, it is your Moon that knows it and your Sun that can't say it. The wordless ecstasy, the mute sorrow, the secret dream, the esoteric picture of yourself that you can't get across to the world, or that the world doesn't comprehend or value—these are the products of the Moon. When you are misunderstood, it is your Moon nature, expressed imperfectly through the Sun sign, that feels betrayed. Things you know without thought—intuitions, hunches, instincts—are the products of the Moon. Modes of expression that you feel truly reflect your deepest self belong to the Moon: art, letters, creative work of any kind; sometimes love; sometimes business. Whatever you feel to be most deeply yourself is the product of your Moon and of the sign your Moon occupies at birth.

Mercury

Mercury is the sensory antenna of your horoscope. Its position by sign indicates your reactions to sights, sounds, odors, tastes, and touch impressions, affording a key to the attitude you have toward the physical world around you. Mercury is the messenger through which your physical body and brain (ruled by the Sun) and your inner nature (ruled by the Moon) are kept in contact with the outer world, which will appear to you according to the index of Mercury's position by sign in the horoscope. Mercury rules your rational mind.

Venus

Venus is the emotional antenna of your horoscope. Through Venus, impressions come to you from the outer world, to which you react emotionally. The position of Venus by sign at the time of your birth determines your attitude toward these experiences. As Mercury is the messenger linking sense impressions (sight, smell, etc.) to the basic nature of your Sun and Moon, so Venus is the messenger linking emotional impressions. If Venus is found in the same sign as the Sun, emotions gain importance in your life, and have a direct bearing on your actions. If Venus is in the same sign as the Moon, emotions bear directly on your inner nature, add self-confidence, make you sensitive to emotional impressions, and frequently indicate that you have more love in your heart than you are able to express. If Venus is in the same sign as Mercury, emotional impressions and sense impressions work together; you tend to idealize the world of the senses and sensualize the world of the emotions to interpret emotionally what you see and hear.

Mars

Mars is the energy principle in the horoscope. Its position indicates the channels into which energy will most easily be directed. It is the planet through which the activities of the Sun and the desires of the Moon express themselves in action. In the same sign as the Sun, Mars gives abundant energy, sometimes misdirected in temper, temperament, and quarrels. In the same sign as the Moon, it gives a great capacity to make use of the innermost aims, and to make the inner desires articulate and practical. In the same sign as Venus, it quickens emotional reactions and causes you to act on them, makes for ardor and passion in love, and fosters an earthly awareness of emotional realities.

Jupiter

Jupiter is the feeler for opportunity that you have out in the world. It passes along chances of a lifetime for consideration according to the basic nature of your Sun and Moon. Jupiter's sign position indicates the places where you will look for opportunity, the uses to which you wish to put it, and the capacity you have to react and profit by it. Jupiter is ordinarily, and erroneously, called the planet of luck. It is "luck" insofar as it is the index of opportunity, but your luck depends less on what comes to you than on what you do with what comes to you. In the same sign as the Sun or Moon, Jupiter gives a direct, and generally effective, response to opportunity and is likely to show forth at its "luckiest." If Jupiter is in the same sign as Mercury, sense impressions are interpreted opportunistically. If Jupiter is in the same sign as Venus, you interpret emotions in such a way as to turn them to your advantage; your feelings work harmoniously with the chances for progress that the world has to offer. If Jupiter is in the same sign as Mars, you follow opportunity with energy, dash, enthusiasm, and courage; take long chances; and play your cards wide open.

Saturn

Saturn indicates the direction that will be taken in life by the self-preservative principle that, in its highest manifestation, ceases to be purely defensive and becomes ambitious and aspiring. Your defense or attack against the world is shown by the sign position of Saturn in the horoscope of birth. If Saturn is in the same sign as the Sun or Moon, defense predominates, and there is danger of introversion. The farther Saturn is from the Sun, Moon, and Ascendant, the better for objectivity and extroversion. If Saturn is in the same sign as Mercury, there is a profound and serious reaction to sense impressions; this position generally accompanies a deep and efficient mind. If Saturn is in the same sign as Venus, a defensive attitude toward emotional experience makes for apparent coolness in love and difficulty with the emotions and human relations. If Saturn is in the same sign as Mars, confusion between defensive and aggressive urges can make an indecisive person—or, if the Sun and Moon are strong and the total personality well developed, a balanced, peaceful, and calm individual of sober judgment and moderate actions may be indicated. If Saturn is in the same sign as Jupiter, the reaction to opportunity is sober and balanced.

Uranus

Uranus in a general way relates to creativity, originality, or individuality, and its position by sign in the horoscope tells the direction in which you will seek to express yourself. In the same sign as Mercury or the Moon, Uranus suggests acute awareness, a quick reaction to sense impressions and experiences, or a hair-trigger mind. In the same sign as the Sun, it points to great nervous activity, a high-strung nature, and an original, creative, or eccentric personality. In the same sign as Mars, Uranus indicates high-speed activity, love of swift motion, and perhaps love of danger. In the same sign as Venus, it suggests an unusual reaction to emotional experience, idealism, sensuality, and original ideas about love and human relations. In the same sign as Saturn, Uranus points to good sense; this can be a practical, creative position, but, more often than not, it sets up a destructive conflict between practicality and originality that can result in a stalemate. In the same sign as Jupiter, Uranus makes opportunity, creates wealth and the means of getting it, and is conducive to the inventive, executive, and daring.

Neptune

Neptune relates to the deepest wells of the subconscious, inherited mentality, and spirituality, indicating what you take for granted in life. Neptune in the same sign as the Sun or Moon indicates that intuitions and hunches—or delusions—dominate; there is a need for rigidly holding to reality. In the same sign as Mercury, Neptune indicates sharp sensory perceptions, a sensitive and perhaps creative mind, and a quivering intensity of reaction to sensory experience. In the same sign as Venus, it reveals idealistic and romantic (or sentimental) reaction to emotional experience, as well as the danger of sensationalism and a love of strange pleasures. In the same sign as Mars, Neptune indicates energy and intuition that work together to make mastery of life—one of the signs of having angels (or devils) on your side. In the same sign as Jupiter, Neptune describes intuitive response to opportunity generally along practical and money-making lines; one of the signs of security if not indeed of wealth. In the same sign as Saturn, Neptune indicates intuitive defense and attack on the world, generally successful unless Saturn is polarized on the negative side; then there is danger of unhappiness.

Pluto

Pluto is a planet of extremes—from the lowest criminal and violent level of our society to the heights people can attain when they realize their significance in the collectivity of humanity. Pluto also rules three important mysteries of life—sex, death, and rebirth—and links them to each other. One level of death symbolized by Pluto is the physical death of an individual, which occurs so that a person can be reborn into another body to further his or her spiritual development. On another level, individuals can experience a "death" of their old self when they realize the deeper significance of life; thus they become one of the "second born." In a natal horoscope, Pluto signifies our perspective on the world, our conscious and subconscious. Since so many of Pluto's qualities are centered on the deeper mysteries of life, the house position of Pluto, and aspects to it, can show you how to attain a deeper understanding of the importance of the spiritual in your life.

Forecasts

By Terry Lamb

Aries . . . . Page 28
Taurus . . . . Page 51
Gemini . . . . Page 74
Cancer . . . . Page 97
Leo . . . . Page 120
Virgo . . . . Page 143
Libra . . . . Page 166
Scorpio . . . . Page 189
Sagittarius . . . . . Page 212
Capricorn . . . . . . Page 235
Aquarius . . . . Page 258
Pisces . . . . Page 281

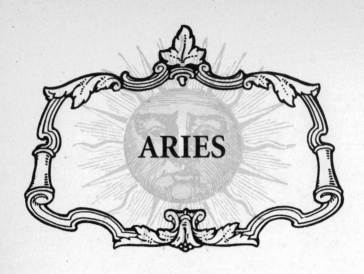

ARIES

The Ram
March 20 to April 19

♈

Element:	Fire
Quality:	Cardinal
Polarity:	Yang/Masculine
Planetary Ruler:	Mars
Meditation:	I build upon my strengths.
Gemstone:	Diamond
Power Stones:	Bloodstone, carnelian, ruby
Key Phrase:	I am
Glyph:	Ram's head
Anatomy:	Head, face, throat
Color:	Red, white
Animal:	Ram
Myths/Legends:	Artemis, Jason and the Golden Fleece
House:	First
Opposite Sign:	Libra
Flower:	Geranium
Key Word:	Initiative

Your Ego's Strengths and Shortcomings

If you ever feel like you're full of fire and rarin' to go, you're just feeling your fire side. Fire is the element of Aries; it's how the ancients chose to characterize your passion, vigor, and bravery. Like your element, your direction of motion is upward: you aspire to greater heights and new horizons. You seek adventure and love the thrill of exploration. The unknown holds no fear for you—rather, it piques your interest. You have the courage to tread the wilderness, live on the edge, and survive moment to moment. You don't need others' approval as you walk your path—you may barely notice their existence as you head toward your objective.

However, like fire, you really do need others. Fire needs fuel and air to exist, and so you draw your light from other people's sustaining belief in you. Your inspiration comes from the unexpressed needs of others as much as your own. As you search for your identity, you need to see yourself reflected in their eyes; this is how you come to know yourself—the most important objective of your path of personal growth.

What you lack in tact, you make up for with sincerity. No one can ever doubt your word, but your perception of reality may be twisted if you cannot see anything beyond your own perspective. You and your projects could risk being irrelevant if you don't take other people's ideas and needs into consideration. By disciplining yourself to stick around long enough to really listen to others, you can create a better balance of drive and receptivity, becoming more successful in all your efforts.

If you are long on enthusiasm but short on follow-through, that's because you're a better starter than finisher. Those in the avant garde can't be expected to cover the flank as well. Rely on your strengths of drive and initiative and bring others in on your schemes to make sure the work gets done.

Shining Your Love Light

Sometimes you wonder if you want a partner, especially since it seems so complicated to consider someone else's needs in addition to your own. Yet, somehow you can't live without another person in your life, because there's a mystery there. The more you learn about the other person, the better you know yourself. Somehow it brings out the best in you. With another Aries you'll find a natural affinity, but don't expect your partner to pick up after you! Taurus provides a steadying influence for your adventures and flights of fancy, but he'll feel left behind if you can't slow down to match his pace. Gemini is as inquisitive as you and enjoys exploring new realms. Don't be surprised, however, if she wants to stick around to socialize when you're ready to be off on your next wild ride. Cancer's emotional world may baffle you, but she will also teach you to honor the feelings that affect you from just beneath the surface of your being. Leo speaks your fiery language of "act first, think later," so you'll have loads of fun together, but don't forget to temper your mutual joy in life with some common sense. Virgo supplies a missing piece of the puzzle for you—rational analysis and organization, while you help to override this sign's worries with clear-sighted action. You'll see your greatest weaknesses reflected back to you through Libra, but if you dare to face them you'll gain the greatest rewards. While Scorpio shares your zest for action as a response to life, these signs are motivated by their determination rather than their enthusiasm, as you are. Sagittarius will match you, step for step, as you tilt after your latest windmill; however, with two of you willing to live on life's skinny branches, you need to agree to get grounded together or hire a nanny to take care of you both. Capricorn may seem too serious to hold your interest, but if you give these signs room in your life, they'll give you the keys to success—and their hearts. Aquarius shares your aloofness when it comes to social involvement, but he is really a political animal that needs to feed on human interaction without being tied down. The motivations of Pisces may be hard for you to grasp, but this sign shares your forward-thinking attitude toward life.

Making Your Place in the World

You are best when it comes to getting things going, Aries, and there are many ways to play up this fine quality. You are a great team leader for any project, but especially ones where fast action and ground-breaking techniques or procedures are required. Any situation where you have to go it alone works for you, too—from on-site customer service, training, installations, and repairs to delivery services. You have the "get up and go" required to be top of the market in sales—especially direct sales with your own territory and product line. The ultimate motivator for you, though, may be entrepreneurship, because then you can use your competitive spirit to positively affect your bottom line. And, with your natural athletic talents, don't forget sports.

There's one pitfall that could make it all come crashing down, however, and that's a lack of team spirit. In the business world, the emphasis is on human relations, on connecting with others. Even if you work a solo job you must have successful contacts with customers, clients, and colleagues. If you can focus on leaving behind smiles when you go, you'll make the best of your skills.

Putting Your Best Foot Forward

Even in the best of us there are weaknesses that we can learn to overcome in order to improve our effectiveness, happiness, and success. Your drive, ambition, optimism, and ingenuity are marvelous qualities in themselves, but they can be overdone, and others may feel you are overbearing or exhausting at times with your ebullience. They tendencies are best expressed as complements to the qualities of others or to other traits in your own character. Balanced against receptivity, realism, logic, and the ability to follow through, your leadership skills will shine like fine diamonds and provide the spark needed to keep everyone motivated and energized. A key skill to activating these qualities, whether in yourself or in a group, is to consider other points of view. This means listening to what people have to say, as well as learning to understand what *isn't* said through body language and the actions people take. Asking the right questions can make others feel more comfortable about letting you know their true thoughts, but you must truly listen and respond to what you hear from them to become convinced that you value their input. It also helps to slow down your responses when you feel like taking action. Although action may be called for, others who don't move as quickly as you may be left behind otherwise. By slowing down, they will feel more included.

Tools for Change

With the planets where they are this year, you will benefit from applying industry and consistency to your efforts, especially in your private life. One of the best ways to do this is to develop a greater awareness of your inner world—emotions, impressions, intuitions, instincts. While this may be an unfamiliar and sometimes bewildering world, everyone needs to do the work of understanding this side of their nature. There are ways to approach this process to make it fascinating rather than tedious. One of the best ways is to learn to remember your dreams. It also helps to keep a journal if you enjoy writing to reflect your feelings back to you. However, the simplest and most effective thing is to spend time with yourself and your own thoughts without external distractions. When you are at home, driving alone, or exercising, spending the time in silence will support a spontaneous introspective process. Meditation will also support the unfolding of your inner being and activate your senses as well as your psychic ability. Yoga induces the union of mind and body, and with your natural attunement to physical movement and athletics it fits your style to a "T." The same can be said about martial arts, which direct your physical power in a disciplined manner. It will also help you if you can learn to function as part of a team in every area of your life, from work to family to social activities. You may find it quite pleasant to do so in the context of team sports. Travel abroad, or at least to places foreign to you, will broaden your perspective and take you outside yourself. This will give you a better sense of who you are and what you have to offer, as well as a deeper dedication to helping others in need. You may also find higher educational pursuits to be particularly useful now, because they will empower you for years to come. A decision to study further can come at no better time in your life, no matter what personal sacrifices you have to make. Foreign languages and cultures, philosophy, religious studies, the sciences—all will lend objectivity to your viewpoint, a powerful adjunct to the passion you naturally bring to all you touch.

Affirmation for the Year

I accept the support of those around me
and affirm their importance in my life.

The Year Ahead for Aries

Your road to success is paved with opportunity in 2005, Aries! With Jupiter in Libra and your Seventh House for most of the year, your key to wealth and happiness lies in your relationships with others, both personal and business. Cultivate them with care and consistency for maximum benefit. You may have lots of opportunities to choose from where partners are concerned, so make the best of this year! After October 24 Jupiter moves into Scorpio and your solar Eighth House, bringing a year of reward for the past eight years of diligent effort—if you don't spread yourself too thin due to your great optimism.

After two years of flying below the radar with many of your efforts, including responsibilities that have drawn you close to home, you'll enter a time of greater freedom, energy, and creativity on July 17 when Saturn moves from Cancer, your solar Fourth House, to Leo, your Fifth House. The more you can apply yourself with persistence and practicality (I know it's not your strong suit), the greater the plums you will pick over the coming twenty years. In deciding where to cast your hook into the waters, you may benefit by looking back to ten years ago, for now you are getting results from those efforts.

Chiron also changes signs this year: after almost four years in Capricorn, it enters Aquarius and your solar Eleventh House on February 21. You'll experience a corresponding shift of transformative healing energies from the realm of your career to that of your social milieu and group affiliations—from organizations to political parties to socio-economic "class." Since early 2001 you've been healing your image of authority figures, your notions of leadership and responsibility. Now you have a greater sense of true inner worth—and perhaps a reluctance to take leadership positions, since your awareness of how important responsible action is to the success of any leader has grown. It's time to take this new wisdom and apply it to your groups. By offering structure and responsible insight, you will assist them in reaching their goals as well as your own.

Uranus is spending its third year in Pisces and your Twelfth House. It may bring unexpected circumstances out of the woodwork yet again. These experiences are designed to awaken you to the essentially irrational nature of our universe—the unseen, inner world that is the source of all truth. Contrary to what the outer world teaches us, the randomness of events in our visible life is ordered and purposeful when seen from inside. Uranus takes us there in fits and starts, shocking us when we stray from this awareness until it becomes a part of us. You are two years into this journey of new awareness, and new adventures await in 2005.

Slow-moving Neptune is in Aquarius and your Eleventh House of group affiliations, as it has been since 1998. It has been dissolving old, unnecessary social patterns and needs so that you can fulfill a higher, finer role in society—whatever that means for you. This year continues that process, and it may mean giving up old associations and forming new ones.

Pluto remains in its most recent and familiar location: Sagittarius and your solar Ninth House of exotic places and ideas. You may find yourself transformed once again in mind and body as you encounter foreign concepts and contexts. Travel, higher education, occult or religious studies, a remote perspective, acquiring a foreign language—many are the opportunities which can bring you the deep change you need to fulfill who you really are.

The eclipses affect you just as deeply this year as they ignite your drive to succeed, to follow your path of self-development. You'll find new fascination in your close relationships, which will reflect your true qualities, both positive and negative, so that you can grow. You may part with some who are close to you even as you form new bonds.

If you were born from March 20 to April 2, Saturn in Leo will be making an exact contact to your Sun from your solar Fifth House. This is a constructive transit, which will help you build new creative structures. If you are involved in a creative field you may take on a large project that requires planning and hard work. Regardless of your profession, you may find that structuring your plans for the future will bring great rewards in coming years—although not right away. It is important to think in terms of what you really want from life, not just what will provide quick results or easy money. You may also find that commitments to children are on the increase, requiring more of your time and resources. You may also be more risk-averse than usual, and this is wise: Saturn wants you to work with a system, not move on intuition. If you like to speculate or gamble, your hunches may work less successfully than those decisions made through study and the use of statistics. On the whole, this is a harmonious transit that will allow you to sift through the activities in your life and cut away those that are not satisfying to you in some way. Far fewer obstacles than usual should block your way. Critical dates in this process are July 16 through 23 and November 22.

If you were born from March 23 to April 1, Uranus in Pisces creates an awkwardness in your life that may inconvenience you or focus you on feelings of discontent. You may experience a general malaise that challenges you to look for deeper meaning, or you may even become ill. We often feel confined during Uranus transits. This may be due to actual circumstances, as with recovery from surgery, or it may be an artifact of a particularly intense work cycle. Chances are good that you will identify something from which you will want to break free. However, the time may not be right—at least from a rational point of view. It may be wisest to take the insight you gain from your new awareness and work constructively toward a new reality. You may also find that psychic or spiritual experiences become more prominent in your life. You may want to start meditating or changing your spiritual practices. Psychic abilities and events may increase in number and intensity. Your dreams may be especially vivid and offer you guidance in cracking the code of the inner you that is currently being revealed. Related events will occur around February 25, June 14, August 31, and November 15.

If you were born from April 3 to 8, Neptune will prominent in your life for the coming year, creating opportunities in your Eleventh House matters—your affiliations with organizations and groups, including your family and your social milieu. In any of these environments you are likely to find yourself feeling more sensitive—more aware of the emotional, energetic, and psychic dynamics of those around you. You may find it difficult to be in crowds or events that draw large groups of people because of the chaotic undercurrents that they generate. You may also be drawn to groups that have overt spiritual goals or humanitarian ideals. The groups you are attracted to may serve the underdog in some way, providing support to the underprivileged or to those with extra challenges in life. The role(s) you are attracted to may require some sacrifice on your part, something you will feel good about. Some old associations may dissolve, to be replaced by ones you consider more meaningful. Less happily, you could be drawn into groups where drugs or insidious influences are the basis of the association. You may discover such "toxic" influences as subtle manipulation and sabotage. Generally, however, this contact provides opportunity and inspiration, not difficulty. Key events will arise on or near February 2, May 19, August 8, and October 26.

If you were born from April 9 to 21, Saturn's final months in Cancer will bear special significance. You've had two years to observe and learn from others as they experience a restructuring of emotion and intimacy in some area of their lives. Now it's your turn to experience this in your home and private life—the area ruled by your solar Fourth House. The challenges related to this contact became more intense in November 2004, and they will continue on the same trajectory through March 21. Resolution will come swiftly after that, and the pressure will release in mid-July. You may be finding now that you feel "heavier" than usual, more burdened by the obligations in your life. You may be concerned about having the things you consider essential—a safe and pleasant home, a secure job, or emotional fulfillment. Someone or something at home may be requiring your focus or presence, and this is not necessarily a bad thing. For instance, you may have decided to embark on a home improvement project that demands your hard work, or you may be a new parent, bursting with the joys—and demands—that a new infant brings. Whatever draws your attention inward, attending to it now promises future rewards. You'll experience Saturnian events around January 13 and March 21.

If you were born from April 11 to 14, Pluto has its eye on you, but in a kindly way. Chances are, you've been feeling a powerful force within you, drawing you in a new direction that now must be heeded. You may feel yourself imbued with new inspiration based on uncovering long-buried ideals and realizing anew how important they are to you. You may find yourself exposed to new ways of thinking about the world through travel or study—something that brings you in contact with completely new perspectives. You may find that your old way of seeing things has been "stood on its head," and that you are now on the inside looking out. This will change your path accordingly, but it does not follow that it will be in a dramatic or difficult way. It is more likely to flow with grace and enthusiasm from your heart in a way that will dovetail with the path you are already following. The more you can get a sense of what path you are on—and that you are on a path in the first place—the more you will be in tune with Pluto's song. You will probably have the opportunity to take on a greater task than you have in the past—one with more responsibility and power than previously. You will empower yourself if you dare to dream in the loftiest terms, for those are the realms that Pluto inhabits. As long as you serve a higher purpose instead of yourself, you will use this energy well. A pattern of events related to the things Pluto symbolizes will occur on or near March 26, June 13, September 2, and December 15.

Aries/January

Planetary Hotspots

The spotlight is on home and career this month, Aries, and you may feel like you're in survival mode as Saturn and Chiron assume center stage. Patterns that emerged on November 12 last year are now demanding your attention around January 13. Illness could be a factor, especially if you've been living on the skinny branches, and it could be more serious than just a passing cold. Take care of yourself.

Wellness and Keeping Fit

Health is on everyone's mind near mid-month, what with the latest viral threat being at its peak, and you need to be more cautious than usual. There are extraordinary pressures on you mid-month, and they will challenge your immune system. Any health imbalances that lurk below the radar can surface on the screen at that time and seriously side-track you just when you least need it. Sleep; eat; be less merry.

Love and Life Connections

With Mars contacting Pluto on January 28, the potential exists for explosive relationship situations. While such experiences will have their seeds in the past, they will essentially be new and need to be looked at with fresh eyes. There is a lot of positive potential here— educational prospects, travel, reaching your goals—if you can avoid overreacting over whatever emerges around this time.

Finance and Success

As the Sun arcs through your solar Tenth House, this seems like a time to shine in your career, but you may think that your personal life is holding you back. "If only" doesn't count. Do what you can with what you have, and accept your current limitations with grace. After March 21, things will improve.

Rewarding Days

7, 8, 11, 12, 15, 16, 20, 21, 25, 26

Challenging Days

2, 3, 4, 9, 10, 22, 23, 24, 30, 31

Aries/February

Planetary Hotspots

Whether it's business or personal, partnership is the special feature in this month's entertainment as Jupiter is emphasized in your solar Seventh House. If you enjoy a competitive edge with this significant other, the balance of wins and losses between you may be shifting in some way. You may feel inspired and challenged this month to work toward altruistic goals, especially within the groups you belong to. You'll be committing yourself in these areas around February 2 and 25.

Wellness and Keeping Fit

If for some reason you have the lingering aftereffects of illness left over from last month, they could come back to bite you toward the end of the month. Stay on your antibiotics until the end, and continue to seek treatment until symptoms are completely gone. Resume your physical fitness routine only when you feel robust.

Love and Life Connections

As Jupiter and the eclipses highlight your solar Seventh House, there's never been a more important year for relationships in your life, Aries. The events you experience around February 1 are key. You could feel someone slipping away from you, heading off into the sunset or just actively involved in pursuing success. Or this could simply be a time of extra challenges, but in a good way. Any setbacks will be overcome by early June.

Finance and Success

Don't let someone else's "get rich quick" scheme hook you—you will be a little more vulnerable than usual around February 2 as the Sun contacts Neptune in your Eleventh House of acquaintances. It will be a fine month for making new contacts, but commitments are better put off until after February 5.

Rewarding Days
3, 4, 7, 8, 11, 12, 13, 15, 16, 21, 22

Challenging Days
5, 6, 18, 19, 20, 26, 27

Aries/March

Planetary Hotspots

All that hard work begins to show results after mid-month, as Saturn is favorably highlighted. Whatever you've been working on since last July is now coming to fruition. It's good the pressure's off at home, because it's heating up elsewhere. Pluto's grabbing the focus from your solar Ninth House, increasing your passion for reaching goals and highlighting ways in which you feel confined. It's time to go for freedom, whatever that means for you!

Wellness and Keeping Fit

Your health is more stable than it's been so far this year, but you still need to take care of yourself. However, Mercury turns retrograde in your solar First House on March 19, once again emphasizing your health and well-being. This is not as serious as the planetary events of January and February, but the pressure will be on you to perform in some way. If you listen to your body and respond to what it tells you, you will not suffer any setbacks.

Love and Life Connections

You'll figure out that your relationships need to go through adjustments this month, and you may end up having to eat crow. It never hurts to apologize, especially if you're responsible. Even if you're not, an apology for *something* opens the door to reconciliation.

Finance and Success

Early in the month, relationship, home, and career collide in a critical mass, but it's short-lived—a crescendo of awfulness before the release that relaxes most, if not all, of the tension. Finally, you'll be freer to go after the gold, even if it means long hours at the office.

Rewarding Days

3, 4, 7, 8, 11, 12, 15, 16, 17, 20, 21, 22, 30, 31

Challenging Days

5, 6, 18, 19, 25, 26, 27

Aries/April

Planetary Hotspots

Relationship tensions reach their peak around April 3 as Jupiter and the eclipses spotlight your interactions with others. You may feel torn between your own plans and direction and that of others important to you. Negotiation is the key, and perhaps a little sacrifice. The tension will die down after April 12, but if you haven't dealt with the underlying situation it will come back again later.

Wellness and Keeping Fit

You can finally get back to your normal diet, sleep, and exercise routine, and you may be tempted to cut corners in these areas. After the health challenges you've faced so far this year, maybe it's time for a new normal, including adjustments that will prevent such incursions into your well-being in the future. At first, it may be difficult to adjust, because you have so much to pay attention to this month, but after a few weeks you'll have the pattern established.

Love and Life Connections

The changes you're contemplating in your routine and lifestyle inevitably involve those close to you. If you stop eating junk food, you're also asking those at home not to serve it, or perhaps not to eat it at all. This can cause upheaval, albeit healthy, in others' lives in addition to your own. The drag this places on your own progress is only temporary—they'll get used to it in time as you stick with the new program.

Finance and Success

Blessedly, this part of your life is on autopilot this month. With Venus in your Second House of personal finance, you are on an even keel—perhaps even quite content with your bottom line.

Rewarding Days

3, 4, 7, 8, 12, 13, 17, 18, 26, 27, 30

Challenging Days

1, 2, 14, 15, 16, 22, 23, 28, 29

Aries/May

Planetary Hotspots

Groups and organizations require more focus this month, perhaps in challenging ways, as both Chiron and Neptune increase the heat in your solar Eleventh House. You may find yourself taking on a new project or task to enhance the effectiveness or activities of the group—some project that goes right to the core of a key difficulty the group faces. It may feel like a fool's errand, but you are the ideal candidate for the role because of your willingness to pioneer new efforts, even if they are unpopular.

Wellness and Keeping Fit

With all the attention coming your way, it could be overwhelming if you're one of the shy Aries types. Either way, pressures continue, and your health could still be at risk while Mars transits your solar Twelfth House. Give yourself a break: make a conscious effort to relax, and spend some time working in the background, where your focus will not be fragmented by others vying for your time and skills.

Love and Life Connections

It's time to lighten up and enjoy the companionship of others in an inquisitive way. Explore the world around you: take in a museum or play, go shopping together. Brothers and sisters may feature prominently at this time.

Finance and Success

The most important factor in our success is our contacts and associations with others, and it is particularly true this month. If you invest time and interest in your relationships with colleagues and business associates, as well as professional organizations, you can take best advantage of the prevailing planetary winds.

Rewarding Days

1, 5, 6, 9, 10, 14, 15, 23, 24, 25, 28, 29

Challenging Days

11, 12, 13, 19, 20, 26, 27

Aries/June

Planetary Hotspots

Jupiter, Pluto, and Uranus each have something important to say in June. At the same time, your efforts at fulfilling personal goals—perhaps including education and travel—are demanding more of your time as the efforts you put in since mid-December begin to bear fruit. On the other hand, new situations mean new dilemmas as they collide with old ways of doing things. Around June 14 you'll become acutely aware of something that needs your attention and raises issues of principle, and you'll benefit from the application of forethought and wisdom.

Wellness and Keeping Fit

You could be accident-prone this month or experience headaches and inflammations as Mars travels through your solar First House. Cooling exercises—and a cool head—will override these tendencies.

Love and Life Connections

After four months of adjusting your role and the give-and-take of your significant relationships, a new balance has been reached. After June 5 you'll feel like you can breath easier, but that doesn't mean you can relax into old patterns. Continue to honor the changes that have been so hard-won.

Finance and Success

You'll need extra effort to fulfill tasks that work toward building a better future for yourself, but it has never been better timed. The planets give their full support, especially around June 13, even if they also present a quandary. A time of great challenge is also a time of great potential.

Rewarding Days

1, 2, 5, 6, 7, 10, 11, 12, 20, 21, 24, 25, 28, 29

Challenging Days

8, 9, 15, 16, 17, 22, 23

Aries/July

Planetary Hotspots

Saturn enters Leo on July 16, relieving the pressure on your home and private life. This is also one more step out of obscurity after a few years of being overlooked. It's had its advantages, though, because fewer people noticing you has meant you could work unhindered toward your objectives. You may notice a shift almost immediately; others will seem to suddenly realize how talented you are and give you something to do, especially around July 22. While you may prefer to avoid it, it's time to start giving back to others after this time of inward preparation and relative protection.

Wellness and Keeping Fit

You're back to your old high energy level now, and enjoying the benefits of the new approach you're taking to your health. July will be a time of continued stability, although children's health issues may be in the picture.

Love and Life Connections

Children and romantic ties assume center stage, especially from July 21 to 31, as a series of contacts suggest a need to focus on this area of your chart. You may feel overtaxed by others' needs, but fortunately you have the strength to manage it this time.

Finance and Success

Spending may go up in response to a situation that arises at the end of the month. This is a temporary state of affairs, however, and to be expected from time to time as a part of life's flux and flow.

Rewarding Days

3, 4, 8, 9, 17, 18, 21, 22, 25, 26, 27, 30, 31

Challenging Days

5, 6, 7, 13, 14, 19, 20

Aries/August

Planetary Hotspots

The gap between your ideals and reality may become apparent around August 8, especially in your social world. Your role in groups and organizations needs to be adjusted to mesh with the demands of your personal life. On August 31, new insights come to light which will help you deal with all issues that arise in your life. It has to do with your perspective and attitude. A subtle change in the way you approach anything that comes up is the easiest, yet most profound, way to get the results you want.

Wellness and Keeping Fit

If you haven't stayed on top of the health issues that arose in January, they will rear their ugly heads around the end of the month. A pre-emptive strike early in the month—or better yet, remaining true to your new regimen throughout the year—will ensure the best experience this month.

Love and Life Connections

Issues with young people clear up after August 15, and if you've handled the situation well, everyone has learned something. You've learned to give a little more, while they've learned to expect a little less. It doesn't hurt to take a little time off this month to enjoy yourself and spend time with friends.

Finance and Success

Everything is status quo at work—enough so that you can get away for at least a few days. You'll probably fare better if you plan such happy events to occur between August 15 and 30. Don't let what happens in your extended business circle affect your self-esteem. If you assert your values around August 28, your assertions may fall on deaf ears, but later the value of what you say will sink in.

Rewarding Days
4, 5, 14, 15, 18, 19, 22, 23, 26, 27, 28, 31

Challenging Days
1, 2, 3, 9, 10, 16, 17, 29, 30

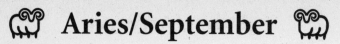 Aries/September

Planetary Hotspots

Hard on the heels of August's month-end surprise, Pluto dishes out its rewards for your efforts of the past nine months. You've seen progress in reaching your goals, perhaps completing educational or travel objectives as well. The fulfillment continues after the release on September 2.

Wellness and Keeping Fit

This is a great month to give your lifestyle choices an extra perusal. Get a thorough physical examination—a good annual habit, because while the Sun is in this house (which it is every year at this time) your symptoms will be front and center where they can be detected and addressed. Massage treatments, acupuncture, or any other method you can use to boost your body's strength will be especially valuable. Along the way you may discover that some of your habits need changing in order to improve or maintain your current well-being.

Love and Life Connections

Relationships flow more smoothly all month long, especially if you make the effort to think of the other person and what he or she is experiencing. Consistent effort will show him or her that you mean what you say.

Finance and Success

The training and experience you gain now will feed your career later, so don't skimp in trying to accomplish what you think will work best for you. After September 11 monies come in which you have been waiting for, and you'll need them, as financial needs will arise—perhaps unexpectedly—by the end of the month.

Rewarding Days
1, 2, 10, 11, 14, 15, 18, 19, 22, 23, 24, 27, 28, 29

Challenging Days
5, 6, 7, 12, 13, 25, 26

Aries/October

Planetary Hotspots
After the relative calm of September, October is full of action and distraction. Mars and Chiron are spotlighted early in the month, while Neptune's subtle softening of circumstances will be felt around October 26. A solar eclipse draws your attention to relationships once again on October 3, while a lunar eclipse does the same on October 17.

Wellness and Keeping Fit
Despite all the pressures on you this month, if you've done your work where health is concerned you'll sail through this time unscathed. Just try to be gentle on yourself if you're stressed out: eat well and get lots of sleep.

Love and Life Connections
The big push is on in your relationships, including those with close associates at work, especially around October 3 and 17. Even if it seems like it's about the work, it's not. Everything has a personal side to it, and thinking of it in those terms will help you understand what's really going on so you can address the real problem. With the eclipses involved, it will take time to completely remedy the situations that arise, but that means you also *have* time. Don't panic and think it's all over.

Finance and Success
You're feeling financial pressures these days as expenditures exceed income. If you've been saving money for such times as these, it's no big deal. But if your savings account reflects too much of a "live for today" attitude, you'll be more challenged to manage what arises. The issues you experience may be ongoing through mid-December, slowly dissipating after that.

Rewarding Days
7, 8, 11, 12, 13, 16, 17, 20, 21, 25, 26

Challenging Days
2, 3, 4, 9, 10, 22, 23, 24, 30, 31

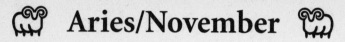 Aries/November

Planetary Hotspots

Mars is creating intensity in everyone's life, but nowhere more than in your Second House of personal finance. You may discover that you've been your own worst enemy when it comes to spending. It's time to pull in the reins big-time and handle some of those expenditures that aren't fun but necessary. Mercury assumes a greater profile when it turns retrograde on November 14, signaling a need for attention to your aspirations and principles. You may find travel to unfamiliar places difficult between then and December 3. On November 22, Saturn gives you feedback on the added responsibilities you'll be expected to handle over the coming five months—issues to do with children, creativity, risk-taking activities, and romance.

Wellness and Keeping Fit

Around November 15 you'll get a progress report on how you're doing with potential long-term health issues. Even if you're not getting a check-up at this time, your body will do the talking. If you've been sticking to your healthier regimen, the messages will be good.

Love and Life Connections

If relationship concerns arise, it will be with your kids or romantic partner, as Saturn is emphasizing activity in your solar Fifth House. Now is the time to take a constructive attitude about what needs to change, whether it is within you or in the objects of your affections (probably both). Taking the long, slow route of gradual progress, proving your intentions with actions, not words, is the most effective now.

Finance and Success

You may be tempted by an offer that comes in around November 7. If it seems too good to be true, that's because it is. You could be conned around this date, so waiting a few days will clarify the situation and make it easier to see beneath the surface.

Rewarding Days

3, 4, 5, 8, 9, 12, 13, 16, 17, 18, 21, 22, 23

Challenging Days

6, 7, 19, 20, 26, 27

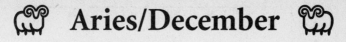 # Aries/December

Planetary Hotspots
Mercury's direct communication with you about what you need to repair and remedy ends on December 3, and the pressure Mars has put on your finances is relieved after December 9. With Pluto's new yearly cycle starting on December 15, the feel of new beginnings is in the air. By dreaming big, you'll be able to maximize the benefits you gain from each of these planets.

Wellness and Keeping Fit
Your health should hold up this month, in spite of the pressures that lie elsewhere in your life. Stick to your exercise routine, perhaps softening it when your emotions run high. Sleep is Aries's secret ingredient to maintaining strength—the thing you need most and are most willing to forego when stresses are high.

Love and Life Connections
Discipline is the key to success in your relationships this month, but it is much more effective when exerted on yourself instead of others. If you don't practice what you preach, those you are trying to influence will not be swayed—even your own children. The most effective parent is one who sets the example he or she wants the kids to follow. On December 24 Venus begins a six-week sojourn in retrograde motion, bringing focus on your role in groups. The question is, do your values match theirs?

Finance and Success
Lack of discipline could cost you this month, especially around December 17. On December 5 a planetary event that also occurred on June 25 will bring back something unresolved from that time, perhaps causing a large cash outlay either into or out of your pocket.

Rewarding Days
1, 2, 5, 6, 9, 10, 14, 15, 18, 19, 20, 28, 29

Challenging Days
3, 4, 16, 17, 23, 24, 30, 31

Aries Action Table

These dates reflect the best—but not the only—times for success and ease in these activities, according to your Sun sign.

	JAN	FEB	MAR	APR	MAY	JUN	JUL	AUG	SEPT	OCT	NOV	DEC
Move						11-28	6, 7					
Start a class					28-31	1-11						
Join a club	30, 31	1-16										
Ask for a raise		2-26	22-31	1-15								
Look for work	10-30								4-31	1-8		
Get pro advice	24, 30, 31	26, 27	25-27	21-23	19, 20	15-17	13, 14	9, 10	5-7	2-4, 30, 31	26, 27	23-25
Get a loan	5, 6	1, 2, 28	1, 2, 28, 29	24, 25	21, 22	18, 19	15, 16	11-13	8, 9	5, 6	1, 2, 28-30	26, 27
See a doctor		16-28	1-31	1-30	1-12				4-30	1-8		
Start a diet									4-20			
End relationship			25-27									
Buy clothes						28-30	1-23	16-31	1-4			
Get a makeover			5-31	1-30	1-12							
New romance						28-30	1-23	4, 5				
Vacation	1-10	3, 4	3, 4, 30, 31	26, 27	23-25	20, 21	17, 18	14, 15	10, 11	7-31	1-26	1, 2, 12-31

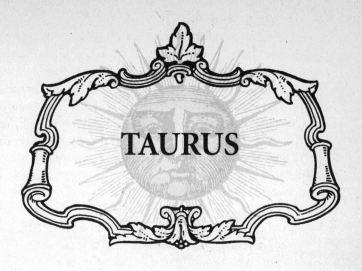

TAURUS

The Bull
April 19 to May 20

Element:	Earth
Quality:	Fixed
Polarity:	Yin/Feminine
Planetary Ruler:	Venus
Meditation:	I trust myself and others.
Gemstone:	Emerald
Power Stones:	Diamond, blue lace agate, rose quartz
Key Phrase:	I have
Glyph:	Bull's head
Anatomy:	Throat, neck
Color:	Green
Animal:	Cattle
Myths/Legends:	Isis and Osiris, Cerridwen, Bull of Minos
House:	Second
Opposite Sign:	Scorpio
Flower:	Violet
Key Word:	Conservation

Your Ego's Strengths and Shortcomings

Taurus, you're as strong and steady as your elemental counterpart, the Earth. Just like the planet we live on, you are enduring, patient, and bear all that is put upon you. You are a source of energy, fertility, and abundance. If you are drawn to gardening or nurturing growing things, it is because you are dedicated to all developmental processes. You want to help things grow, heal, and improve. Sometimes you express your earthy nature by building and beautifying. Whether you are decorating a home, designing a web page, sewing a dress, or putting in cabinets, you have an eye for what can be improved to meet people's needs more completely. Far from frivolous, your ameliorations always have a practical side. You may often hear words like "sensible" and "patient" used to describe you, because these are also qualities associated with this element.

On a deep level, you are motivated to keep things as they are—to conserve, preserve, hold steady, or create things that last. This ties in with your element's nature, which is to remain still and provide support. This can be unbalancing in extreme form, for sustaining steadiness can become stubborn immobility. You can get stuck in a rut, unable to change. It's important to keep moving and to realize that change is fundamental to life. When something has worked for a long time, it doesn't mean that it will be good forever—in fact, it's probably overdue for updating. You need others in your life to spur you to action and create the inspiration you need to undertake the next project. However, if you're not an idea person, you are the heart of any undertaking, since without you the bulk of the work would not get done. It's important for you to watch your moods and stay physically active. When you become immobile for too long the weaknesses of your earthy side may take over. You could become depressed, listless, and mired in old ways of thinking. By exposing yourself to new ideas and active people you will find it easier to maintain your elemental balance. It will also help to focus on your inner feeling of beauty and harmony and strive to make every step you take an expression of that harmony.

Shining Your Love Light

Your steadiness is a great asset to any relationship, but just as you withstand its ups and downs with strength and loyalty, so it takes you time to be convinced that a partnership is worth such steadfast devotion. It may take time for you to prepare yourself for a partnership, but when you're ready, you're there with all your heart and soul, and it is just as difficult to shake you loose. No matter where you are with your relationships, it's important to let your partner know where you are in the process of growing and changing so that he or she knows something is happening.

With Aries to spark you, you can create great things together— just be sure to value your fiery friend's vigor, even if you don't always keep up. A fellow Taurus will be easy to understand, and you'll be of one mind about how to approach life. Gemini will draw you out and get you to express yourself socially and verbally, but don't forget to contribute your valuable common sense. Cancer's warmth and need for emotional security will be easy to understand—the perfect blend for a long-term bond. Leo will challenge and perhaps irritate you with his apparent self-involvement, but then his unaffected generosity and enthusiasm will warm your heart. You'll feel well understood by Virgo, whose capability and "can-do" way of life provides the perfect support for your own efforts. Libra has a special attunement to beauty, just as you do, and together you can create great harmony if you recognize the value of her more abstract ways of expressing it. Scorpio reveals your shadow side by showing you the need for decay and destruction in order to build and grow. Together you can fulfill the cycle of life: death and rebirth. Sagittarius will lighten your step and lead you into untrammeled new territories of world and culture. Capricorn adds the statesman to your architectural inclinations—you can make great designs of grand scale, even if only in your own lives. You may be uneasy with Aquarius's eccentricities until you try them on and see how much fun they can be, and how they bring you a new objectivity. Pisces brings out your sensitive side by helping you see the inner, energetic world, while you provide essential pragmatism.

Making Your Place in the World

With your steadfastness and practicality, you are well suited to many career paths. One of the most successful may be in working with money and finance, whether in banking, brokering, financial planning, accounting, or trading. If your interests run more to the world of three dimensions, you may find your niche in a construction trade (such as carpentry, framing, or masonry), architecture and design, or gardening and horticulture. Fine crafts could also attract you, from art restoration, weaving, and dress and costume design to sewing, or needlework. You will generally tend to feel more comfortable in positions where your income is a known factor and is given to you in predictable ways and regular intervals. However, this can be a stumbling block to reaching for higher income levels; if you are willing to accept a little more risk and sporadic tendencies in the timing of your paychecks, you will be more financially successful.

Putting Your Best Foot Forward

To be at your best, Taurus, you need to loosen up. This does not mean you should become less precise in what you do, but rather become more adventuresome. First, you will benefit by learning to handle risk. Risk is all in the eye of the beholder: what seems risky to you now may seem stodgy and conventional to others. What we don't understand appears risky; so new ideas, ventures, and projects may seem to introduce an unacceptably high risk level into your life. However, once you understand what's involved, know the procedures and protocols, acquire the skills and support, and lay your foundation, your tasks will be achievable without triggering high levels of insecurity in you. Second, you may literally need to loosen up; do some stretching—yoga, ballet, or calisthenics. When our body is inflexible we feel less able to deal with what comes up in the course of our daily activities. If your body is supple your mind will be more supple too. Third, you will be more successful in all life's avenues if you loosen up your attitude. Become more open to possibilities, think in terms of choices when newness is on the menu. Let yourself explore novel ideas and experiences, and give yourself the time you need to adjust and to make the right decision when a choice confronts you. Even in small decisions we establish a subtle atmosphere of openness or closed-ness that has an effect the next time a choice comes up. If we are more adventuresome—even a little—it opens doorways of potential that may seem inconsequential at first but will eventually result in expanded awareness and options.

Tools for Change

One of the most important things you can do in your life is to keep yourself moving and fluid. As an earth sign this is not natural, but movement is the natural antidote for becoming too fixed and limited. It is important, above all, that you find pleasure in the activities you choose. This means having a handful of options from which you choose on any given day. It is helpful if you have a schedule or routine to use as a guideline. That way you don't get caught in the trap of having to think about whether you want to exercise today—if you have the energy, or if you're too busy, or if there's enough time before your next commitment, etc. It doesn't matter what type of exercise routine you develop, as long as it's not the same thing every day. It's important to vary your pattern of muscle use so that you are stretching your body's capacity. Another technique you can use to overcome a typical Taurean trap is to vary your routine in life as well. It's okay to have a schedule and stick to it for the most part. Living in a rhythm allows us to get more done more efficiently. However, consistency should not become constriction; your life should be flexible enough to permit spontaneous activities. This means not scheduling every minute of your day, nor overcommitting yourself to any activity, whether it's work, family, or your latest project. The key is balance and moderation. Finally, as you go through the types of changes required in your life now, it's important to be generous with others. Even in times of relative lack there is something you can give without unbalancing yourself, and this brings you into the world of interdependence on others. When you give to others you will also feel more comfortable relying on them in times of need. As you go through the inevitable changes that arise, you will find this of critical importance. Broadening your mind is an important focus for you right now as well, and that can be enhanced by taking classes. This will get your social, as well as your mental, circulation going.

Affirmation for the Year

I am flexible in body, mind, and soul.

The Year Ahead for Taurus

You've put in years of hard work, and you're about to emerge into the light because of it. It starts with Jupiter, which spends most of the year in Libra and your solar Sixth House. You'll find it easy to get your life in order. You're optimistic about getting everything done, turning over a new leaf in the way you handle your health, work, and daily routines. You may focus on habits that aren't in your best interest and choose this time to eradicate them, particularly in the area of health and diet. Generally your health will be good, but that doesn't mean that you can ignore it or indulge in excesses because previous aches and pains have gone away. After October 24 you'll begin to be noticed—that's when Jupiter enters Scorpio and your solar Seventh House. You can expect your work to be recognized as an effort worthy of praise over the next three years, and relationships blossom as well.

You'll feel a shift in mid-July as Saturn changes signs from Cancer to Leo. Before that time, while Saturn is in Cancer, you'll continue to focus on restructuring your ways of thinking, connecting, and communicating. You may have discovered some shortcomings in your way of communicating with others, and developed a more thoughtful style. Once Saturn enters Leo on July 16 you may feel drawn inward. You are examining your level of fulfillment in your personal life; things that seemed acceptable before feel less bearable, and now you want to change them. It's best to acknowledge whatever you are feeling and begin steps toward the alterations you need to make your life deeper and more meaningful.

Chiron is moving across the top of your chart now and will make the shift from your solar Ninth House to your solar Tenth House when it moves from Capricorn to Aquarius. The last four years have been a time of preparation, perhaps understanding how you need to "tweak" your life plan. You may find that the pursuit of material comfort and wealth is not enough to make you happy—you need a sense that your efforts are improving the world as well. This year, you can begin to create the opportunities you need to see that realization manifested positively in your career or calling.

Uranus has been waking you up to the power of your social and professional contacts for the past two years, and this process continues throughout 2005. You may find yourself more outgoing now, as you see that the power of your relationships with others can make your life richer and more enjoyable, as well as help you reach career goals. In examining the groups you spend your time with, you may find it necessary to shift emphasis, backing off in one affiliation while putting more energy in another. You may want to break away from some of your associations altogether, because you are looking for more depth than they offer.

Neptune is traveling through your solar Tenth House for yet another year and leading you to continue your quest for deeper meaning in your career. You want to feel connected, to work in an environment that is friendly rather than cold and competitive. As is possible with Neptune, you may find that the work that you once did is changing out from under you, dissolving in response to the changes in the surrounding world. If so, it is important to be attuned to those changes and to watch for your opportunity to make alterations yourself.

Pluto is driving through your solar Eighth House, which rules the aspects of life and society that have the power to change us— money, unconscious influences, and death among them. Since 1995 Pluto has been slowly transforming your relationship with the outer world and the way in which you draw its resources to you. If you have mismanaged that relationship, you may have too much debt, or poor prospects for meeting your financial goals. Since clinging to the past only makes the change more difficult, take a deep breath and then begin the steps you need to develop true stability.

The eclipses are finally about to leave you alone, after two years of changes that have affected you personally while they were in Taurus and Scorpio. Your personal life as well as your relationships have gone through surprising plot twists to put you on a new, more stable plateau. Now you can cultivate your inner life, in spiritual contemplation or just "in your cave," as the eclipse points move through Aries and Libra, your Sixth and Twelfth Houses.

If you were born from April 19 to May 2, Saturn in Leo is making waves in your life this year from your solar Fourth House. Your home, inner emotional life, family—anything you consider private—will require more care and closer examination over the year beginning July 16. At that time, you're likely to awaken to the importance of something in your life that perhaps you've been putting off. Now it's time to face the music, and if you do, rewards will eventually be yours for your efforts. It is likely that you've been holding on to something or someone too tightly, and you may be stifling both yourself and your loved one. This is a burden for you as well as for him or her. It is also possible that someone else is holding on to you more than you want, and it may be necessary for you to work it through with that person. Someone may be ill, the home may need repairs, or we may suddenly become fascinated by our heritage and spend hours on the Internet researching our ancestry. Whatever it is, we are likely to feel pressured to carry on with our previous obligations, especially those that draw us out of the home. It may be desirable to cut away some other activities or responsibilities to lighten your load in order to maintain health and happiness during this time. Related events will occur around January 13 and March 21.

If you were born from April 22 to May 1, the impulse to light up your life with new and unusual social ties may fill you. This is because Uranus is contacting your Sun from your solar Eleventh House of group affiliations. You may have felt this building up—a need to free yourself of old ties that don't work for you anymore. Now, as the contact becomes exact, you can see what you need: a deeper connection with the people you spend time with. You're paying more attention to the inner purpose of a group and how well the group is fulfilling that purpose. You are looking for an alignment of goals with actions—a reflection of what you are searching for in your own life. You're less willing to suffer fools, and you may be more comfortable attending meetings without belonging, or even representing a "rebel faction" in a group. You could become a member of the loyal opposition in an effort to improve its efforts to serve its membership. As long as you don't blind yourself to the alienation that you may create in the process, keep on with your efforts at reform, both in your own life and the organizations you belong to. Key events will occur on or near February 25, June 14, August 31, and November 15.

If you were born from May 3 to 8, you have reached an important juncture in your career life as Neptune reaches the degree of your Sun from your solar Tenth House. You may have noticed changes occurring in your work environment: your industry or company may be shifting, even dissolving around you. Your job may be changing: perhaps work is shifting away from you and your position has become less relevant, or you're finding that more sacrifice is required. Most importantly, however, you may feel disenchanted or disillusioned with what you've been doing. You may be more willing to examine the effects that the company or business has in the world around you, positive or negative, and less able to ignore your own feelings of fulfillment or lack thereof. Neptune leads us to look for something deeper and more spiritual, to do good in addition to doing well. You may be willing to make sacrifices of income or status in order to take a job that holds more meaning for you. You may become involved in artistic, healing, or helping professions, or focus more on the humanistic side of the business you already know. No matter what new truths you discover inside yourself, this is the year to make changes in response to them. A progression of events important to this process will arise near February 2, May 19, August 8, and October 26.

If you were born from May 9 to 20, Saturn in Cancer will make a harmonious contact with your Sun from your solar Third House. Since Saturn helps us identify weaknesses in our nature, you may have decided over the past two years that you needed more training in some capacity, and you should be near the completion of that effort now. You could be preparing yourself in some way for new career or business successes through outreach or communication, or even through writing your magnum opus for publication. No matter what surface form your efforts take, on the inner level you are learning how your thoughts limit your life and keep you from being free to make the best choices for yourself. You may be getting a new perspective on what your possibilities are, even if it's coming from regrets over past choices. Whatever the stimulus, there's no time like the present to change. This is one of the easiest areas in which to transform our lives, because the changes involve a simple shift in perspective—perhaps all that is needed for true happiness. Through this realization you may be recognizing how rigidity curtails your emotional fulfillment, and you may wish to express your revelation to those in your personal world in order to develop greater intimacy. Key dates for the final resolution of these issues are January 13 and March 21, with substantial relaxation of tension regarding these issues when Saturn enters Leo on July 16.

If you were born from May 12 to 15, Pluto is making contact with your Sun from your solar Eighth House. The time of transformation is finally upon you, after several years of feeling it bubble within. It may come to you in several ways simultaneously, possibly because you've uncovered a core problem in your life that needs a complete revolution and will turn your life upside down. While ultimately this is a spiritual change, it may come to you through your finances, or even through the loss of something or someone you hold dear. This is not necessarily bad or even unpleasant, but you may experience sadness because you are accustomed to the way things were. You may also fear the newness because it is unfamiliar and you don't like the risk that changes involve. As with all transformation, you will have to spend time in an undefined, ambiguous reality as you transition from old to new. You may unconsciously cling to the old form to avoid this feeling of chaotic unboundedness, but that will only make the transition more difficult. By focusing on your goals and being willing to endure temporary uncertainty, you will make the most of this time. March 26, June 13, September 2, and December 15 bring critical turning points.

Taurus/January

Planetary Hotspots

You'll be back in the saddle right away after the holidays as activities you committed yourself to last July become more demanding. You may feel overwhelmed as Saturn's yearly cycle reaches its peak on January 13, and communications assume especial importance—from a book you're working on to catching up on back orders. On January 16 you begin a new Chiron cycle in your solar Ninth House by noticing what is missing in your life as you search for a deeper sense of purpose.

Wellness and Keeping Fit

You can greatly enhance your health by being generally more active. More than just developing an exercise routine (which is good), just giving yourself a chance to walk across the parking lot or to climb the stairs rather than taking the elevator is the way to increase the energy circulating throughout your body. From a trimmer physique to a more alert mind, you'll benefit tremendously.

Love and Life Connections

Although obligations call, this is also a good month to get away from it all. It doesn't mean that you have to be alone, only that you need to be in a place and with people where you can replenish yourself and recharge your batteries. Even if you can't get away, don't feel obligated to spend time with people you don't want to be around.

Finance and Success

You're generally in a preparatory period right now, getting ready for the day, not too far off, when you will be called upon to fulfill obligations cast for you by others. The demands placed on you will be greater as you approach the end of the month, so put in your time on your personal projects and catch-up work before January 27, because after that time you'll be more visible to others.

Rewarding Days

1, 9, 10, 13, 14, 17, 18, 19, 22, 23, 27, 28, 29

Challenging Days

5, 6, 11, 12, 25, 26

Taurus/February

Planetary Hotspots

The early part of the month is full of activity, as Jupiter emphasizes your Sixth House of work, health, and habits around February 1; a new yearly Neptune cycle begins on February 2, bringing your dreams and visions of the ideal career to light. On February 25, Uranus awakens you to the ways you can break free of social convention when its yearly cycle starts in your Eleventh House.

Wellness and Keeping Fit

The amount of work you attempt to complete on a daily basis has more impact on your health than almost anything else, which is why these two areas of life are symbolized by the Sixth House. As Jupiter travels here, you will do well to be careful about how much you take on, since Jupiter's motto is "Only too much is enough."

Love and Life Connections

Your associations with others—particularly groups, organizations, and colleagues—are highlighted from February 16. As February 25 approaches you will be rethinking the ways in which you are affiliated with these groups, and you may even be thinking of giving up some of your memberships or obligations to them. When you think about it, other associations may be more useful to you now.

Finance and Success

With Jupiter emphasized in your house of work, you may feel overwhelmed by your workload. To overcome this, you can do two things. First, let those who are responsible for giving you the work know that you have too much to do and ask them what they want to you do first. Second, you can, if it is within your power, delegate tasks to others. If there is a question about how much work you should be able to do, it never hurts to document exactly what you are doing to dispel any sense that you are not pulling your weight.

Rewarding Days

5, 6, 9, 10, 14, 15, 18, 19, 20, 23, 24, 25

Challenging Days

1, 2, 7, 8, 21, 22, 28

Taurus/March

Planetary Hotspots

Mars creates heat this month as it contacts Jupiter and Saturn on March 3 and 7, respectively, bringing out challenges in the ways you make ideas useful in everyday life. You may simply have too much to do—too much success, producing a near-frenetic activity level. March 19 through 26 are peppered with significant planetary events that will change your perspective and modify the direction of your life, when Mercury, Saturn, and Pluto all change directions.

Wellness and Keeping Fit

A pile-up of worry and a lack of time off could result in you con- tracting a virus around March 19, when Mercury turns retrograde. Plan some time off—not to do some additional activity, but to relax and do nothing. This is the best health palliative for you now.

Love and Life Connections

Issues that have come up with brothers and sisters seem to be on the way out by March 21, and you can let go of your concerns about their well-being.

Finance and Success

In whatever ways you earn your income, those situations may be in a state of slow transformation. You will notice this in particular around March 26, when Pluto draws your attention to changes in your access to other people's money. This can include your partner's income and spending as well. You'll have five months to work out the kinks in the new system, with peak dates on June 13 and Sep- tember 2.

Rewarding Days

5, 6, 9, 10, 14, 15, 18, 19, 20, 23, 24, 25

Challenging Days

1, 2, 7, 8, 21, 22, 28

Taurus/April

Planetary Hotspots

On April 3 you'll reach the halfway point in the yearly Jupiter cycle, which started last September 21. Since then you've put a lot of effort into laying the foundation for future successes, working in the background where you can get the most accomplished. You'll begin to see the light at the end of the tunnel this month, and you'll have the eclipses on April 8 and 24 putting booster jets behind your efforts. Don't expect it to be all smooth sailing, though. Not only do the eclipses raise new issues, but Mercury in retrograde until April 12 will show you the obstacles in your way and how to fix them.

Wellness and Keeping Fit

It remains important to maintain the best of all regimens when it comes to your health, because the pressures to complete a number of initiatives are still high. Resist the temptation to engage in emotional eating in an attempt to de-stress.

Love and Life Connections

After a couple of years of focus on relationships, they stay in the relative background now while your mind is busy with other areas of your life. The exception is the final eclipse in your house of partnerships on April 24, which will allow you to put the finishing touches on changes you've made for the better.

Finance and Success

Around April 13 you may be at the brunt of a drive by someone to "snow" you, perhaps even to undercut your efforts in some way. No reason to be paranoid—only be alert, and don't believe everything you hear or see. Others will see the truth in time, and it's best if you do from the start.

Rewarding Days

1, 2, 5, 6, 9, 10, 11, 14, 15, 16, 19, 20, 21, 28, 29

Challenging Days

3, 4, 17, 18, 24, 25, 30

Taurus/May

Planetary Hotspots

Business, career, and affiliations are highlighted this month as Mars, Chiron, and Neptune are activated in your solar Tenth House. Chiron's change in direction on May 8 brings to your awareness a critical inadequacy in the way you do business or fulfill your career path. If you are to enjoy the best of success, that will need to be overcome. On May 19 your dreams for the future are challenged. You may see a need to modify them in light of new information—the result being a more realistic set of goals and one that suits you better. Mars triggers Uranus on May 15, bringing a surprise to you from the realm of your group associations. This doesn't have to be unpleasant—it could be an award or recognition.

Wellness and Keeping Fit

Every year on your birthday is a time of new beginnings, when your energies are renewed and you feel like starting fresh. You can use this renewed vitality to regenerate your fitness routine. Look critically at what you've been doing: what didn't work should be corrected and what did work can be continued or used as the foundation for the next step.

Love and Life Connections

This month, especially until May 9, is a good time to share your heartfelt emotions with those you care about, as Venus transits your First House of self-expression. When Mercury enters this house on May 12 you can be sure your communications are clear.

Finance and Success

With so much happening in a visible way in your career life, you may be tempted to ignore the parts that need maintenance. Don't forget to massage the clients and associates who continue to give you support; keep the bills paid and the paperwork organized.

Rewarding Days

2, 3, 4, 7, 8, 11, 12, 13, 16, 17, 18, 26, 27, 30, 31

Challenging Days

1, 14, 15, 21, 22, 28, 29

Taurus/June

Planetary Hotspots

Planetary activations occur on June 2, 5, 13, and 14, making June a very busy month for you, Taurus. Mars contacts Pluto on June 2, bringing an explosive issue to the surface, perhaps related to events occurring on January 28. June 5 sees the end of your Jupiter-related expansive efforts in the workplace—perhaps a project is substantially complete now. Events on June 13 and 14 could shake up your sense of foundation, but that doesn't mean it's a bad thing.

Wellness and Keeping Fit

With the spurt of energy and inspiration you're feeling, you could become overeager and overtrain this month, especially after June 11 when Mars enters your solar Twelfth House. Allow your exuberance to play a role in fulfilling your new routine, but don't get carried away. Building slowly will give the best results.

Love and Life Connections

Surprising social events that occurred at the end of February will tie in with those that occur around June 14. If you take note of what occurs now, you will be able to create a more positive outcome in November. Look forward to the turning-point date, August 31.

Finance and Success

Long-term financial difficulties reach critical mass around June 13, and you feel compelled to act. While it may be necessary to take a stand, dragging your heels until the dust settles may help your cause, not hinder it. Look to make a big change, but slowly. You have time to think it through.

Rewarding Days

3, 4, 8, 9, 13, 14, 22, 23, 26, 27, 30

Challenging Days

10, 11, 12, 18, 19, 24, 25

Taurus/July

Planetary Hotspots

The yearly Chiron cycle culminates and a new Saturn cycle begins on July 23. Before then, you'll feel a subtle shift as Saturn moves into Leo and your solar Fourth House. It's time to buckle down and take care of any neglected responsibilities in your home and private life. This will pull you away from your recent focus on career, but it doesn't have to happen immediately. You have three years to carry out your directives here.

Wellness and Keeping Fit

Mercury turns retrograde on July 22 in your Fifth House of games and sports, suggesting that you may be accident-prone when it comes to activities around and for three weeks after that date. The key is not to overdo it or take an inordinately high risk for your fitness level.

Love and Life Connections

Communication lines could get crossed with your romantic partners or children in the latter half of the month as Mercury turns retrograde on July 22. Key to the debate is how to handle the balance between obligations at home and work. You may not be able to remedy the problem right away, but you can at least see it now, and that is the first step toward overcoming it—which you will do in large part over the coming year.

Finance and Success

On July 23 you're turning the corner on the problems that have arisen in career and business, even if it seems like they've only gotten more challenging. Try to breathe deeply and take time away from the responsibilities that face you now. It will be easier to do so after that date.

Rewarding Days

1, 2, 5, 6, 7, 10, 11, 12, 19, 20, 23, 24, 25, 29, 30

Challenging Days

8, 9, 15, 16, 21, 22

Taurus/August

Planetary Hotspots

You could feel disillusioned about your prospects for success and fulfillment in career or business as Neptune's yearly cycle reaches its peak on August 8, but difficulties in your personal life clear up somewhat after August 15, making life more livable. You get an end-of-summer surprise when Uranus is spotlighted on August 31, juicing up your social life.

Wellness and Keeping Fit

Your persistent efforts at improving your habits will begin to show a result after August 15, as Venus enters your solar Sixth House. It's not an invitation to get lazy about your routine, however, because you'll lose ground.

Love and Life Connections

The more time you can find to put into your private life and family relationships, the more satisfied you'll be with the results. You're now entering a three-year period of focus in this area, and it might as well be fun. Bring your attention to what's working, not what isn't, for starters. In that context, you can tackle what's wrong as a group, where everyone's voice is heard. If young children who can't speak for themselves are involved, listen to what their actions tell you.

Finance and Success

You don't have to surrender success in order to please those in your personal life, but you do need to let go a little bit more at work. You've put in a gigantic effort over the past nine months, and now it's time to give back to those who supported you during that time. Chances are you can delegate more than you have in the past, or just say "no." If you have control over the situation, eliminate projects or clients that aren't producing.

Rewarding Days

1, 2, 3, 6, 7, 8, 16, 17, 20, 21, 24, 25, 29, 30

Challenging Days

4, 5, 11, 12, 13, 18, 19, 31

Taurus/September

Planetary Hotspots

The month starts off with a bang, Taurus, as Pluto is highlighted on September 2. You've been working through a financial dilemma whose shape began to unfold last December. With critical events near March 26 and June 13, now there's a relaxation of the tension: you may actually be seeing some hard-fought gains. Although there's still more to accomplish, the wave has crested. As the month unfolds, Mars slows its speed in preparation for its biennial retrograde, this time in your own sign. This suggests a natural period of self-examination and self-correction.

Wellness and Keeping Fit

With Mercury traveling through your Fifth and Sixth Houses, your health and fitness routines rise to the surface of your awareness. You will have the time to regularize your schedule again, after months of being at least occasionally overwhelmed by events.

Love and Life Connections

This is a good month to invest extra time into your romantic relationship. This may surprise your partner, but it certainly won't be unwelcome. If you have a family, this may include more quality time with your children—special events at school, a spontaneous trip to the beach or a museum, or just kicking a soccer ball around together.

Finance and Success

With your financial fires extinguished and Mars highlighted in your own sign, you have time to look at the deeper causes of your current dilemma and ask yourself the hard questions of how to prevent them in the future. If your job situation is unstable, face the music and start looking. Whether you get a new job easily has as much to do with your self-esteem as your skills and the economy, so start by boosting your confidence.

Rewarding Days

3, 4, 12, 13, 16, 17, 20, 21, 25, 26, 30

Challenging Days

1, 2, 8, 9, 14, 15, 27, 28, 29

Taurus/October

Planetary Hotspots

Mars turns retrograde on October 1 for eleven weeks, spotlighting your personal growth and well-being, since it is in your home sign of Taurus. With eclipses on October 3 and 17 drawing focus to your Sixth and Twelfth Houses of health and service to others, you are sure to be looking for ways to improve your physical well-being. Questions about your direction in life move toward resolution, if only by default, when the cycles of Chiron and Neptune move into their final stage on October 5 and 26; yet life springs eternal as a new Jupiter cycle of expansion and enterprise begins on October 22.

Wellness and Keeping Fit

You may be facing some painful truths about your overall health now. It's important, if you haven't done it for a while, to get a thorough physical exam. You could be accident-prone, especially in the early days of the month—a tendency that can be reduced by staying completely focused when engaged in sports, driving, or handling equipment. Tiredness could also be a factor, so get plenty of sleep.

Love and Life Connections

Your relationship life gets a boost on October 25, when Jupiter enters Scorpio for a year's stay in your Seventh House of relationships. You will draw more attention from others and appear more attractive, whether for business or personal partnerships. Opportunities for liaisons will increase and make your life more fruitful in many ways because people bring opportunity with them.

Finance and Success

Now that the fog has cleared, you can see the problem and you want to do something about it. However, now doesn't appear to be the time, and you may feel frustrated. In the meantime, lie low and gather your forces. Waiting will bring good luck.

Rewarding Days

1, 9, 10, 14, 15, 18, 19, 22, 23, 24, 27, 28, 29

Challenging Days

5, 6, 11, 12, 13, 25, 26

Taurus/November

Planetary Hotspots

Your Eleventh House of organizations and groups enters the limelight as Uranus enters the final stage of its yearly cycle on November 15. Meanwhile, on November 14, Mercury's three-week retrograde brings out any further glitches in your ongoing financial renewal process. Family and private matters, which you began working with in mid-July, become critical around November 22, revealing to you the problems that need to be remedied in this inner world.

Wellness and Keeping Fit

You may be called upon to take care of personal matters that pull you away from work around November 7, perhaps even because of an illness or surgery. If you feel that you are compromising your efforts in your career, let go of your fears. You must take care of yourself, and if you can't do that without compromising your job, then the perspectives of both you and your business associates need to change.

Love and Life Connections

Events on the home front may keep you distracted from other activities in your life, especially from November 18 through 22. Whatever occurs at this time reveals a situation that needs work. It could be a home repair, or reparations in a relationship. Perhaps someone is ill at home and needs care. This is the time of maximum effort because the situation is new, and while it can be bewildering because of its unfamiliarity, you will overcome it and reach a new normal.

Finance and Success

With Mercury retrograde in your Eighth House of finances, you may experience cash flow difficulties from about November 10 through December 3. While it adds to your feeling of discomfort, there are ways you can minimize the impact, and in the long run it will be a small blip on the scale of your life, so it's best to see it that way now.

Rewarding Days

6, 7, 10, 11, 14, 15, 19, 20, 24, 25

Challenging Days

1, 2, 8, 9, 21, 22, 23, 28, 29, 30

Taurus/December

Planetary Hotspots

Situations you've been dealing with all fall will ease in the early part of the month, as Mercury and Mars resume their normal direction of travel on December 3 and 9, respectively. They have made you conscious of ways to improve how you present yourself to others. A new Pluto cycle starts on December 15, initiating a new year of activity in the healing transformation of your finances. Venus enters the spotlight on December 24 as she draws attention to your career growth.

Wellness and Keeping Fit

Health issues assume a much lower profile now as the planets point to other areas of your life. Lifestyle changes in response to your experiences may be needed to ensure that your new health status remains stable and leads to greater improvement.

Love and Life Connections

Home, work, and partnership relationships are the source of greatest concern for you this month, Taurus. The delicate balance between them is disrupted on December 17, and Venus's increased prominence around this time suggests that you are questioning the value of your ties with those in your career path. As you re-evaluate those bonds, you may decide to renegotiate your agreements with others, whether written, spoken, or implied. This may involve cutting away from those who are undermining.

Finance and Success

Although you may have allowed sentiment to dictate some of your business activities in the past, you can no longer afford to do so. This doesn't mean that you can't maintain ties with people you like—on the contrary, it means letting go of those who don't really support you so that you can invest more time and energy in the people willing to work with you on a level playing field, without manipulation.

Rewarding Days
3, 4, 7, 8, 11, 12, 13, 16, 17, 21, 22, 30, 31

Challenging Days
5, 6, 18, 19, 20, 26, 27

Taurus Action Table

These dates reflect the best—but not the only—times for success and ease in these activities, according to your Sun sign.

	JAN	FEB	MAR	APR	MAY	JUN	JUL	AUG	SEPT	OCT	NOV	DEC
Move						28-30	1-22	16-31	1-4			
Start a class		16-28	1-5, 9, 10			11-28	6, 7					
Join a club		26-28	1-22	15-30	1-10							
Ask for a raise	30, 31	1-16										
Look for work									20-30	1-30		
Get pro advice	5, 6	1, 2, 28	1, 2, 28, 29	24, 25	21, 22	18, 19	15, 16	11-13	8, 9	5, 6	1, 2, 28-30	26, 27
Get a loan	7-9	3, 4	3, 4, 30, 31	26, 27	23-25	20, 21	17, 18	14, 15	10, 11	7, 8	3-5	1, 2, 28, 29
See a doctor			5-19	12-30	1-28				20-30	1-30		
Start a diet									20-30	1-8, 16, 17		
End relationship				24, 25								
Buy clothes							25-31	1-17	3-20			
Get a makeover				15-30	1-10, 12-28							
New romance							25-31	1-17	3-5			
Vacation	9-31	1, 2, 5, 6	5, 6	1-3, 28, 29	26, 27	22, 23	19, 20	16, 17	12, 13	9, 10	5-30	1-14, 30, 31

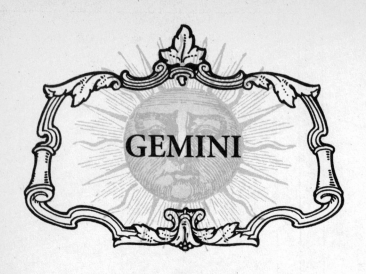

GEMINI

The Twins
May 20 to June 21

Ⅱ

Element:	Air
Quality:	Mutable
Polarity:	Yang/Masculine
Planetary Ruler:	Mercury
Meditation:	I explore my inner worlds.
Gemstone:	Tourmaline
Power Stones:	Ametrine, citrine, emerald, spectrolite, agate
Key Phrase:	I think
Glyph:	Pillars of duality, the Twins
Anatomy:	Hands, arms, shoulders, lungs, nervous system
Color:	Bright colors, orange, yellow, magenta
Animal:	Monkeys, talking birds, flying insects
Myths/Legends:	Peter Pan, Castor and Pollux
House:	Third
Opposite Sign:	Sagittarius
Flower:	Lily of the valley
Key Word:	Versatility

Your Ego's Strengths and Shortcomings

Gemini, there's a part of you that captures the essence of your element, air: light, breezy, uplifting, and free-spirited. However, there's more to you, and your element, than meets the eye. You are a connector. Like the breeze that blows warm air into the cold mountains, you bring new insights from one person to another. You're always telling people what you heard someplace else, giving vital information to assist them on their way. You are a veritable fountain of knowledge, at the ready for whoever may benefit by it. Sometimes the gift you bring is the gift of gab—lifting someone's spirits by telling a joke or helping him see the humor and hope in his own situation. When you're done, you're on your way to the next contact, just like the wind that gives you its energy. One of your best qualities is your ability to relate to all people equally, without judgment or rancor, no matter who they are. You are able to see both sides of a situation equally, to "connect the dots," but you may have difficulty reconciling divergent concepts or positions, and experience inner conflict as a result. As with the air, your movement is lateral, across the land, and you travel from place to place as the mood and need takes you. Where your thoughts go, so go you; to see something new is to want to explore it. One of the pitfalls of this fine quality is that you may be so busy moving that you don't stay in one place long enough to truly experience all it has to offer you. You may miss out on rewards or some of the deeper treasures hidden within. You may become shallow if you only explore things at a superficial level. You will benefit more if you find a few things to pursue with some depth over a longer period of time.

Shining Your Love Light

With your social skills and ease at conversation, you find something in common with everyone you meet; however, meeting that special someone takes more time and care. You want a companion that you can share your ideas and experiences with freely—someone as curious about life as you are—but you also need someone who is balanced and sensible. You may be uncomfortable with a partner who dwells in feelings a lot of the time, but emotions are an important part of your make-up. As much as you love to talk, you may exhaust a partner that does not have your mental stamina—and not get anywhere. Remember that there are other modes of communicating—through feelings, touch, and shared inspiration.

Aries inspires you and introduces you to new places, people, and ideas—just what you love. Taurus keeps your feet on the ground and puts you in touch with the real world, helping you achieve your goals. You're like two peas in a pod with another Gemini, the veritable twins exploring your exciting world together. You'll find your emotional side with caring Cancer, and help him to find an objective viewpoint. Leo's passion for life will invigorate your senses and fill you with joy, but someone will still have to pay the bills. You'll find mental common ground with Virgo: her analytical skills are a good complement to your breadth of knowledge. Libra knows how to find peace between the conflicting parts of your inner being and understand your dilemmas. Scorpio can bring depth to your perspective on life, but this sign's intensity will challenge you. Sagittarius can see the unifying factors in the multiple realities you perceive, a perfect reflection of your inner nature. Capricorn helps you see the big picture out of the details you apprehend, but he may need your help to lighten up his serious attitude. You'll find a kindred spirit in Aquarius—although she is more political than you, you both enjoy social interaction even if for different reasons. The world of subtle feeling that Pisces inhabits may seem a mystery to you, but you will benefit if you explore it just as you would any other unfamiliar turf.

Making Your Place in the World

Careers that involve communication and commerce are your forte, Gemini. Your curiosity will be fully satisfied as an investigative reporter. You may find any job that involves writing to be your cup of tea, but especially a situation that has variety and involves interaction with others. You'll also be in your element in sales or customer service, where social contact is a key feature, but you may enjoy planning meetings or social events—weddings, parties, events. Counseling fields may also attract you, where you get to rely on your communicative skills to support others' growth. You may also enjoy a career where you use your hands, such as hairstyling, since your manual dexterity is exceptional. Whatever you do, you will be more successful if you can stick with it. It takes time to build regard and earn rewards, and if you're always job-hopping you won't make the most of your skills. Instead, select a type of job or work where variety is built into the position—then you won't get bored.

Putting Your Best Foot Forward

Although you are a great talker, it never hurts to learn how to communicate better. Since you are probably relying on this skill a great deal in your life, you will be able to travel your path to success more easily if you learn to manage your verbal communications with skill and compassion. Taking a course to develop your verbal skills, or a program to understand how words and psyche intertwine, such as psychology, is like cutting a rough diamond into a fine gemstone— the potential was always there, but when developed it will shine forever. Another way you can increase your potential for success is to focus on being consistent. Although your versatility is an asset, when taken to extremes it can make you appear fickle and insincere. While you don't want to quash your natural flexibility, you want to use it when it will enhance a situation or experience, not undermine it. When you are consistent, others will have more confidence in you and your ability to follow through. Finally, you will benefit if you can learn to face situations that are challenging rather than avoiding them. If you observe carefully, you'll find that avoidance does nothing to solve a problem, and it may make matters worse. Sometimes it is good to have space to develop our thoughts, and this can benefit the other person involved as well; however, when the time comes, taking responsibility for your role and making apologies where necessary will often be the key to resolution.

Tools for Change

As an air sign, you may spend so much time in your head that you forget about the rest of you. The result is a body that is out of shape, tired, overwrought, and unable to support the things you want to do. One of the best antidotes to this difficulty is the practice of yoga. Yoga uses not just the body but the breath to bond the mind and body. It develops a link between the inner being and the outer being so that you are more aware of your body and how it feels. You will be able to manage pain when you experience it, and you will often be able to avoid it altogether—especially the pain that comes with body armoring, which you may experience. Body armoring comes as a result of nervous tensions, which are translated into muscles that are tensed in anticipation of the need to defend oneself. Over time, the muscles forget what it is like to be relaxed. Yoga retrains the muscles to relax, even as it helps us find our center. Yoga also encourages attunement to the inner, spiritual world, but it is not required. You can increase that attunement through meditation, and this is a highly effective way to overcome or avoid the effects of aging, as well as to live a happier life. With either of these, the use of the breath is vital, and you will benefit by any practice or technique that focuses on your breathing. Another tool you can use to develop your nature is travel. Nothing will broaden your perceptions of yourself, your culture, and the human species as moving among those who grew up in a foreign environment will. This will add depth and authenticity to your self-expression, and you will find that you have more to give others, making you better able to grease the wheels of society. Finally, one of the greatest and most powerful tools you can use is silence. Although you are good at talking, the effective use of silence is essential. All good speakers know how to use pauses to draw attention and to gain power. When you fill in the gaps in conversation with chatter you are giving away your power to others. On the other hand, if you wait until you have something to say, using silence to empower your perspective and find your center, you will find others listening to you more closely and your thoughts will be expressed with more clarity and impact when you are ready to release them to others.

Affirmation for the Year

Silence is power.

The Year Ahead for Gemini

This is a year of empowerment, Gemini, as you find yourself at the fulcrum of change. Jupiter lends its support as it sweeps through your solar Fifth House of creativity. You can capitalize on its energies by lending your creative finesse and sense of beauty to projects and processes that you hold dear. You may become more involved with children, sports, games, or any activity that you consider fun. You may take that special vacation you've been planning for years or find a new hobby that is especially enthralling. You may want to take greater risks than usual, feeling even more optimistic than your usual upbeat attitude, but this should not blind you to the statistical realities of the activities in which you engage. You are also likely to discover new interests that you may want to incorporate into your life path in a more serious way. Once Jupiter leaves Libra, don't let your optimism about achieving your goals dim, because your insights into what inspires you are authentic. Jupiter moves into Scorpio on October 25, and you will enter an especially fruitful period, when your interest in putting your life in order will be at a peak. It's a good time to make plans and get organized in order to set a good foundation for your long-term goals.

Saturn starts the year in Cancer and your solar Second House, where it has been encouraging you to limit your use of resources so that you can achieve a greater, long-term goal. On July 16 it moves into Leo and your Third House, setting your curiosity on edge. You're likely to find it advantageous to apply yourself in a new area of study, whether for career advancement or simply the fun of it. You'll be looking more deeply within, sharpening your mind and opening it in some way to new sources of happiness.

Chiron moves from Capricorn to Aquarius on February 21, completing a four-year period of spiritual transformation and financial limitation. Now you'll feel a sense of liberation as you shift your focus to more ethereal pursuits, from studies of the occult to Eastern mythologies. Most importantly, you're likely to find yourself drawn down a new path in some way in the quest for meaning in your life. You may decide to add new skills to your career repertoire in order to fill in weak areas, or you may decide that you want to help others more. This could eventually lead to a career change in about five years, if you so desire.

Uranus remains in Pisces for its third year, bringing continued excitement and opportunity for innovation in your career, business, or profession. You may feel confined, doing what you've done before, and want to introduce more creativity or original thought into your activities. You may wish for greater potential for growth, more freedom, or more independence of thought. Although you may want to make the changes happen yesterday, a more gradual transformation could be easier to handle.

Neptune in Aquarius continues to heighten your ideals and imbue you with insight from your solar Ninth House. Over the past several years you've been going through a subtle shift in your life direction. You may be interested in new philosophies, spiritual pursuits, or teachings. Your definition of happiness may be changing, or you may feel more and more like dedicating yourself to a type of work where a certain amount of self-sacrifice is required. These changes in perspective and path will continue this year.

Your relationships with others have been filled with intensity as Pluto has made its way through Sagittarius and your Seventh House. You have become aware of the impact your personality can have on others, and you may have felt used or manipulated by them. Others may react strongly to you now, but it may be more a reflection of them than of you. Still, it's important to engage in a process of self-examination and reflection to make sure that your intentions and efforts are free of error.

The eclipses are bringing forth changes in your social life this year, as they move through Aries–Libra and your Fifth–Eleventh House axis. Romance may be in the air, and a sense of newness or rejuvenation infiltrate your life. You may find more children around you, or joy in a new pastime.

If you were born from May 20 to June 3, Saturn in Leo is connecting with your chart from your solar Third House. Your thoughts will turn to more serious matters than usual, and you may notice lacks in your education, your understanding—even your ways of thinking. You are likely to take a more structured approach to these areas; perhaps you'll take a course, begin a writing project, or engage in activities that expose you to new concepts. Your projects may keep you close to familiar territory, as you turn your efforts inward to self-improvement and self-expansion. Your close relations—brothers, sisters, cousins—may become more important as well, or even burdensome. It is a good time to seek out weaknesses in these areas and improve them. Your persistent efforts now will begin to show benefits in about three years, with more substantial returns in seven to ten years. Although you are rarely at a loss for words, you may find that you want to choose them more carefully as Saturn travels through this area; you may realize anew that communication is a fine art that can always be improved by adding a dose of sincerity, which is Saturn's forte. By facing your responsibilities squarely in these areas, you can avoid unwelcome restrictions. Critical dates for this process are July 16 through 23, and November 22.

If you were born from May 23 to June 2, Uranus is connecting with your Sun from its position in Pisces and your solar Tenth House. You've probably felt increasingly caged and dissatisfied with the fulfillments of your career over the past couple of years, at least as far as your current job is concerned. You may be looking down the tunnel of the future and foreseeing the disquietingly grim reality that will be yours in the coming years, and you want to bail. The depth of the change you enact will depend on the distance you find yourself from the path you want to be on. It is important to become aware and take heed of your hidden motivations and urges, because to ignore them is to invite unpleasant and untimely disruptions. Others could force you into a position not of your choosing if you do not take a proactive approach: in the worst-case scenario you could find yourself without a job at all when you least expect or can accommodate it. You may also find that you have more difficulty kowtowing to those who take an authoritarian stance. You may instinctively rebel, absolutely refusing to be controlled or pressured by those who do not treat you as a free agent. You may also find that the authority of government, religion, or law enforcement is less palatable as well, although just as important to accept. Major events related to these issues will occur around February 25, June 14, August 31, and November 15.

If you were born from June 4 to 8, Neptune will transit your Sun from its position in Aquarius and your solar Ninth House. From the time it entered this area in 1998 you've probably felt a gradual shift in your life direction to a more spiritual or at least a more meaningful direction. You may feel that self-sacrifice or help for those in need should play a role in that direction, in a field such as social services, the healing professions, or the rarefied realms of higher education. You may find it desirable to take up a course of study that will lead to qualification in this new direction. You could also feel inspired by travels and other ways of contacting other cultures and ways of thinking. It is important, however, to use an ounce of common sense in making decisions in these areas, since you may tend to be unrealistic. If you do travel to unfamiliar places, you may be vulnerable to parasites and other insidious difficulties. You could also be taken advantage of even if you do not lack experience with the currency, language, and culture. You will benefit by relying on someone who has already earned your trust and by becoming as informed as possible prior to your new experience. Important dates for this process are February 2, May 19, August 8, and October 26.

If you were born from June 9 to 21, Saturn's final months in Cancer will have special significance for you, as it aspects your Sun from your solar Second House until July 16. Issues in that area (the limitation of resources) became more prominent last autumn. You may have discovered that austerity measures were necessary to cover unexpected expenses, or you want to save more money than before to fulfill a special need. It could also be that your spending habits need modification in order to ensure a secure future. You may have been living from paycheck to paycheck, not holding back funds for the extra needs that inevitably arise. It is possible that the difficulties are more serious, that you've gotten into serious debt and it will take a long time to recover. Saturn's transit can signal the time to face responsibilities we have avoided, giving us the chance to recover, but it takes courage, persistence, and patience to see the problem through. We may also go through a change in values under Saturn's influence in the Second House. Even if it is because you get used to a more modest lifestyle due to your forced limitations, any influence that helps us find more meaning in what is truly important is of the greatest value. Key dates are January 13 and March 21.

If you were born from June 12 to 15, your life will be touched by Pluto this year, leading you to transform your relationships. Whether you embark on these changes of your own free will or others instigate the changes for you, you will find your perspective, even your daily life, dramatically altered by your interactions with those you are closest to. All your closest relationships are likely to be transformed: your intimate relationships, business partnerships, close friendships. Although you may receive frequent and vivid feedback from them, those interactions are really a reflection of what is happening inside you as you try out new ways of expressing yourself. You may notice that others are less willing to indulge your more extreme behaviors, but at the same time you will become conscious of the fact that they are taking your actions more seriously, perhaps relying on you more for leadership. You may also become sensitive to the manipulations and power plays that you greeted with indifference in the past—and others may actually become more autocratic. Regardless of the actual events that manifest this year, your relationships will be deeper and more authentic as the inner changes that have been transpiring for years finally break through the masks that you and your loved ones wear for each other. You'll notice these issues in the forefront around March 26, June 13, September 2, and December 15.

Gemini/January

Planetary Hotspots

Issues related to finances arise this month as Saturn and Chiron are active in your Second and Eighth Houses. On January 13, Saturn reaches the halfway point in its yearly cycle. Ways of managing your personal resources that arose last mid-July come to a head and place an extra burden on you now. On January 16, shift your focus to how you can overcome the problem by increasing your income.

Wellness and Keeping Fit

You could be thrown off your normal routine this month by distractions in your financial affairs, especially in mid-month. Try to stay on your routine by flexing the type of exercise you do or food you eat to fit the situation.

Love and Life Connections

On January 28, an incident may occur which affects your partner. Even if it does not involve you directly, it affects you indirectly, as you will need to respond. Your partner's way of managing finances may be creating difficulties for you. It won't work to address the surface manifestations, say, of overspending. You will get a positive result if you look for why the overspending is occurring—what's triggering it. It may be a call for attention or a cry for help that needs to be addressed over time.

Finance and Success

Chances are that your finances need an overhaul. You may be spending too much; your partner may be spending too much. You may simply have accrued too many debts together. Whatever the diagnosis, the cure must be approached as a team. Setting financial goals and developing a plan for reaching them will improve the odds of overcoming the challenges you now face.

Rewarding Days

2, 3, 4, 11, 12, 15, 16, 20, 21, 25, 26, 30, 31

Challenging Days

1, 7, 8, 13, 14, 27, 28, 29

Gemini/February

Planetary Hotspots

Two events brighten your experiences early in the month: Jupiter draws attention to your solar Fifth House of romance, children, and creativity on February 1, and a new yearly Neptune cycle starts on February 2, inspiring you with new ideals and aspirations for the future. On February 25 a new Uranus cycle begins, awakening you to new prospects and possibilities in your career.

Wellness and Keeping Fit

Although your attention is pulled to the outer world this month, it's best to maintain your fitness routine despite the temptation to go full bore into the battle fray. Try activities that test and build your strength, get plenty of sleep, and eat a low-sugar and low-fat diet.

Love and Life Connections

A vacation would be both pleasant and good for your relationships anytime after February 2. If you have a partner, planning a trip that pleases you both will lead to a memorable experience together. If you are on your own, you may meet someone with whom you will have a good time, with the possibility of future contact. Romances started up to this point enter a period of testing on February 1. The question of how far the relationship will go will be answered over the next four months.

Finance and Success

Your Ninth House of goals, education, and aspiration is spotlighted this month by Chiron and Neptune. Around February 2 you'll be thinking about what is meaningful to you and how you can bring it closer to you, and with Chiron entering this house on February 21 it may feel far from what you're doing now. While there may be a reality gap between what you see and what you have, at least you know where to go.

Rewarding Days
7, 8, 11, 12, 13, 16, 17, 21, 22, 26, 27

Challenging Days
4, 5, 9, 10, 23, 24, 25

Gemini/March

Planetary Hotspots

Tensions rise this month as Mars squares off with Jupiter and Saturn, and Mercury, Saturn, and Pluto change direction. Activities peak in your social life in the first week, prompting a desire to spend extra money. Mercury's retrograde begins on March 19, and, as it approaches, your organizational activities increase. After five months of working on it, you've made some progress in improving your financial affairs that becomes evident by March 21.

Wellness and Keeping Fit

If you didn't get that vacation last month (or even if you did), a trip focused on sports or active pursuits will fit the flow starting March 20. This is more likely to be a trip you take on your own.

Love and Life Connections

Your social life is full right now as group activities pick up. Some special tasks come your way as March 19 approaches, and tensions may rise, leading to hasty words. The increased level of social interactions will last for about three weeks. During that time you can use your innate mediation skills to heal the situation.

Finance and Success

Your finances may be stretched to the edges of your budget due to increased social activities early in the month, but sticking to your plan is especially important during times of stress. You need to develop ways of coping without overspending under all circumstances. Your burden lightens up after March 21, but it's not completely eradicated, so don't drop your vigilance.

Rewarding Days
7, 8, 11, 12, 15, 16, 17, 20, 21, 22, 25, 26, 27

Challenging Days
3, 4, 9, 10, 23, 24, 30, 31

Gemini/April

Planetary Hotspots

Your creative energies are flowing strong as Jupiter reaches the peak of its yearly cycle on April 3. This may be in response to group activities. Romance may be in the air as well, as you meet more people. Eclipses bring out new possibilities and obstacles in partnerships and work, perhaps also revealing new health imbalances.

Wellness and Keeping Fit

If you travel this month, you'll get a chance to gain a new, deeper perspective on your life. You'll be able to see the big picture and discern what really matters to you—which is a cure for many a stress-related illness and a recipe for happiness.

Love and Life Connections

Existing situations come to a head in your social life, with peak events for Jupiter and Mercury, as well as an eclipse, occurring in your Fifth–Eleventh House axis. The potential for a new romance is high in the first half of the month. You could fall prey to a con artist or thief while on the road if you are traveling on April 13.

Finance and Success

Peak events in your house of associations open up new prospects because of these contacts, so your extra efforts over the past few weeks will not be wasted. You'll have the coming year to cultivate these opportunities, so take your time and think in terms of the full range of possibilities that may arise. This may involve letting go of previous commitments to make room for new tasks. If creativity plays a role in your career or business, you will find your creative juices flowing well for most of the month. If you can't make use of every inspiration now, take a few notes for later use.

Rewarding Days

3, 4, 7, 8, 12, 13, 17, 18, 22, 23, 30

Challenging Days

5, 6, 19, 20, 21, 26, 27

Gemini/May

Planetary Hotspots

It's time to get busy working toward your new goals as Chiron and Neptune move into the active phases of their yearly cycles on May 8 and 19. You may find that you need to explore new subjects or situations you've never dealt with before. You may need to travel or study something new, or even go back to school.

Wellness and Keeping Fit

Meditation and more inward-turned activities will serve your well-being this month, as Mercury moves through your Twelfth House and Venus through your First House. It's time to replenish your energy stores, or perhaps even do a physical cleansing.

Love and Life Connections

You'll have more allure than usual this month as Venus moves through your First House. You may decide to change your look a little—a new hairstyle or fashion change. Others will invite you to parties and events, and you'll enjoy lots of social contacts. If any rifts exist between you and others, you can resolve them more easily this month.

Finance and Success

Although your plans for the future will have an impact on your career path, they should also satisfy something deeper, create a feeling of greater meaning in your life, and energize and inspire you. Your new path should feel spiritually significant as well as mundanely practical. In the coming three years you'll have plenty of time to adjust and reach your goals, so go for what you really want. Over the coming five months you'll have the chance to factor in the other needs you have in your life. A surprising event on May 15 will spur you on.

Rewarding Days

1, 5, 6, 9, 10, 14, 15, 19, 20, 28, 29

Challenging Days

2, 3, 4, 16, 17, 18, 23, 24, 25, 30, 31

Gemini/June

Planetary Hotspots

Tensions rise again this month, especially on June 1 and 2, and around June 13, when Pluto is activated in your solar Seventh House of partnerships. With Jupiter also spotlighted in your Fifth House of creative endeavors, children, and romance, your attentions will be focused on your ties with others. Near June 14 you'll become aware of ways to inject more life into your career or business, as Uranus moves into the active phase of its cycle.

Wellness and Keeping Fit

You will enjoy sports, especially team sports, this month, as social houses in your chart are highlighted. Your energy level is naturally high, since this is the start of your new birth year.

Love and Life Connections

The ongoing revolution in your relationship life is in your thoughts this month, especially near the peak date of June 13. The challenge is to find the right balance between yourself and your partner. Often, where Pluto is involved, outside support, such as a therapist or business consultant, is helpful in getting your relationship on track. Career events will have an effect on your partnership on June 2. You now know where your current romantic relationships—those not yet formed into long-term commitments—are headed, and you will decide early in the month how you want to continue them.

Finance and Success

As June 14 approaches you may become aware of the need for change in your business or career life. Unexpected events could occur around this time to get the ball rolling, whether instigated by you or someone else. Often things go wrong to prompt such a change, but these events should be viewed as providing guidance, so look for clues within them to get your sense of direction.

Rewarding Days

1, 2, 5, 6, 7, 10, 11, 12, 15, 16, 17, 24, 25, 28, 29

Challenging Days

13, 14, 20, 21, 26, 27

Gemini/July

Planetary Hotspots

The interaction of Saturn and Chiron this month makes your need for a new direction in life even more evident. Although this has been happening for two years, it is especially strong this month in your Third and Ninth Houses. Saturn starts its new cycle on July 23 after entering Leo and your Third House on July 16. Also on July 23, Chiron's yearly cycle reaches its culmination, challenging you to examine the progress you've made toward your goals. To make sure you've got it right, Mercury turns retrograde on July 22, bringing attention to ways in which you need to change attitudes and communicate differently.

Wellness and Keeping Fit

Improving your attitudes toward your experiences changes your reality, including your health. Since it's our reactions to events that trigger stress responses in the body, and not the events themselves, our attitude is the core of our well-being. A change in how we perceive something is the most profound change we can make to our health picture. This is the ideal month for such changes.

Love and Life Connections

You still have a few more months of Jupiter in your creative-romantic Fifth House, so make the most of them. Get out to social events that place you with like-minded people. This could include classes, clubs, and gatherings related to a subject you enjoy, from gardening to baseball to art.

Finance and Success

The pressure's off your world of personal finance at last, but that only means that you've had a chance to develop better habits that will last a lifetime. By continuing to be inventive in finding ways to avoid spending money, you'll continue on the road to financial health.

Rewarding Days

3, 4, 8, 9, 13, 14, 21, 22, 25, 26, 27, 30, 31

Challenging Days

10, 11, 12, 17, 18, 23, 24

Gemini/August

Planetary Hotspots

A moment of disillusionment arises on August 8 as Neptune reaches the culmination of its yearly cycle of interaction with the Sun. Since February, you've been working on developing a new life path for yourself, part of a longer term process that began in 1998 when Neptune entered Aquarius. Now that Chiron has also entered this sign and your Ninth House, you can make more concrete progress toward your goals because you can see more easily what's wrong, and Mercury is also assisting with the process until August 15. On August 31, Uranus reaches its peak moment for the year, and you must refine the balance between personal and public life.

Wellness and Keeping Fit

Your activity level is likely to be higher than usual until a little after August 15, but don't use that as an excuse to avoid eating well, exercising, and getting enough sleep. If the day has left you frazzled, engaging in mild exercise—yoga or gentle Pilates—will keep your energy centers aligned and your nervous system relaxed.

Love and Life Connections

Brothers and sisters could have become more important in your life of late, especially this month. It's important to make sure that you don't commit yourself to something that you later regret around August 8—it may be more than you can live up to.

Finance and Success

So long as you don't overspend, you can safely put your financial affairs on the back burner this month while you attend to other things. Uranus's prominence on August 31 falls in your career house, so you can expect a high level of activity both there and at home to conflict and keep you very busy. Compensate by taking a break before the fun starts, around mid-month.

Rewarding Days

4, 5, 9, 10, 18, 19, 22, 23, 26, 27, 28, 31

Challenging Days

3, 4, 10, 11, 16, 17, 30

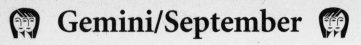 Gemini/September

Planetary Hotspots

On September 2, Pluto enters the final stage of its yearly cycle. Since December, you've taken a few more steps in the process of refining the way you relate to others that has been in development since 1995. Now that the period of critical growth is passing, you can tie up loose ends and consolidate the gains you've made. As you can see, building good relationships takes constant vigilance and self-improvement, whether in your personal, your professional, or your daily life.

Wellness and Keeping Fit

A health problem could be lurking in the background, and, if so, it is likely to emerge in the next month as Mars slows down in preparation for its retrograde period starting October 1. You may find that inexplicable symptoms arise this month, and you'll need to decide how to deal with them. Generally, subtle, non-life-threatening symptoms may be more easily understood within the context of a holistic approach, since your solar Twelfth House is involved.

Love and Life Connections

Your relationships show signs of overt improvement at the month's start, even entering a playful, free, and easy mode as the month progresses. It's important to invest time into your love ties when the going is easy, because that's how the trust and respect are built that see you through the hard times. Plus, it's comfortable and fun.

Finance and Success

Things at work become more relaxed starting September 11, when Venus enters your solar 6th house. You may also find your relationships more friendly than usual, since you have more time to smile and converse. This is a good way to forge better bonds for the future.

Rewarding Days

1, 2, 5, 6, 7, 14, 15, 18, 19, 22, 23, 24, 27, 28, 29

Challenging Days

3, 4, 10, 11, 16, 17, 30

Gemini/October

Planetary Hotspots

Mars turns retrograde on October 1 in your solar Twelfth House of hidden influences and universal ideas. Add to this two eclipses, an emphasis on Chiron and Neptune, and Jupiter's new cycle, and you've got the recipe for an active month full of important events.

Wellness and Keeping Fit

If you have health issues that need to be dealt with, you will know about them by October 1. Chances are, however, that even if you are in perfect physical health, your spiritual health could stand some improvements. You may be off center, your energy field cluttered with others' thoughts and feelings. You may be scattered, undisciplined, or unproductive. These are states that can be overcome with spiritual attunement, which can be gained through energy healing, subtle therapies, meditation, or retreat.

Love and Life Connections

Children and romance receive focus as the eclipses light up your Fifth and Eleventh Houses. Once again, you may find it easy to meet new prospective love matches if you take advantage of the social activities available to you. Since the eclipses establish a six-month focus, this is the beginning of a time of development rather than a one-shot opportunity.

Finance and Success

Jupiter enters Scorpio and your solar Sixth House on October 25, just after starting its new yearly cycle on October 22. This opens a year of increased activity and opportunity in your efforts to provide service to others. Since in a spiritual sense we are all here to serve, the more we can do this, the more benefits accrue to us at other times. While your efforts may fly below the radar now, you will be noticed much more in the years ahead.

Rewarding Days

2, 3, 4, 11, 12, 13, 16, 17, 21, 22, 25, 26, 30, 31

Challenging Days

1, 7, 8, 14, 15, 27, 28, 29

Gemini/November

Planetary Hotspots

A Mars-Neptune contact on November 7 will help you gain insights from your internal searching and will influence the goals that you have been working toward. Mercury turns retrograde on November 14 in your Seventh House of relationships, ramping up the volume on messages from others. Uranus also enters the spotlight on November 15, starting a period of resolution where situations in your career are concerned. Around November 18 to 22, Saturn's new tasks for you become evident.

Wellness and Keeping Fit

As Mars continues to works its way backward through your Twelfth House of seclusion and hidden matters, you will uncover more inner challenges to overcome. Your internal well-being continues to be the focus and the most profound source of your health now. If you feel enervated now, it's because so much energy is turned inward.

Love and Life Connections

You may notice that you want to talk less, now that Saturn is in your solar Third House. You'll have a tendency to be more thoughtful, taking more time to observe the effect that your words have on others, as well as the effect others' words have on you. You may develop an interest in psychology, astrology, or any other science that opens the door to understanding human nature. Around November 18 you'll encounter a challenge that makes this process noticeable.

Finance and Success

As if in response to your need to be focused in other areas, your money seems to be taking care of itself this month. That doesn't mean you should ignore your bills, but that the funds are coming in without your direct attention. You only need take care of your customary obligations.

Rewarding Days

8, 9, 12, 13, 16, 17, 21, 22, 23, 26, 27

Challenging Days

3, 4, 5, 10, 11, 24, 25

Gemini/December

Planetary Hotspots

With both Mercury and Mars returning to forward motion on December 3 and 9, respectively, you'll feel as though you can move forward unimpeded. However, there is one more hurdle you need to clear before that is true. Venus turns retrograde on December 24, presenting one last additional perspective on your new path, so that you can be sure you've got it right. The Sun's contact with Pluto on December 15 creates a temporary intensity and starts a new cycle of growth in relationships.

Wellness and Keeping Fit

Although the prevailing virus may threaten you before December 9, if you take care of yourself you'll sail smoothly through the holiday season. The danger is overcommitment or attempting to go outside your energy zone to complete your work, so don't skimp on sleep.

Love and Life Connections

As yet another year of working on relationships begins on December 15, you are becoming an old hand at the issues that arise. You may find at some point that your new understanding brings you into contact with others who present opportunities to you. If your work involves counseling or consulting in any way then this is an especially significant long-term process, since it is teaching you how to empower others as you empower yourself.

Finance and Success

Your future success relies on your ability to lay a good foundation of service to others over the coming year, as Jupiter makes its way through your Sixth House. Although you can overdo it by taking on too much, you can also greatly enhance your prospects by choosing the right projects now. Many things will present themselves to you as opportunities, but you don't have to accept all of them.

Rewarding Days

5, 6, 9, 10, 14, 15, 18, 19, 20, 23, 24, 25

Challenging Days

1, 2, 7, 8, 21, 22, 28, 29

Gemini Action Table

These dates reflect the best—but not the only—times for success and ease in these activities, according to your Sun sign.

	JAN	FEB	MAR	APR	MAY	JUN	JUL	AUG	SEPT	OCT	NOV	DEC
Move									3-20			
Start a class						28-30	1-22	16-31	1-4			
Join a club			5-19	12-30	1-12							
Ask for a raise			22-31	1-15	10-31	1-3						
Look for work	1-9	16-28	1-5									
Get pro advice	7-9	3, 4	3,4,30,31	26, 27	23-25	20, 21	17,18	14, 15	10, 11	7, 8	3-5	1,2,28,29
Get a loan	9, 10	5, 6	5, 6	1-3, 28, 29	26, 27	22, 23	19, 20	16, 17	12, 13	9, 10	6, 7	3,4,28,29
See a doctor	1-9				12-31	1-11				8-31	1-13	13-31
Start a diet					23, 24					8-30	14, 15	
End relationship												
Buy clothes								17-31	1-11, 20-30	1-8		
Get a makeover					10-31	1-11						
New romance								17-31	1-11	3, 4		
Vacation	11,12,30,31	1-26	7, 8	3, 4, 30	1, 28, 29	24, 25	21, 22	18, 19	14, 15	11-13	8, 9	5, 6, 16-23

The Crab
June 21 to July 22

Element:	Water
Quality:	Cardinal
Polarity:	Yin/Feminine
Planetary Ruler:	The Moon
Meditation:	I have faith in the promptings of my heart.
Gemstone:	Pearl
Power Stones:	Moonstone, chrysocolla
Key Phrase:	I feel
Glyph:	Crab's claws
Anatomy:	Stomach, breasts
Color:	Silver, pearl white
Animal:	Crustaceans, cows, chickens
Myths/Legends:	Hercules and the Crab, Asherah, Hecate
House:	Fourth
Opposite Sign:	Capricorn
Flower:	Larkspur
Key Word:	Receptivity

Your Ego's Strengths and Shortcomings

Just like the fish in the sea, yours is a watery world, because Cancer is a sign of the water element. To you, we are suspended in an ocean of emotion. The energies of feelings float and flow, in and around and through all of us, and you can feel and report them in graphic detail. You are the emotional barometer in any setting, at the ready with your insights into what everyone is feeling and how to meet their needs as well as your own. You fulfill the nurturing aspect of your element, giving and sustaining life through nourishment and care, ensuring that those in your fold want for nothing. The challenge you face is in making sure that you are fulfilling their needs in a balanced way—neither draining yourself nor smothering the object of your care. As people's needs change, the amount and type of nurturing you give must be altered in response. You are as enfolding of those in your "family" as the water in a bath, surrounding them with the unseen energies of kindness and warmth. Your definition of family may extend beyond those with whom you share mitochondrial DNA. Your family extends to whomever you feel should come under your protection. Water moves downward, taking the shape of its vessel, and just like water, you are molded by your surroundings—and especially by people. Your mood may move downward, but it swells upward as well, in the inevitable flow of the river of your consciousness. In extreme form, your emotional energy could become too inward and downward focused, leading to self-involvement, hypersensitivity, or over-emotionalism. When you learn to ride that river, remaining buoyant as you glide over the waves of life, your emotions will remain steady in the midst of the highs and lows of events.

Shining Your Love Light

Your nurturing ways serve you well in relationship, Cancer, and others are drawn to your tender ways of showing love. You are especially good at creating a family feeling—whether you cook, entertain, or just listen well, your welcome mat is always out, and others feel healed in this bath of kindness. Partnership and marriage are very important to you, and once you form a partnership you are exceptionally loyal. You expect your commitment to last a lifetime through thick and thin. You are keenly aware of what it takes to sustain love, and you fully expect to experience ups and downs over the lifetime of your bond, but to you that only deepens the love.

With Aries, your life will be filled with thrills and excitement, but you'll be able to keep pace with this sign as the pursues his latest scheme. Taurus is much like you, concerned about security and survival, and her stability and common sense are fantastic complements to your high emotional IQ. Gemini stirs your verbal capabilities and leads you on quests for greater knowledge, as you supply the focus on heart and feelings. Another Cancer is a good candidate for a long-term match—you'll instinctively understand each other. Leo will bring lightheartedness and enthusiasm to your outlook, while you'll help him get in touch with his intuitive side. Virgo brings practical skills and a desire to contribute that you really appreciate, while your emotional warmth adds welcomed support. Libra challenges you to think with objectivity and balance about your relationship, while you remind her of the importance of compassion. Scorpio understands the power of emotions as you do and injects intensity into your bond. Sagittarius's passion for the road ahead lifts you out of your homebody ways and inspires you to transcend the mood of the moment. You'll teach Capricorn to come out of his shell and display his true warmth, while this sign will help you contain and filter your emotions for a more professional demeanor. Aquarius will expose you to new ideas and people with this sign's love of all humanity, while you will help in the exploration of emotional frontiers. Pisces shares your compassionate approach to life, a source of mutual support and sustenance.

Making Your Place in the World

You love nothing more than to assist and support others, Cancer, and any career that allows you to do that is right up your alley. With your appreciation of homes and their importance to others' happiness, real-estate sales and services provide an ideal place for your fulfillment and success. You may also be drawn to providing health care as a nurse, doctor, therapist, or alternative health practitioner, since you love caring for those in need and have a healing touch. Yet the noble art and science of motherhood may be the strongest attraction, since you find nothing more rewarding than the thrill of seeing your children develop into their own uniqueness. If you do not have children, nurturing the youngsters of other parents, including animals, may be your choice. With children you can allow your own childlike nature to come out, support their emotional growth, and explore the world afresh as they grow. With your strong instincts and intuitions you can also be happy and successful as a psychic counselor.

Putting Your Best Foot Forward

With your loving approach to life, no one can find fault with how much you care. However, giving love and care to others is a fine art that you must balance if you want to have healthy relationships with those you love. This can be very complex from a mental perspective, because we have to pay attention to the changing needs of the person in question: What does she need today? Am I satisfying a need that he can and should fill himself? Am I helping her grow or stifling her development by assisting her? Paying attention to these issues will help you get it right when reaching out to others. It will make it easier for others to come to you, because they know you won't smother them. A key to this is to wait until you are asked for help before giving it. By using a blend of intuition and education you can keep your giving in balance. In addition, sometimes it is hard to discern whether you are responding to someone else's need or your own. Sometimes you try to help others so that you feel needed. When support comes with strings attached, people instinctively reject it, even if they need the help. It works better to ask for the help and support you need from others and then give your assistance freely.

Tools for Change

You may be delving with special vigor into your past and focusing on self-development more than usual this year. One way you can support this process is to study human development—especially that of the child. Many things happen when we are children that we are not equipped to understand, so we rely on others to interpret them for us. To become adult, we have to develop our own independent interpretations of our past experiences so that we can understand our current experiences objectively and respond with a true awareness of our choices. It is important to understand the processes of childhood so that we can see where we might have gotten stuck in our development due to misunderstood events. Then, you can use conscious recall to explore the events unique to your childhood and discover misinterpretations and misunderstandings. This will help you master your responses to events that occur in the here and now. Think about times in your past when difficulties arose, including adolescence and adulthood. These can be reinterpreted using your new knowledge, plus the help of others if needed, to give you more power over your emotional responses. Another tool you can use to enhance your Cancerian expression is to get in touch with your own needs and find ways to fulfill them. Sometimes you will be able to do it yourself, other times you will need or want to ask your loved ones to fulfill them, and still other needs may require help from those outside your circle of family, friends, and relatives. Paying attention to your needs and seeing that they get met in responsible ways will prevent you feeling needy or unconsciously expecting others to fulfill them. When you feel needy, it may be more difficult to get others' support. It is also more difficult to maintain the energy you need to care for others if you are not nurturing yourself. It's also important to take time away from your caretaker roles and just have fun. This can include spontaneous play, enjoying a form of entertainment, or engaging in an artistic pursuit of your own. Although you may be carrying an extra burden this year in some way, giving yourself a break will lighten your load and revitalize you for the next round of giving.

Affirmation for the Year

By nurturing my self, I can give to others.

The Year Ahead for Cancer

You've been under pressure for the past two years, but in 2005 you'll feel the pressure shift and lift and your opportunities grow. Jupiter is in Libra until October 25, your solar Fourth House. After three years of self-cultivation and internalization, you've been slowly putting your dreams into forms others can see. Although they're not quite ready for prime time, you have the satisfaction of knowing that they are likely to bear fruit. You'll probably spend more time at home during this period (if that's possible), or you may expand your home by remodeling and enlarging it, or by moving to larger or happier quarters. If you are in real estate, your business will boom. Your household may grow as well: you may have another child, acquire more pets, or a grown child may move back home. Once Jupiter enters Scorpio, your solar Fifth House will be lit up. You'll be more active and creative than before, perhaps shifting gears in your life path and taking on some new pursuit that is a joy rather than an obligation.

When Saturn moves from Cancer to Leo on July 16 you may feel as though a burden has lifted. Perhaps you've felt depressed, tired, or without hope as difficult situations seem to persist relentlessly despite your best efforts. While Saturn is still in Cancer you will need to carry on with your patient efforts at overcoming the problems that have dogged you for the past two years. Whatever problems arise are likely due to limitations in your own perspective. These are the easiest problems to fix because reparations do not rely on anyone but yourself. When Saturn enters Leo in July the focus will turn to your values and resources—especially physical ones such as your time, money, land, and possessions—and you may adopt austerity measures to achieve new goals.

Chiron has been in Capricorn and your Seventh House of relationships for the past three years, reflecting the wounds in your bonds with others. You may have discovered that some people are too dependent on you, or that you have come to rely on others too much in some ways. Sometimes we collect others around us to act as a shield against something or someone we don't want to face. Once Chiron enters Aquarius and your solar Eighth House in February you may discover weaknesses in your finances that are tied to the people in your life. This could be the indiscretions of your partner or your own poor money management, which is injuring your financial standing with others. In the next six years you'll have the opportunity to resolve those issues.

Uranus is in its third year in Pisces and your solar Ninth House. It is taking you to the top, buoying you up and leading you to think about "what if" instead of "why not." Your doubts about your ability to accomplish exceptional tasks will be at an ebb—if you can settle down long enough to apply yourself constructively. You're full of truly new ideas and novel approaches to old problems, so go ahead: share them with others.

Neptune has been in Aquarius and your Eighth House since 1998, dissolving your previous ways of handling your shared resources. You may have found that you don't feel as secure with your financial portfolio as you'd like, so you've been making some changes. An interest in the occult or spiritual studies may have led you to embrace deeper values. This taps the true message of Neptune in the Eighth House, which is that true security comes from within, and not from any physical resources we can collect in our name.

Pluto continues its transformation of your solar Sixth House from its position in Sagittarius. You may have found since 1995 that your way of handling your daily life has been eating away at your health. Since then you've been working steadily toward improving your habits—from the ways you handle stress on the job to how much time you put in at work to what you eat. It is important to be consistent with these changes: when you falter, get back on your feet and carry on as before.

The eclipses are challenging you to find a balance of commitment in home and career that works for you. You may find that some changes need to be made, which may either be voluntary or forced on you by others. You'll be more strongly motivated to enact them this year.

If you were born from June 21 to July 3, Saturn is contacting your Sun from your solar Second House starting July 16. You'll notice a shift in emphasis from your personal development to improving your use of resources. This may involve financial retrenching, curtailment of expenditures, or merely a change in priorities. However, limitation is usually required in order to achieve a larger goal. Your financial portfolio may need to be restructured, or renewed concerns about your physical security may lead you to increase your insurance coverages and retirement fund. While we think of money, land, and possessions when it comes to resources, time and skills also fall into this category. You may find that you want to use your time in a new way or rely on skills that currently lie dormant in your nature. On a deeper level, you'll be challenged to reassess your values. When you feel your motivation flagging, it's a sure sign that you are engaging in activities in which you find little value. This is the time to examine moods of resistance and procrastination for the seeds of discontent that signal this loss of meaning. Your experiences on July 16 through 23 and November 22 will be Saturnian in nature.

If you were born from June 23 to July 3, your Sun is being boosted by Uranus's beams, which come from Pisces and your solar Ninth House. Sparks are flying, and you feel uncharacteristically optimistic, even daring, in your approach to life and its quest. Changes you scarcely dared think about before now seem not just possible but necessary. You may be inspired by a new, freeing ideology that overrides older, more traditional ways of thinking to which you previously adhered. This could come from higher education, contact with foreign cultures, a spiritual study, or even a strange new religion. Your mind moves quickly over the range of your experience, generating completely novel concepts that uniquely solve problems in the world around you. At a deeper level, you may be searching for a path with greater meaning, where you consider taking risks you have not previously entertained. You could find yourself considering a change in career as you look for your life purpose in new terms. Don't be surprised if you take exception to the tried and true, perhaps even displaying irreverence in hallowed territory. Although a bit unsettling, this is generally a harmonious energy that you should enjoy if you allow the spunk and adventurousness of your nature come through. Uranus energy will be highest on February 25, June 14, August 31, and November 15.

If you were born from July 4 to 10, Neptune in Aquarius is dissolving away old patterns and false images from your Eighth House matters: shared resources and influences that overpower us, such as death, the movements of society's masses, and the occult. Most likely you will find something that needs fixing in your use of others' monies. Perhaps you've borrowed too much money, or you find that you're being underpaid for the work you are doing. Or perhaps the burst of the financial bubble seriously eroded your bottom line and it's time to build it back up. Your partner may be eroding your wealth with poor spending habits. Since Neptune is a sign that insidious influences may be at work, you may discover that others have been working against you—even deceiving you. You may also find that you do not want to participate in the shared value system of the culture in the same way you unquestioningly did in the past. Your investigations of the occult or the unconscious motivations that run through human nature may lead you to question the "standard version" of reality, and you may begin to see people and events from a deeper level where hidden urges become clear. Whatever Neptune uncovers for you, you'll understand the truth in a new way when this year is complete. You'll feel most Neptunian around February 2, May 19, August 8, and October 26.

If you were born from July 11 to 22, Saturn is in direct contact with your Sun until July 16 from your solar First House. You've already been scrutinizing your own nature for flaws for two years, but the pressure is on now as you put daily effort into resolving an issue that arose last fall—one that falls squarely on your shoulders. If you are wise, you will take responsibility where you must, but it is important not to do so in areas that are another's domain. This would create an imbalance that you will resent, and it will take its toll on your health. Even though this process is well under way, you will yet uncover factors that hold a key to their resolution, so it is not merely a matter of carrying on stubbornly, but of facing whatever new insights present themselves. When Saturn is in our home sign, self-examination is top priority. This means that you must be willing to admit to your errors and correct them, even if they are large and will take a long time to rectify. Still, persistent effort in the right direction guarantees lasting results. Peak events related to this process will occur on or near January 13 and March 21.

If you were born from July 14 to 16, Pluto in Sagittarius is challenging you from your solar Sixth House, the house of lifestyle, daily routines, work, eating patterns, and organization, as well as health and illness. All of these areas have been undergoing a transformation that may require a major change in your habits and daily activities. Top on your list of priorities for the year should be a thorough physical examination by whatever professionals you value, from regular doctors to acupuncturists to holistic practitioners. This does not absolutely ensure that no problems lie hidden within your body, but it's a start. Chances are good that you will find something to correct or improve. Then the challenge is to overcome your own resistance to a change in habits—always a demanding task for Cancers. The most important thing is respecting yourself: when you respect yourself, you will take better care of your body, and you will be able to surmount the natural petulance that we all feel when we must give up cherished old patterns. By staying with the situation now you will be able to avoid or at least postpone greater problems, which could arise as Pluto progresses further through the sign. Pluto will be prominent in your experiences around March 26, June 13, September 2, and December 15.

Cancer/January

Planetary Hotspots

You're pulled in several different directions at once, as Saturn's yearly cycle reaches its peak in Cancer. A workload faces you just as you get back from the holidays, and it may not be just at work. Your relationship life is one of those areas needing extra care, but you could miss the signs if you don't pay attention. The issue there will be spoken quietly now, and in louder tones later in the year. These energies culminate around January 13.

Wellness and Keeping Fit

Health matters could be front and center this month, and if so, news of them will come from someone else. This could mean hearing about your health from a doctor, or hearing that someone else is facing a challenge. Either way, you'll need to make or continue lifestyle changes to accommodate this trend in your life. January 16 and 28 are key dates.

Love and Life Connections

Your relationships continue to need extra attention, as they have for the past two years. Although a shift is coming, it's not here yet. In the meantime, it's important to go the extra mile to show you care without compromising yourself. Be alert on January 16, for that is when a seed event will occur for the coming year.

Finance and Success

It's hard to stretch yourself to take care of financial matters right now, what with all the work you have, so delegate the tasks to someone else, if only for a while. If you feel insecure about it, have him or her report back to you regularly about how it's going.

Rewarding Days

1, 5, 6, 13, 14, 17, 18, 19, 22, 23, 24, 27, 29

Challenging Days

2, 3, 4, 8, 9, 15, 16, 30, 31

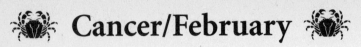 Cancer/February

Planetary Hotspots

Come February 1, you'll be at your most active and dynamic as enterprising Jupiter takes center stage. Your focus will be on home, family, and private life—perhaps you'll move house. Harmonizing with this effort is the vision of your financial future and how you want to work toward it this year, tied to Neptune's yearly cycle, which starts February 2. On February 25 you'll be awakened to new possibilities by Uranus, as its new cycle begins.

Wellness and Keeping Fit

Although you are busy now—distracted—you need to stay in tune with your body. Listen to what it tells you, and shift gears when it says you've been at something for too long. Under stress, you may tend to overeat or eat poorly. You can use Saturn, now in your sign, to access your self-discipline, and once you've done so, good habits will reinforce themselves.

Love and Life Connections

Financial ties with those you love have involved ongoing sacrifice since 1995, and this year is no exception. It's important, however, to factor in your own needs and goals for the future. After February 5, you'll find people more aggressive toward you as Mars moves through your house of partnerships. This means that friends may be looking out for you, offering you good advice and support, so listen closely.

Finance and Success

You are generous to a fault, but it may not help those close to you. You understand the need for a budget, but unless you impart that knowledge to your loved ones through actions as well as words, the lesson may go unlearned. Set limits on what you'll give and make them known ahead of time—then stick to them.

Rewarding Days

1, 2, 9, 10, 14, 15, 18, 19, 20, 23, 24, 25, 28

Challenging Days

5, 6, 11, 12, 13, 26, 27

Cancer/March

Planetary Hotspots

Mercury turns retrograde on March 19, requiring some backtracking in your career. Saturn's backwards motion ends on March 21, and you get the chance to relax a little more and celebrate a job well done. On March 26, Pluto moves into its five-month retrograde period, and you can anticipate a need to make further changes in your daily routines and rhythm of work—part of a long-term progression toward greater effectiveness and health.

Wellness and Keeping Fit

The ways you maintain your health become more important around March 26, with Pluto emphasized in your Sixth House of well-being, daily routines, and service to others. Cutting away activities that clutter your life is just what it takes to work through your personal Pluto issues.

Love and Life Connections

You may feel a sense of urgency, even a crisis, in your personal life, as a conflict arises during the first week of March. Even more uncomfortable, you may not be able to completely resolve it at that time—it may have to wait until after March 19 to discuss it more fully, and a few weeks beyond that to clear it completely. It's important to realize that sometimes people need time to think things through, and this may be one of them.

Finance and Success

Events in the days leading up to March 19 have you rethinking your current career situation. You may not be feeling fulfilled by what you're doing, and you may be getting negative feedback to boot. Be sure to examine where your feelings are coming from, because that will tell you more accurately what will solve the problem. You'll gain lots of insight for about three weeks after March 19.

Rewarding Days

1, 2, 9, 10, 13, 14, 18, 19, 23, 24, 28, 29

Challenging Days

5, 6, 11, 12, 25, 26, 27

Cancer/April

Planetary Hotspots

Home and career developments consume your time and focus early in the month as Jupiter reaches the peak of its yearly cycle on April 3. As if that weren't enough, a solar eclipse on April 8 invigorates the process and sets out your prime directive for the next six months, which will be related to these areas. Mercury's retrograde period ends on April 12, sweetening the deal, because now you know more about where you're headed and how to achieve it.

Wellness and Keeping Fit

One of the best things you can do this month is to take some time off to get away from it all. If possible, travel out of town to someplace where you have no ties to your obligations—perhaps a spa or a spiritual retreat, or even a wilderness area.

Love and Life Connections

Your social life picks up this month, Cancer, as you are called out of your shell to attend group functions and gatherings. Although this is awkward with the efforts you need to exert at work and home, it's essential to laying the groundwork for future success.

Finance and Success

With the lunar eclipse in your Fifth and Eleventh Houses, your career will be served by social contacts you make this month, even if the benefits don't reveal themselves right away. You're still thinking about what you want to do next to further your career—especially after some disappointing events last month. After April 1 you'll begin to see the possibilities, and by April 12 you'll be ready to take action.

Rewarding Days

5, 6, 9, 10, 11, 14, 15, 16, 19, 20, 21, 24, 25

Challenging Days

1, 2, 7, 8, 22, 23, 28, 29

Cancer/May

Planetary Hotspots

Both Chiron and Neptune change direction, starting the retrograde stage of their cycles and making clearer the challenges you face in your financial dealings with others. On May 15 you can get a glimpse of "what if" and decide if you want to pursue the possibilities.

Wellness and Keeping Fit

You've been so busy over the past few months, you need some time to recharge your batteries. With Venus entering your Twelfth House on May 9, this is an ideal time to retreat from the world you know, even if you were able to do so last month. It is rejuvenating to take time to appreciate the present moment—to go where your past and future don't exist. Whether you meditate at home or sit outside a café telling fish tales on the south coast of France, you will get the most from this type of activity at this time.

Love and Life Connections

The challenges in your personal life fade into the background for the time being this month. It doesn't mean they've gone away, but it gives everyone a welcome break to get priorities straight.

Finance and Success

You may find, with Chiron and Pluto active, that you need to adjust the way you deal with some components of your financial portfolio. You may need to consolidate your investments, rather than diversify. You may also find that your debt burden has become uncomfortably high without your being entirely aware of what was happening. As these situations reveal themselves, you can begin to rectify the situation in two ways: fill in the gaps and institute preventive guidelines to make sure this doesn't happen again. In a few months you'll be substantially on your way toward healing the situation.

Rewarding Days

2, 3, 4, 7, 8, 11, 12, 13, 16, 17, 18, 21, 22, 30, 31

Challenging Days

5, 6, 19, 20, 26, 27

Cancer/June

Planetary Hotspots

Planetary events throughout the month make June a time of high activity. On June 5, Jupiter is spotlighted. Four months of intensive activity are over as you work to fulfill the goals you set last September for your home and family life. Pluto's cycle reaches its crescendo on June 13, spotlighting any remaining adjustments you need to make to your plan for fulfilling your work and health plans. On June 14, Uranus adds fuel to the fire when it enters its retrograde period, highlighting your goals and sense of direction.

Wellness and Keeping Fit

Health imbalances could reach a crisis point near June 13 as Pluto's position in your Sixth House of health is triggered. By being sensitive to how you're feeling, and then responding as necessary, you'll weather the storm. If you can, it is a great time to focus on personal pleasures and beautifying yourself as Venus moves through your solar First House.

Love and Life Connections

Although the pressures are high this month in general, Venus in your First House also smooths your way and gives you the support and warm attentions of others. Romantic adventures may come your way mid-month.

Finance and Success

You'll feel pulled between home and career around June 25 as the challenges you've been dealing with all year come to a head. You may feel conflicted as new opportunities develop that pull you away from your home life. Although you may feel you have to choose, it is only a temporary situation. By explaining this to your loved ones, you'll reassure them of your long-term priorities.

Rewarding Days

3, 4, 8, 9, 13, 14, 18, 19, 26, 27, 30

Challenging Days

1, 2, 15, 16, 17, 22, 23, 28, 29

Cancer/July

Planetary Hotspots

Finally, Saturn moves out of your sign, Cancer! On July 16 it begins its occupation of Leo and your Second House of personal finance. The seeds of the initiatives of the past two years are now planted, and it's time to begin developing them. You'll be less stretched, less likely to feel overburdened now. Mercury turns retrograde on July 22 in the same area, giving you a glimpse of what you can do to improve your foundation and sense of security.

Wellness and Keeping Fit

Your physical health is showing signs of definite improvement now, with Saturn out of Cancer and your solar First House. Now that the pressure's easing off, your stress level will go down. You have the time now to get some tonic and preventative treatments, such as acupuncture or chiropractic treatments, which will boost your vitality.

Love and Life Connections

It seems as if love and money are intertwined right now, and they need to be disentangled. On July 6 and 7 you can communicate with eloquence and generosity about the situation, but you will also need to listen and stick to your principles. Things get tough during the last two weeks of the month, and anything you can do to clear up difficulties now will reduce the potential for greater challenges from the same quarter in November.

Finance and Success

You're sorting through your situation with debt, income, and expenditures, and you're discovering some factors that you hadn't been fully aware of before. This examination is essential to righting the boat, so don't shy away from it and the communications you must have with others to resolve conflicts. It will be easier in the first half of the month.

Rewarding Days

1, 2, 5, 6, 7, 10, 11, 12, 15, 16, 23, 24, 28, 29

Challenging Days

13, 14, 19, 20, 25, 26, 27

Cancer/August

Planetary Hotspots

Two planets reach the halfway point in their yearly cycles in August. Neptune brings more clarity to your financial picture around August 8, as something that has been obscured comes to light. Around August 31, Uranus's peak brings out your wanderlust, and you may want to make a break for freedom in some way.

Wellness and Keeping Fit

Vacationing fits your need for freedom this month, and now you may have the time to do it. If your finances dictate a curtailed adventure, just stay closer to home or make your trip shorter, but do get away from it all.

Love and Life Connections

You don't quite feel like immersing yourself in your family yet, even though they're important to you. Sure, take them on vacation with you, but make no apologies if you need to wander off by yourself periodically. You need to restore yourself as much as possible so that you can really be there for them later.

Finance and Success

With Uranus active in your Ninth House, you want to make your life more meaningful. It isn't enough just to work—you have to feel like you're fulfilling a purpose you believe in as well. This has become a growing conviction for you over the past three years, but now it is feeling more urgent. As August 31 approaches you'll gain more insight into what that purpose is and how to achieve it, even if you don't like what you'll have to change to get there.

Rewarding Days

1, 2, 3, 6, 7, 8, 11, 12, 13, 20, 21, 25, 29, 30

Challenging Days

9, 10, 16, 17, 22, 23

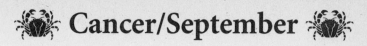 Cancer/September

Planetary Hotspots

Two big events will mark this month in your memory. On September 2, Pluto draws your attention back to your Sixth House of health, lifestyle, and work routines. You've been working on improvements in these areas, and now the moment of truth arrives. You'll also begin to see the potential for difficulty or disruption in your social world, particularly that of business associates, organizations, and the family or ethnic community with which you identify.

Wellness and Keeping Fit

You've been focused on making lifestyle improvements that will heal current health imbalances as well as head off future challenges. One of these challenges is stress. As with everyone, stresses arise when you respond emotionally to your experiences. They wreak havoc on your body when you are unaware of them or unable to release them. This is the real process of growth you've been going through, and on September 2 you get the opportunity to see in some way how far you've come on this journey.

Love and Life Connections

You can finally breathe a sigh of relief and withdraw into your warm, happy family cocoon this month, as the fast-moving planets begin to move through the private, home-oriented part of your chart. Enjoy—you deserve it!

Finance and Success

Carefully watch the events occurring in your circle of acquaintances and colleagues. There may be a problem developing which you can play a constructive role in resolving. Your compassion and listening skills make you a natural confidant. Although it will help if you can assuage hurt feelings this month, the situation won't even completely emerge until next month.

Rewarding Days

3, 4, 8, 9, 16, 17, 20, 21, 25, 26, 30

Challenging Days

5, 6, 7, 12, 13, 18, 19

Cancer/October

Planetary Hotspots

On October 1, Mars change direction for eleven weeks, and you may find yourself in a peacemaker role. However, the bulk of your activities this month are directed toward rekindling your most important relationships—with family, close friends, and your partner—as two eclipses light up these areas on October 3 and 17. Both Chiron and Neptune move into the final stage of their yearly cycle, and relationship and financial issues will finally be resolved.

Wellness and Keeping Fit

If you take the time to restore your strength this month, the dip in your immune system that could come at month's end when Mercury enters your Sixth House of health will be less drastic. Resuming a more rigorous exercise routine will energize you.

Love and Life Connections

This is the key area of your life this month, Cancer, as the planets collect in your Fourth and Fifth Houses, the most private and personal areas of your chart. Jupiter enters this house on October 25, starting a year-long cycle when you can pour attention into this most important area of your life. This will go a long way toward healing a rift in your relationship life as well.

Finance and Success

It's quite all right to withdraw from regular social activities in your more public life right now. You won't miss anything, and you'll be back in the saddle in a couple of months. On October 26, Neptune enters the last phase of its yearly cycle, helping you turn the page on some financial matters that have been left unresolved.

Rewarding Days

1, 5, 6, 14, 15, 18, 19, 22, 23, 24, 27, 28, 29

Challenging Days

2, 3, 4, 9, 10, 16, 17, 30, 31

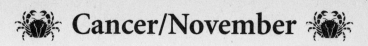 Cancer/November

Planetary Hotspots

Three planets hit the spotlight this month: Mercury on November 3, when it turns retrograde; Uranus on November 15, when its retrograde ends; and Saturn on November 22, the beginning of its retrograde. Mercury could bring a temporary dip in your vitality that results in viral infection as it travels through your Sixth House of health. The changes you have been seeking to create seem to move palpably forward now that Uranus is near the end of this year's cycle, and you're one step closer to a more meaningful life. Saturn's first cycle in your solar Second House may be challenging, as it also ties in with events in your Eleventh House of organizations and social groups through a challenging contact with Mars.

Wellness and Keeping Fit

Sleep is an essential component to your well-being this month, yet you may feel like skimping on it because of the demands you face. Worry, even if it doesn't keep you awake, may increase your stress level needlessly. Meditate, rest, and continue to get exercise.

Love and Life Connections

Partners will be exceptionally understanding this month as Venus moves through your Seventh House of relationships starting on November 5. However, it is wise to be alert for areas that might need renegotiating in your partnership, since Venus will turn retrograde late next month and reveal areas for growth and adjustment.

Finance and Success

It's time to accept the challenge and map out a plan for overcoming the financial limitations you currently face. You may have too much debt, or you may merely need to revamp your investment portfolio. Whatever the challenge, expect that it will take time to resolve, since Saturn is involved.

Rewarding Days

1, 2, 10, 11, 14, 15, 19, 20, 24, 25, 28, 29, 30

Challenging Days

6, 7, 12, 13, 26, 27

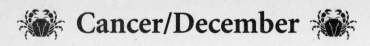

Cancer/December

Planetary Hotspots

Planetary events pepper the month like so many stars in the sky, as Mercury, Venus, Mars, and Pluto are highlighted. Most significant is the start of the yearly Pluto cycle on December 15, which begins another round of clearing your life of unwanted clutter and irrelevant activity.

Wellness and Keeping Fit

Getting and keeping your life in order also creates physical health, because the inner world reflects the outer. Call it feng shui, call it what you like—it's important. Taking this part of your life in hand and eliminating unneeded papers and objects, even if they have sentimental value, is worth it. Although you may not be able to do it all at once, it's not a bad project for the coming year.

Love and Life Connections

Come December 24, your relationship agreements, conscious or unconscious, are up for renegotiation, with an emphasis on money and financial management. It helps if you set financial goals with your partner, so that the two of you are in agreement on what you want to accomplish. Then it's easier to agree on what measures to take to reach them—they'll feel less like restrictions.

Finance and Success

Your relationships are tied into your financial life this month, and what you agree on will shape your security for the next eighteen months. Bring in a professional if you have trouble agreeing or have questions on how to manage some aspects of your portfolio. When Mars goes back to its normal direction of travel on December 5, the tension relaxes in your external social world. That doesn't mean the problem is solved, however, and if not, it still deserves attention.

Rewarding Days

7, 8, 11, 12, 13, 16, 17, 21, 22, 26, 27

Challenging Days

3, 4, 9, 10, 23, 24, 25, 30, 31

CANCER ACTION TABLE

These dates reflect the best—but not the only—times for success and ease in these activities, according to your Sun sign.

	JAN	FEB	MAR	APR	MAY	JUN	JUL	AUG	SEPT	OCT	NOV	DEC
Move									20-30	1-8		
Start a class									3-20			
Join a club					12-28							
Ask for a raise				15-30	1-10	3-28						
Look for work	1-30		5-19	12-30	1-12							
Get pro advice	9, 10	5, 6	5, 6	1-3, 28, 29	26, 27	22, 23	19, 20	16, 17	12, 13	9, 10	6, 7	3, 4, 30, 31
Get a loan	11, 12	7, 8	7, 8	3, 4, 30	1, 28, 29	24, 25	21, 22	18, 19	14, 15	11-13	8, 9	5, 6
See a doctor	1-30				28-31	1-28				31	1-13	13-31
Start a diet	1-9									31	1-13	13-31
End relationship						22, 23	19-21					
Buy clothes									11-30	1-8	1, 2	
Get a makeover						3-28						
New romance									11-30	1-8	1, 2	
Vacation	13, 14	9, 10, 16-28	1-22	5, 6	2-4, 30, 31	26, 27	23, 24	20, 21	16, 17	14, 15	10, 11	7, 8

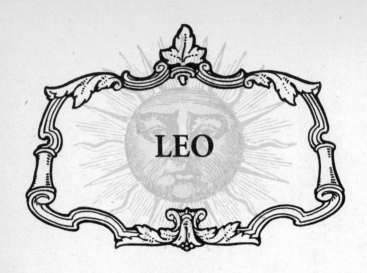

The Lion
July 22 to August 22

♌

Element:	Fire
Quality:	Fixed
Polarity:	Yang/Masculine
Planetary Ruler:	The Sun
Meditation:	I trust in the strength of my soul.
Gemstone:	Ruby
Power Stones:	Topaz, sardonyx
Key Phrase:	I will
Glyph:	Lion's tail
Anatomy:	Heart, upper back
Color:	Gold, scarlet
Animal:	Lions, large cats
Myths/Legends:	Apollo, Isis, Helios
House:	Fifth
Opposite Sign:	Aquarius
Flower:	Marigold, sunflower
Key Word:	Magnetic

Your Ego's Strengths and Shortcomings

Just as fire sends its flame out to light the world, so do you send the rays of joy and love to others. Fire is your element, and you exude the warmth of the Sun in all that you do. Your fire burns long and steady, sustaining life through giving your inspiration and vigor to others, and you're high on motivation and low on pessimism as you aspire upward like the flames of your element. You have plenty to give, to share, but only if you have a fuel source—something that keeps you going. You may rely on others to feed you with their attention, or you may simply rely on someone who has faith in you and the value of what you bring forth—and if you desire an audience, it's just because your experiences are richer for the sharing. Your optimism and ebullience provide the grease that turns the gears of progress, providing a steadying motivation to see a project or initiative through to the end. When spirits flag, you are there, generating the heat of enthusiasm to reach your goal.

Yours is a social, group-oriented energy, like a fire that warms the hearth in a gathering place, and just as people collect to warm their toes, so do they congregate to bask in the glow of your generous spirit. So much brightness can have a downside: if you seek attention for its own sake rather than as a part of a shared process of giving and receiving, others will tire of it and move on. If your giving is from the heart rather than driven by inner emptiness, however, it will be well received. You will be weakened if your creative inspiration is driven by a desire for others' approval. Instead, it should be expressed according to what moves in you—a natural expression of your inner life.

Shining Your Love Light

You're never happier than when your heart is engaged in feelings of love and romance, Leo. You are the original romantic, giving candy and flowers by candlelight. You want a playmate, someone who shares your sheer enjoyment of life and its lighter, more creative side. Once you give your heart, you are steadfast in your love: you will not break a relationship commitment lightly. Your generous spirit is appreciated by your partner and friends, but it can be draining if you give with an objective in mind. When you give freely, you receive freely—that's the signal that you're in balance on this score.

You are meant to love all, but be sure to focus special attention on your beloved so that he knows he's Number One.

You'll find a true companion in Aries, whose fiery nature matches your own as you seek fantastic adventures together. Taurus understands your need to sustain and support the processes of growth and development, but your mutual stubbornness could get in the way unless you each learn to bend. Gemini gives voice and mobility to your inspiration, while you help her find focus and direction. You'll receive loving care and a rich family life with Cancer, and your optimism will lift his mood. A fellow Leo is as energetic and fun-loving as you, but you could become too competitive with each other. Virgo shares your loyalty, so you know she'll be true to you—and she'll keep you organized. Libra loves the glamorous life just like you; together you'll trip the light fantastic and keep up on the latest in entertainment and style. Scorpio brings depth and intensity to match your enthusiasm and vitality, while passion runs strong for both of you. Sagittarius lifts your sights to new, higher goals, sparking your initiative with fire of its own. Capricorn adds structure and responsibility to your inspirational leadership style, creating a very effective combination. Aquarius shares your interest in groups and group dynamics, although this sign prefers aloofness and independence to your immersion approach. The tenderness of Pisces could get in the way until you realize how valuable sensitivity is when added to your passion for life.

Making Your Place in the World

Leo, your warmth and generosity are factors of success in many fields. Although all the creative arts and pursuits of culture are your delight, you may thrill especially to acting. The lights, the audience, the chance to dress as a king or a priestess, to play the role of another person—these put you in top form. Even if it is not your career path, performance activities can make life worth living no matter what your day job. You may enjoy another type of performance activity: teaching. Standing in front of people and inspiring them through greater knowledge satisfies your desire to give to others and contribute to their development. You will also be good in sales of whatever type, as long as you believe in what you are selling. You could stumble on your road to success if you ignore the details of the work you do. Staying organized and adding attention to the minutiae in addition to the big picture will keep you on track.

Putting Your Best Foot Forward

With your love of others' attentions, you instinctively seek to be at the center of things. However, there are times when you will need to take to the sidelines in order to let others have their day in the Sun. Not only does this keep you in balance with the others in your life, but it keeps you in balance with yourself. You can't be "on" all the time, anymore than anyone else can. Everyone needs times to be receptive and to let others take the lead. If you are confident of yourself and your abilities, you will find it easier to take a back seat in order to stay in balance with those around you. The more you can do to build your love of yourself—your self-esteem—the easier it will be to do this. In the same vein, the less you blow your own horn (and the more real talent and skill you have), the more an audience will gather around you. One more way to be at the center is to be in your *own* center—to maintain inner balance. When you are inwardly centered you will always speak from your heart, and that has the most impact on those around you.

Tools for Change

The more you can do to increase your skills at whatever you do, Leo, the more effective you will be in garnering the attention you seek and giving your own unique expression of love and creativity to the world. This means that when you learn something, you need to learn it well. Get the best education you can from the experts— and then keep learning. One of the best ways to ensure that you keep your edge in your field, or any area of life, is to teach what you know. Keeping a step ahead of your students will sharpen your own expertise and give you a chance to integrate the knowledge you have. Another way to keep your mastery honed is to make sure that you take time out periodically to play. You're not usually one to be accused of overwork, but it's good to remember the importance of random and spontaneous acts; by not spending all your time at one activity, you are able to add more creativity to anything you do. Participating in games, sports, and performances is more effective than observing them when you need to spur your own genius.

Another way to keep yourself centered is through regular exercise. In particular, activities involving balance work well—from gymnastics to yoga to skating. Becoming involved in volunteer service or charitable causes can be especially valuable to your long-term direction this year. In doing so you create goodwill with others, and you get the chance to give, which opens your heart and fills your spiritual bank account with the kind of gold you *can* take with you. Dramatic role-playing, performance, or production are purely Leonine therapies, because through them you can express your passions and participate in a dynamic energy exchange—the type you live for.

Your spine and heart, ruled by Leo, are most important to your overall health. Stay in shape with aerobic activities so that your heart muscle is strong; then eat fats in moderation—healthy, non-saturated fats—and plenty of fresh fruits and vegetables. For your spine, you must work to keep it supple and strong. Strengthening exercises such as yoga or Pilates back-bends, moderate weight training targeting the back, and calisthenics are highly effective. For flexibility and stretching, forward-bending postures and exercises are ideal.

Affirmation for the Year

I live and give from my heart.

The Year Ahead for Leo

The pressure's on, but so is the potential for greatness, Leo, as the planets poise themselves to activate your special qualities. Jupiter supports you from its position in Libra and your Third House. This is an opportunity period for you, one that allows you to assess where you stand in your world and decide what paths you want to tread next. You'll feel like exploring new options and experimenting with new ideas. You will feel even more social than usual. You may spend more time about town, attending events, and circulating with friends and family, or you may take a class or two, broadening your mind and skill set. If you are so inclined, you could take on a writing project—especially one which you intend to publish. Once Jupiter goes into Scorpio on October 25 you may feel like staying closer to home and enjoying the fruits of your labors in a more sedentary or private way. You may also feel like improving your home by enlarging it or moving to something bigger or richer in style. You could even add a member to your family during the coming year, whether a child or another relative or house mate.

Saturn starts the year in Cancer and your solar Twelfth House, where it will give you more time to bring hidden issues to the surface. Sometimes when Saturn is in this house we feel confined or restricted in some way. However, as with all circumstances, we can put these limitations to good use and come out stronger and better prepared for future obstacles. Once Saturn enters your home sign of Leo, life becomes more definite. There's something you can use to define your existence, and you can take action once again: in fact, you may wish for quieter days. Typically, with Saturn in our Sun sign we are working doubly hard, even to the point of carrying two jobs. This is because we want to accomplish something, and Saturn is obliging us by giving us the avenues for doing so.

Chiron crosses the boundary between Capricorn and Aquarius twice this year before it makes its final pass into Aquarius on December 5. As it does so, it moves between your Sixth and Seventh Houses. While Chiron is in Capricorn you'll continue the thrust of the last three years, when you've been dealing with critical health and work matters. This year you may feel a need to hurry toward your goals to complete them before Chiron finally enters Aquarius. By the year's end your concerns will morph into an examination and discovery of your relationship wounds. You may find that past hurts are coloring current ties, or someone in your life may be wounded in such a way that it affects your relationship. Chiron will help you work out these issues over the next five years.

Uranus is in Pisces again this year, your solar Eighth House. You are awakening to the realities of how you look financially to the rest of the world, and it may not be a pretty picture. If you need to clean up your act, Uranus will provide support, but if you resist, Uranus will send shockwaves into your life that are really of your own making. This can also be an excellent time to explore the realms of the occult, for you are finding that there's more to life than what you can see.

Neptune in Aquarius remains in your solar Seventh House, enshrouding your relationships in an air of mystery. You may be attracted to partners who are enigmatic or spiritual. They could also be unavailable, whether because of other commitments or because they lack interest in commitment. Occasionally this could represent a partner who will take advantage of you and your good faith. Although it suggests relationships with a lack of definition or hidden influences, it can also bring a partner with whom you feel a deep soul bond or spiritual feeling. You may find it difficult to figure out exactly which, if any, of these scenarios is true, but ultimately Neptune reveals the inner truth of whatever it touches, and you will know more about what you are dealing with.

Pluto can be found once more in Sagittarius and your solar Fifth House. This is a comfortable position (if any position of Pluto can be called that), where it empowers your creative efforts. Even if you are not in the arts, you may seek to blaze a trail with an invention or innovation in your chosen field of study, a hobby, or your career. Whatever it is, this inspiration comes naturally to you with your dramatic flair.

The eclipses are in your Third and Ninth Houses this year, supporting a harmonious period of growth and reaching toward your goals. They reinforce what is already a year of relatively easy progress—if you can keep yourself motivated when the pressure is off. They suggest that you will be positively stimulated through travel and contact with new ideas and studies.

If you were born from July 22 to August 4, Saturn in Leo is in direct contact with your Sun from your solar First House. Although this contact will not be "official" until July 16, you have been feeling the culmination of this long-term cycle coming for at least a few months—or maybe years. This is a time of hard work and diligence that, if you fulfill its potential, will be richly rewarding for years to come. Don't be surprised if you decide to set a new course, for this is the beginning of a thirty-year cycle related to accomplishing a task that is, for you, heroic. It will stretch you to your limits and force you to dig deep within to find the strength to fulfill it at times, but the more challenging it is, the more you will grow, and the more deeply satisfied you will be by the results. This is not only because you will accomplish more, but because you will know that you have given it your all. You may pass through a phase of discovering what you don't want and cutting those things away from your life, from habits to people to activities. This will clear the way to new activities which will push you to the edge of your potential. You'll be working very hard for the next three years. Important turning points will occur from July 16 through 23, and around November 11.

If you were born from July 25 to August 3, you'll have the opportunity to shake loose from your restrictions as Uranus in Pisces transits your Sun from your solar Eighth House. You may find that you are uncomfortably indebted to others in your life, whether they be bankers or loved ones. More than anything now, you are likely to want to break free from those bonds that tie you down, and you may feel willing to do almost anything as your feelings of confinement mount. Uranus means to shake us loose: it is the first planet to point the way to the ultimate freedom of spiritual life. However, we can do so in an orderly manner if we can cope with our inner turmoil, and where Eighth House matters are concerned that is often the only way we can extricate ourselves. If we ignore our inner urges at this time then Uranus may send lightning bolts into our life, but it only does so when we refuse to heed more subtle signals. By making adjustments now you'll avoid unsettling events. If shocking events do occur, you can count on the ensuing chaos to clear the air and give you the chance to get on a better course. Key dates for you will be February 2, June 14, August 31, and November 15.

If you were born from August 5 to 11, Neptune will be contacting your Sun from Aquarius and your solar Seventh House. You may discover the unfathomable and fascinating mystery of human nature—perhaps through a new relationship, or one that opens up to you in a new way. You may become interested in psychology or seek to understand the spiritual aspects of relationships. You may feel a soul connection with someone or form a relationship that is based on your shared spiritual outlook on life. Your existing partner could start developing more interest in his or her inner world, or even take up a more religious or spiritual path. There are other, darker possibilities as well. You may be unable to see your relationships with others clearly, resulting in false idealism and disillusionment. You could be vulnerable to undermining influences: someone could take advantage of you, or your partner could be using drugs or alcohol in an unhealthy way. It is important this year to listen to your inner voice in regard to your relationships, but it's also important to verify what you hear. Neptune leads us into the truths of the inner world, but they are often twisted on their way into the world we share with others. Key dates for this process are February 2, May 19, August 8, and October 26.

If you were born from August 12 to 22, Saturn in Cancer will be highlighting your growth from your solar Twelfth House. This process began last summer, and it will continue through July 16, when Saturn enters Leo. Now you are in the middle of working toward changes that you initiated in November of 2004. Since Saturn has been in your Twelfth House for more than two years already, you are well acquainted with the issues that it symbolizes in your life. You have probably felt confined by a variety of factors that, when you think it through, have pushed you toward a waiting game. Now, as Saturn triggers your Sun, you may have a clearer picture of what it will take to resolve these issues, but you may still need to wait until Saturn enters your sign in July before you can take clear steps in the desired direction. For now, you have the opportunity to develop patience and consider all your options in following a particular course. You may need to gather resources, or simply make sure it's what you really want. The process you are in now is evolutionary, and your experiences between now and mid-summer will inform the actions that you ultimately take. If you use this time to do some "spiritual weightlifting"—work through all your inner demons and reach a place of peace and clarity—you will truly be making the most of this time. Key turning points in this process will occur around January 13 and March 21.

If you were born from August 14 to 18, Pluto in Sagittarius will be supporting a harmonious process of change in your life from your solar Fifth House. Pluto is drawing you into the depths of your creative nature, and you want to express yourself in ways that you've suppressed in the past. You may feel a sense of urgency to make something that matters, that will leave its favorable mark on society. You could be hung up on the idea of gaining notoriety for your efforts. There is nothing wrong with this: if you use this urge to challenge yourself to stretch your self-expression closer to your true potential, you will accomplish what Pluto sets out for you. Most critical is the feeling that your life must mean something, for our life is our most important creative product. If you have given your energy to others without having a life of your own in the past, that will no longer be tolerable. You will feel compelled to seek self-definition, to engage in activities and to express yourself in ways that are more fulfilling and reveal your true nature, both to yourself and others around you. If you have children, you may find that they are involved in a transformative process themselves. As they mature you may feel freed to explore your own nature, or they may be changing in a way that teaches you about yourself by reflection. Pluto's energy will be strongest around March 26, June 13, September 2, and December 15.

Leo/January

Planetary Hotspots

As Saturn reaches the culmination of its yearly cycle, it has been increasing the activity in your Twelfth House of hidden influences, confinement, and cosmic unity. Chances are, you've been feeling held back in some way, perhaps due to chronic illness, or just due to tiredness. This feeling will peak around January 13. Since you've been working on this process for two years, the level of claustrophobia you feel should be a signal as to how well you're doing at freeing yourself.

Wellness and Keeping Fit

With a new Chiron cycle starting on January 16 in your Sixth House of health, you get one more year to work out how to bring your physical body into a perfect state of balance and vitality. Holistic treatment is especially helpful with Chiron, since much of its operation is within our energy body, so you'll gain great benefits by accepting support from a practitioner who sees the body as a whole.

Love and Life Connections

Kids and romance feature strongly in your focus all month long, but especially on January 28, when Mars contacts Pluto in your solar Fifth House. This challenging aspect can bring conflict to the surface in a volatile way, so it is important to keep your cool and seek help if you need it. Whatever occurs around this date will tell you what you and your loved ones need to overcome over the next two years.

Finance and Success

As Mars travels through your Fifth House it amps up your creativity. You may feel more poetic and dramatic, but you may also want to pour some of that energy into meaningful and productive creative pursuits, especially if you use your creativity in your career. You can be especially productive around January 28.

Rewarding Days

2, 3, 4, 7, 8, 15, 16, 20, 21, 25, 26, 27, 30, 31

Challenging Days

5, 6, 11, 12, 17, 18, 19

Leo/February

Planetary Hotspots

With Jupiter in your Third House of communications and commerce, you've been overflowing with opportunities in this area. Your activity level will become more intense on February 1 as Jupiter enters its four-month retrograde period. Subtle Neptune's new cycle starts on February 2, initiating a new year of growth in relationships. Last but not least, Uranus makes its new beginning on February 25, continuing to motivate a renovation of your financial dealings with others.

Wellness and Keeping Fit

Your immune system may bottom out this month as Mars begins its transit of your Sixth House of health on February 6. You may be more vulnerable to viruses. Not working beyond the point of exhaustion is key to avoiding these difficulties.

Love and Life Connections

You're starting a new cycle in your partnership and other committed relationships on February 2—a part of the ongoing spiritualization of this part of your life. It's likely that you have been making sacrifices that, although you may resent them, are important to you when you consider the alternatives. You can keep your spirits up by keeping those higher principles in mind, and find ways to break away from those sacrifices periodically so that you can have a life of your own as well.

Finance and Success

For two years now, Uranus has been awakening you to greater possibilities in the way you handle financial matters. You may have experienced anything from cataclysmic financial misfortune to an unexpected windfall or inheritance. Whatever the stimulus, it will benefit you to think "out of the box" in moving forward.

Rewarding Days
3, 4, 11, 12, 16, 17, 21, 22, 25, 26, 27

Challenging Days
1, 2, 7, 8, 14, 15, 28

Leo/March

Planetary Hotspots

A few more months, and you'll be free—or at least you'll feel that way around March 21 as Saturn reaches the final turning point of its yearly cycle, which ends on July 23. Mercury turns retrograde on March 19, leading you to revisit—perhaps revamp—your goals and life objectives. On March 26 you'll feel Pluto's intensity in your Fifth House of romance, creativity, and children, where ongoing changes reach critical mass.

Wellness and Keeping Fit

Acute illness or injury are possible from March 3 to 7 as Mars connects with Jupiter and Saturn in your health houses. You may also experience more mundane pressure, which results in a stress reaction or tiredness. If you avoid pushing yourself too hard, the most extreme manifestations can be avoided.

Love and Life Connections

If you have children, at least one of them may be going through a difficult time or transforming in positive ways. Around March 26 this situation will assume center stage through an event or interaction, pointing to what needs to be done over the coming five months to improve matters.

Finance and Success

There are plenty of hurdles to jump from March 3 through March 7 as you deal with a crush of information which generates work for you. As March 19 approaches, you may be reconsidering the path you've chosen for yourself, thinking about ways you can adjust it to make your life more fulfilling.

Rewarding Days

3, 4, 11, 12, 15, 16, 17, 20, 21, 22, 25, 26, 30, 31

Challenging Days

1, 2, 7, 8, 14, 15, 28

Leo/April

Planetary Hotspots

Third house matters—communications, writing, learning, and commerce—reach a peak this month as Jupiter passes the halfway point in its yearly cycle on April 3. The same area of your chart is triggered indirectly when a solar eclipse overshadows us on April 8, increasing the peak effect. Mercury's return to direct motion takes it out of the limelight on April 12, while a lunar eclipse casts its shadow in your Fourth House of home and family on April 24 to round out the month.

Wellness and Keeping Fit

Health and fitness are on the back burner this month while you attend to other situations. It's still important to maintain your healthy routines, and if you can manage a vacation or weekend get-away it will make life all that much more worthwhile, but it is best to avoid April 8 as a travel day.

Love and Life Connections

Your brothers and sisters may be in your life more these days, and if so, they're most prominent in your focus early this month. On April 13 you may feel the sacrifices you're making for love most acutely, but it's best not to take it out on someone else. If you need to talk about something that's bothering you, do it with a calm demeanor.

Finance and Success

Life flows smoothly in your career and finances these days—in fact, these areas are going exceptionally well. All the work you're doing to support your professional success is paying off.

Rewarding Days

7, 8, 12, 13, 17, 18, 22, 23, 26, 27

Challenging Days

3, 4, 9, 10, 11, 24, 25, 30

Leo/May

Planetary Hotspots

Partnerships show up as the hot spot for you this month, Leo, as both Chiron and Neptune cast a bright light into your solar Seventh House on May 8 and 19. Each of these events signals the start of five months of focused attention on healing a rift or overcoming an obstacle to your growth with your partner. This applies to business partnerships as well as love relationships, and to any agreements you have made with others. You may tend to give too much of yourself in team situations—or not enough. The next five months will ferret out the difficulties and create the circumstances to overcome them.

Wellness and Keeping Fit

Team activities may induce you to engage more readily in exercise this month as Venus moves through your Eleventh House of group activities. Take advantage of it.

Love and Life Connections

Whatever you're dealing with in your primary personal relationship, it's been happening for a long time—ever since Neptune entered your solar Seventh House in 1998. Now that Chiron is there, too, you will be able to see the heart of the problem so that you can heal it. As these two planets make their retrograde stations here on May 8 and 19, the window of revelation opens. If your problem is that there *is* no relationship, you'll understand that issue better as well.

Finance and Success

With Mars now in your house of other people's money, you'll have to be more active in dealing with matters here. This could mean pursuing what's owed you, or making altered arrangements for paying your debts. Your income could increase as well through June 11.

Rewarding Days

5, 6, 9, 10, 14, 15, 19, 20, 23, 24, 25

Challenging Days

1, 7, 8, 21, 22, 28, 29

Leo/June

Planetary Hotspots

Your efforts of the past four months are starting to produce results as Jupiter's retrograde period ends on June 5. You've been busy with paperwork, writing, phone calls, and connections, but it will begin to ease off after this date. On June 13, Pluto is at the midpoint of its yearly round through your Fifth House of romance, children, and creativity, bringing out obstacles so that they can be cleared. Uranus enters its five-month retrograde period on June 14, invigorating your efforts to expand your financial strength.

Wellness and Keeping Fit

Your schedule may now permit you to get away from it all, and it's just what you want as Mars enters your solar Ninth House of travel on June 11. Activity in other areas of your life will slow down after June 14.

Love and Life Connections

Sometimes we need a break from our loved ones, even though we love and respect them very dearly. Mercury and Venus are entering the retreat area of your chart—the Twelfth House—so even if this means taking a day hike alone, putzing around in your office with the door closed, or going out of town, taking a little time to yourself this month will increase your mileage with others and desensitize your trigger points for months to come.

Finance and Success

You're taking the plunge now, embarking on the next stage in that new financial venture or in dealing with old debts. The coming five months will be a trial period for the new arrangements you've been able to make. Be prepared to meet the unexpected anytime until mid-November, but especially around June 14.

Rewarding Days

1, 2, 5, 6, 7, 10, 11, 12, 15, 16, 17, 20, 21, 28, 29

Challenging Days

3, 4, 18, 19, 24, 25, 30

Leo/July

Planetary Hotspots

There's a lot of action in your life now as the power areas of your chart are triggered. Saturn enters your sign on July 16 for a three-year stay. Your work begins now. You may decide that the only way to solve a problem is to take on an extra responsibility; if so, the good news is that you can solve the problem just by doing the work.

Wellness and Keeping Fit

Self-discipline is the key to your well-being now, as Saturn moves into your sign. It will bring out any dormant physical difficulties—especially those associated with age. However, that does not mean that you can't overcome them; Saturn is also about the success of consistent effort.

Love and Life Connections

The buck stops with you as Saturn in your solar First House faces off with Chiron in your Seventh House of relationships. You have already been giving and giving to your partner, and it's time to give again. However, even though the balance scales may be tilted in your partner's favor, you can give wisely—in the right way that helps him or her to overcome difficulties but doesn't overtax you.

Finance and Success

On July 28 you'll have to resolve a time-and-effort conflict between career and relationship. This could involve a business partnership. You'll catch a glimpse of the potential issues starting on July 16, but it is a situation that you will be dealing with through the end of January 2006.

Rewarding Days

3, 4, 8, 9, 13, 14, 17, 18, 25, 26, 27, 30, 31

Challenging Days

1, 2, 15, 16, 21, 22, 28, 29

Leo/August

Planetary Hotspots

Relationships continue to be front and center for you in August, Leo, as Neptune reaches its annual peak on August 8. You're looking for ways to balance the burdens you are currently facing. You feel overwhelmed, adrift, but after August 15 you get some assistance and find some answers.

Wellness and Keeping Fit

Reducing stress is the most important thing you can do to support your fitness. Meditation, yoga, and the creative arts will all help. Working out with the tools and settings at hand—at work, in your home or neighborhood, at the park on the way to work—will minimize the time commitment and make your routine both convenient and varied.

Love and Life Connections

An element of surrender is required as events sweep you along. Key dates are August 8, 15, and 31. If you think of surrender not as giving up something but as opening up to inner truth, you'll find guidance and solace in the experience.

Finance and Success

As if the challenges in your partnerships isn't enough, financial matters pressure you at the end of the month as Uranus's cycle culminates. The situation may be related to what's happening in your relationship life. Reach out to others and ask for help—you'll find you're not alone.

Rewarding Days

4, 5, 9, 10, 14, 15, 22, 23, 26, 27, 28, 31

Challenging Days

11, 12, 13, 18, 19, 24, 25

Leo/September

Planetary Hotspots

One lone planetary event stands out in September: the end of Pluto's retrograde in your solar Fifth House. Ongoing changes in the way you use your creativity, your life and relationships with your children, and your romantic life rise to the surface like so much cream. These transformations may be both disturbing and inspiring. More subtle but just as significant is the fact that Mars is getting ready for its biennial retrograde—this time in your Tenth House. You'll be reworking the ways you fulfill your career goals.

Wellness and Keeping Fit

If you can keep your emotions on an even keel this month you'll be in good health, but with your dramatic style, that's no small task. Don't let your flair and passion lead you to make a mountain out of a molehill. Your greatest strength this month is your ability to distance yourself from events and see them in the context of the big picture.

Love and Life Connections

The extra attention required by your partnership has not abated, yet career demands are up. One way you can cope with this is to call upon personal friends and family to help out. With your ongoing natural generosity, others will not hesitate to assist.

Finance and Success

Business and career become a more high-maintenance area of your life as the month progresses. Mars will retrograde in your solar Tenth House October 1, giving you more than three months to handle challenges there. Conflicts may erupt this month, and related issues will need to be resolved by the end of January 2006.

Rewarding Days

1, 2, 5, 6, 7, 10, 11, 18, 19, 22, 23, 24, 27, 28, 29

Challenging Days

8, 9, 14, 15, 20, 21

Leo/October

Planetary Hotspots

On October 1, Mars starts its first retrograde period in two years, bringing out issues in your career, profession, or business. That's not all, however, as two eclipses also mark a fresh start in the way you perceive and achieve in the world. More new beginnings come in your home and family life with the first day of fall, when the new Jupiter cycle begins in your Fourth House.

Wellness and Keeping Fit

Your health should hold up well under the prevailing stressors, in spite of their frequency and intensity. Your chi is up, so you're likely to feel challenged now rather than overwhelmed. Exercise at home or compete against yourself or other individuals as a special break from the routine.

Love and Life Connections

You get a boost on the home front, and you're finding it especially enjoyable to spend time there. You may plan to renovate or repair—even move—but you are looking forward to better times, no matter how you plan to accomplish it. You'll be creating an appropriate foundation for future happiness and successes.

Finance and Success

The key to handling all that is on your plate right now is attitude. Adopting a "can do" calm and capable approach will go a long way toward making your world work better for you. The eclipses on October 3 and 17 will test your ability to manage events, and will open doors for you if you know how to see them as opportunities.

Rewarding Days

2, 3, 4, 7, 8, 16, 17, 20, 21, 25, 26, 30, 31

Challenging Days

5, 6, 11, 12, 13, 18, 19

Leo/November

Planetary Hotspots
Three planetary transitions make this an eventful month. On November 14, Mercury's retrograde starts, and the tension with your children and creative processes increases, leading you to discover better ways to connect with them. On November 15, you'll have completed five months of renovation in your financial affairs, ready to tie up loose ends as Uranus's retrograde ends. You'll become aware of a new challenge requiring work and self-discipline when Saturn enters its five-month retrograde period on November 22.

Wellness and Keeping Fit
As the month wears on, your life becomes more eventful, making it difficult to fit your regular healthy habits into your schedule if they require extra effort. However, this is the very time they are most important. Do your best to eat well, exercise, and get enough sleep.

Love and Life Connections
Even though life is heating up for everyone with all the planetary activity this and last month, you'll find others have time to support you in getting the work done, so be alert to the possibilities. You'll probably have to ask for it, but it will be freely given.

Finance and Success
You've been learning more about how to handle your financial relationship with the world for three years, putting out fires and developing ingenious methods for capitalizing on your circumstances. This may involve cultivating new ways to earn money—some of which are more risky but have the potential for greater return. As Uranus ends its third year in this part of your chart, you're beginning to see what potential will be fulfilled there. The coming four years will see the fruit ripen on the vines. The more you can live in a world of possibility, yet in a grounded way, the better will be the harvest.

Rewarding Days
3, 4, 5, 12, 13, 16, 17, 18, 21, 22, 23, 26, 27

Challenging Days
1, 2, 8, 9, 14, 15, 28, 29, 30

Leo/December

Planetary Hotspots

"Out with the old, in with the new" applies to December as well as the coming new year, as the retrograde periods of Mercury and Mars end and Pluto's new annual cycle starts. Venus's six-week retrograde begins on December 24, opening the door to new relationship agreements and commitments. The fever pitch of action in your life slows down after December 15, but don't let it stop you from paying attention to what happens on that day. You'll get clues to what Pluto's new cycle holds for you in the realm of children, entertainment, and creative pursuits. Although you've been working with these areas for years, each will present a new twist until Pluto completes its time here in 2008.

Wellness and Keeping Fit

You may have felt separated from your sense of play since mid-November, what with all the duties you've faced. You'll find it again after December 3.

Love and Life Connections

By the time Venus retrogrades on December 24 you'll be aware of some areas in your relationship life that need renegotiating. Whatever comes up will go to the heart of your relationship bond, and you may feel as though the discussion will threaten it. The opportunity exists for your relationship to move into new, healthier territory. However, this will occur over the coming eighteen months—and only if it is first identified and acknowledged by both partners.

Finance and Success

As Mars returns to its normal mode of travel, you'll see the tension at work relax. That doesn't mean that all problems are solved, only that people have discovered new ways of dealing with them. Continue on your path of working toward their resolution.

Rewarding Days

1, 2, 9, 10, 14, 15, 18, 19, 20, 23, 24, 25, 28, 29

Challenging Days

5, 6, 11, 12, 13, 26, 27

LEO ACTION TABLE

These dates reflect the best—but not the only—times for success and ease in these activities, according to your Sun sign.

	JAN	FEB	MAR	APR	MAY	JUN	JUL	AUG	SEPT	OCT	NOV	DEC
Move										15-31	1-3, 11, 12	
Start a class									28-30	1-15		
Join a club						5-19						
Ask for a raise				3-13			1-31	1-6	6-30	1, 2		
Look for work	14-31	1-24			16-31	1-4						
Get pro advice	22, 23	18, 19	16, 17	13, 14	10, 11	6, 7	3, 4, 31	1, 27, 28	24, 25	21, 22	19, 20	14, 15
Get a loan	24, 25	10, 21	18, 19	15, 16	12, 13	9, 10	5-7	2, 3, 29, 30	26, 27	23, 24	19, 20	16-18
See a doctor	14-31	1-24				19-30	1-24					
Start a diet	6, 7, 14-31	1-6										
End relationship							31	1				
Buy clothes	7-13										4-26	21-31
Get a makeover							4-24		6-30	1, 2		
New romance												16-31
Vacation	26, 27	8-28	1-4, 12-31	17, 18	14, 15	10-12	8, 9	4, 5, 31	1, 2, 28, 29	25, 26	21-23	19, 20

VIRGO

The Virgin
August 22 to September 22

♍

Element:	Earth
Quality:	Mutable
Polarity:	Yin/Feminine
Planetary Ruler:	Mercury
Meditation:	I can allow time for myself.
Gemstone:	Sapphire
Power Stones:	Peridot, amazonite, rhodochrosite
Key Phrase:	I analyze
Glyph:	Greek symbol for containment
Anatomy:	Abdomen, intestines, gall bladder
Color:	Taupe, gray, navy blue
Animal:	Domesticated animals
Myths/Legends:	Demeter, Astraea, Hygeia
House:	Sixth
Opposite Sign:	Pisces
Flower:	Pansy
Key Word:	Discriminating

Your Ego's Strengths and Shortcomings

Yours is the second earth sign of the Zodiac, and like your partner signs Taurus and Capricorn, you are practical and grounded. Your special niche in the earthy Zodiac is in service to the community. You try to fulfill the needs of the people around you. You are ready to work, ready to be of assistance, willing to support the efforts of the group. More than that, you look for noble causes to support. You are socially conscious, and you're willing to support the efforts of those who will improve the conditions of others. You are alert to flaws in the situations you see around you. You are the expert in your office who knows the problems in workflow, areas of disorganization, and who's not working. You know how to organize an event or a lecture, and your practical skills may extend to crafts and other useful pursuits. This doesn't mean that you keep your own home or office sparkling clean though, because, with your natural curiosity about the world and the value others see in your skills, you have more than enough projects on your plate at any given time.

Another earthy aspect of your nature is the interaction of the physical body with mind, emotions, and spirit. You hold physical health in high regard, and you do your best to keep yourself in good health and good shape. Inner health concerns you as much as outer health, and you value your well-being over your appearance. If your earthy side is expressed in overabundance, you may feel bogged down, depressed, or overly analytic. If you get too caught up in earthly details, you may become anxious, or even impair your immune system. Kept in balance, your common sense and logic are welcome in every environment.

Shining Your Love Light

Although you may lie low when it comes to showing your love to others, you offer that rare combination of loyalty, dedication, and faith in your partner and the relationship that ties you. You may be cautious about the type of partner you choose, but you know that it's better to make a wise choice to begin with than to blind yourself to things that you know will become obstacles later on. Your greatest weakness in love is a tendency to think that doing things for your partner is the best way to show love, but your partner may need other assurances.

You'll be energized by fiery Aries, who takes action based on your plans. Taurus shares your earthy practicality and adds steadiness and calm to your efforts. You'll find much in common with Gemini, who shares your mental approach to life in a breezier way. Cancer's warmth and nurturing is welcome because you have such a hard time asking for support—and in return she will appreciate your dedication and feel comforted by it. Leo brightens your optimism and adds a spirit of generosity and spring to your step, while you contribute pragmatism and efficiency. A fellow Virgo understands your ways without explanation and knows the value of dedicated effort. Libra brings a more objective viewpoint to your cares about the world, while you give Libra insight into the joys of serving others. Scorpio shares your appreciation of human nature and helps you become aware of your deep feelings. Sagittarius's ideals inspire you to achieve altruistic goals and rise above the details, while you support Sagittarius in getting organized. Capricorn is a kindred earth spirit, a companion in building a better world, with you supplying the details and he the big picture. You'll be sparked by Aquarius— even irritated at times—but she'll induce you to see things in a new way, dispassionately, from all sides of a situation. Pisces is a reflecting pool for you, helping you to see your true inner nature and the connectedness of all things, while you ground Pisces and help him manifest his dreams into the visible world.

Making Your Place in the World

In a world where business, organizational, and practical skills are so highly valued, you are generally recognized as an asset on any team. You are capable of leadership because you are so conscientious about how you use the power given to you. Just as valuable, you see leadership roles as positions of responsibility, not glamour, and you strive to fulfill them with a pragmatic view of what is good for the group rather than your own interests. You are also a quick study at almost any subject, especially in the practical arts. Building crafts such as carpentry or domestic crafts such as dressmaking are right up your alley. Your natural efficiency and ingenuity suggest that your talents may be well applied in product or systems design; financial planning and accounting; or business policies, procedures, and workflow.

Putting Your Best Foot Forward

To be at your best, Virgo, it's most important for you to realize that you don't have to be perfect. You often shy away from trying to do what you really want to do—or avoid promoting yourself—because you can see your flaws and shortcomings. You feel you must wait until you're "better at it." If you do that, you'll never fulfill your dreams. So, to overcome this pattern, you need to take the risk of getting others' feedback. That means developing your competency, and then taking the big plunge and practicing the skills you have learned. As you engage with others, you will probably find that you are at least as adept as anyone else at your task, if not better. As you do so, you will build your self-confidence and empower yourself to take new, bolder steps. Another thing you can do is to reduce the size of your "worry room." Virgos tend to have a large worry room, where all your anxieties go. When there are a lot of them, they crowd each other down to size, but when you only have a few, they expand to take up just as much space in your life. If you reduce your worry capacity, you'll be happier and less prone to nervous tensions and disorders—and more resilient when it comes to taking the slings and arrows of everyday life.

Tools for Change

Because yours is an earth sign, your physical body is a "learning environment" for you. Many of your issues come out through health patterns and illnesses, and accordingly it is vital that you focus on your health, for that is the foundation of all your activities and successes. Tools you can use involve those that keep your body working for you instead of against you. First, you need to stay in touch with your inner being. If something you are doing does not resonate with your true path, you may become ill as a signal that you're headed in the wrong direction. If you are following your heart, you will be stronger. Interpreting your dreams and keeping a journal are two ways you can get in touch with your inner self. Also, don't overwork. When you overwork, your body becomes fatigued from being pressed too hard by the mind (and never mind the potential for repetitive motion injuries). With your tendency to focus on details, you may lose sight of the big picture and amplify your worries. This taxes the nervous system, which results in muscle tension—a common Virgo problem. There are many ways to release muscle tension: yoga, Pilates, hot baths, saunas, massage, meditation, and aerobic exercise, to name a few. You may also have a tendency to suppress your emotions, and this can result in physical difficulties as well. Discovering the emotional source of an illness can be difficult, but a holistic health practitioner, acupuncturist, or a chiropractor who practices N.E.T. (neuro-emotional training) may be especially good at giving you the support you need. Another technique you can apply is the "NO" technique: say "no" when you need to—to take care of yourself, to give yourself a break, to make a transition to something new, to stop someone from taking advantage of you. Practice ways of saying it in private so you have several ways that you consider acceptable to say it, depending on the circumstances. After a while it will become a natural part of your vocabulary. Finally, perhaps the most important tool you can give yourself is the help and support of other people. You don't have to go it alone. You can, and deserve to, ask for other people's help. As adults, we are meant to be interdependent, and we disrupt our relationships if we don't allow others to do for us just as we do for them.

Affirmation for the Year

I accept my strengths as well as my weaknesses.

The Year Ahead for Virgo

The value of your social contacts is underscored once again this year, Virgo, as the planets slowly move through the social western hemisphere of your solar chart. Jupiter continues to track the gradual development of plans you made in 2003–04 by moving through your Second House. You are gathering resources and testing the substance of the many opportunities that arose then, for you cannot fulfill them all, and you want to choose the ones that offer the most benefit in terms of wealth and fulfillment. You may be spending more than you're bringing in right now in an effort to bootstrap your initiatives into action, acquiring new skills or investigating the factors and formalities involved in pursuing the various options before you. You see this as an acceptable risk as long as you can maintain your optimism about the future, but if you harbor self-doubt you may become nervous about these gambles. The extent to which you can stay upbeat will determine the success of your efforts in the long run. Once Jupiter enters Scorpio on October 25 your focus shifts to the realms of communication and social contact. You'll be reaching out more to others, and they'll be your next resource in reaching your objectives.

Saturn is moving from Cancer to Leo on July 16 after nearly three years in Cancer and your solar Eleventh House. While Saturn is still in Cancer you'll have a few more months to work on developing a more effective and supportive network of acquaintances and business contacts. You've been questioning your old associations, scrutinizing them to see if they're worth the effort you put into them. It's not that you'll part with your old milieu wholesale, but rather that you'll sort through and weed out the less favorable ones. When Saturn enters Leo in July it will also move into your solar Twelfth House. You may find that you want to remove yourself from the public eye to a certain extent and cultivate more inner peace. You're more likely to consider filling your spiritual bank account than your physical one.

Chiron also changes signs, moving from Capricorn and your solar Fifth House to Aquarius and your solar Sixth. For three years you've been making a transition from one expression of your creativity to another. Chiron in Aquarius will focus you on your ways of handling work and stress. You may find that you are out of balance in some areas, and this could be weakening your health. Now you'll get a chance to make adjustments in your health routines and work habits so that you are more efficient and less tied to your obligations with more time to play and relax.

Uranus in Pisces continues to make your relationship life more exciting as those around you defy your expectations and change. It's also possible that you are yourself changing in surprising ways. This is the way to master this transit: the more you can be aware of and respond to the need for change in your own life, the less it will be necessary for others to intervene.

Neptune will be in Aquarius and your solar Sixth House for another year, continuing to influence your path to better health. With Neptune you are likely to find that dramatic measures do not work as well as gradual approaches in rectifying health imbalances. In addition, you may not even recognize the need for correction if you do not pay attention to subtle signs in your body.

Pluto remains in Sagittarius and your solar Fourth House, extending your opportunities for deep inner change. You've been in constant transition since 1995, until that transition has become a way of life. The renovations in your home and private life progress this year—your long-held dreams of remodeling your home, moving to a new one, or devoting more time to your family may be realized.

The eclipses are invigorating your solar Second and Eighth Houses in the signs of Aries and Libra. Your finances will go through some changes this year. You may change your source of income or the balance of income to expenditure. It could be time for some serious financial planning—and time to make sure that your insurance coverages are solid.

If you were born from August 22 to September 4, Saturn in Leo is connecting with your Sun from your solar Twelfth House starting July 16. It's time to explore your inner world, as you may be prevented in some way, even if it is just by your own interests, from fully engaging with the world outside your home. You could even be confined due to illness or limitations placed on you by others. Your interest in spiritual pursuits could draw you into a prolonged retreat period, during which time you work on developing your merit. You may find that your happiness is based more on inner worth and fulfillment than on external recognition and financial wealth. The inner life may become more fascinating and vivid to you than the mundane world you normally focus on. Your dreams can be a vital tool in this process of self-discovery, and you can encourage them to be more eloquent in their communication to you by paying more attention to them. You will ultimately make changes in your life path based on what you learn, although you may not have the opportunity to follow through on those ideas right away. Key passages in your inner growth process will occur July 16 through 23 and around November 22.

If you were born from August 25 through September 3, Uranus in Pisces will stimulate change in your relationship life—especially your partnerships. You will perceive changes in those around you that will actually mirror changes in your own nature. Throughout this time you'll have piercing insights into how your own actions influence others. You'll see in stark relief how making seemingly minor changes in the way you act can greatly improve your relationships with others. The key is attitude: once you detect a mistaken impression or interpretation of others' behaviors, you can adjust your attitude toward them and your own behavior will follow suit. Others may also need more freedom from the type of bond you've shared in the past—a child may be grown or spend more time away from you, for example. Your greatest pitfall will be a tendency to hang on too long. If you can be sensitive to others' needs without ignoring your own, you will be able to strike the right balance. If you overreact and give up on a relationship or interpret the need for *some* freedom as a need for *complete* freedom, you can experience needless feelings of rejection and disruption in your ties. Peak experiences of Uranus's energy will come around February 25, June 14, August 31, and November 15.

If you were born from September 5 to 11, Neptune in Aquarius is finally making contact with your Sun from your solar Sixth House. Your daily life "in the trenches" may be ripe for change, and you may find a number of factors that indicate a need for adjustment. You may be discontented with the work you do, the stresses you endure on the job, or the amount of time you must devote to routine activities. You may want more emotional and spiritual fulfillment than you currently experience during your daily activities. This is a good time to get a thorough health examination, as imbalances may begin to surface. You may prefer and gain greater benefit from a holistic and natural approach because they incorporate more subtle diagnostic techniques; standard medical tests may be useful, but your health issues may not yet be detectable through them. If imbalances are detected, you may get the results you desire by using such remedies as homeopathics, Bach flowers, energetic healing, and herbs, with the help of qualified practitioners. A gradual, gentle approach may be sufficient to head off greater difficulties later on. Neptune's energies will be strongest on February 2, May 19, August 8, and October 26—all important turning points in your process this year.

If you were born from September 12 to 22, you will receive support from Saturn while it remains in Cancer and your solar Eleventh House. Over the past two years you've been culling through your social experiences, letting go of old, less fruitful contacts in favor of new ties that allow you to reach your revised ideas of where you want to go next. This involves rethinking your life direction and how you plan to fulfill it, as well as redirecting your attentions to new groups and organizations to reflect your revised path. You could find yourself drawn into leadership roles and activities as others recognize your talents, although the tasks may be difficult and time-consuming. This could also be a time when you want to economize on social activities because you are trying to put more effort into other areas of your life, or because you find the usual crowd boring or unsupportive. Once Saturn leaves Cancer on July 16, the urge to make these changes will fade, so now is the right time to complete this process. Key Saturn dates are January 13 and March 21.

If you were born from September 14 to 18, Pluto is making a powerful connection with your Sun from your solar Fourth House—one that will dramatically transform your life. For several years you may have felt that changes were afoot, or that you wanted to make changes but were unable to. Now the time is upon you, and if you do not initiate dramatic alterations in your life then circumstances will do so for you. These changes will occur from the inside out, and others may not notice unless they know you well and personally. You may harbor seething emotions within a calm exterior. Your attention may be diverted for your regular workaday life to activities at home or in your own private world. You may make a great move to a totally new environment or engage in a total rebuilding of your home. Your family may go through a complete restructuring as someone moves out or another person or group begins to live with you. You may focus more on exploring your family tree or delving into early childhood memories. No matter what form this transformation takes, you will probably withdraw from public life to engage in these pursuits. Critical turning points in your transformative process will occur on March 26, June 13, September 2, and December 15.

Virgo/January

Planetary Hotspots
The year starts off with a load of responsibilities as Saturn reaches the midpoint of its cycle on January 13. Your efforts on behalf of the organizations you serve will reach a peak then, but you'll be busy all month with those tasks. On January 16, a new Chiron cycle begins in your solar Fifth House. For three years, you've been working on ways to overcome difficulties with your kids and creative pursuits, ruled by the Fifth House. This year will complete that process.

Wellness and Keeping Fit
The ongoing healing process you're experiencing in your solar Fifth House affects you personally in terms of the way you create your life. Ultimately, this relies on your ability to love yourself and see your value. Since it matters most how you see yourself, the process of creating a joyful, happy life depends on how much you see your talents and assets for what they are.

Love and Life Connections
You may wonder why your romantic life is so filled with wounded characters. No matter where you turn, your potential partners have obvious difficulties that stand in the way of the relationship you want. Creating something that is worth having takes time and work. It helps to remember that, as you heal your own wounds, you clear the way for a healthy relationship. January 28 brings out a hidden aspect of a long-term situation in your home life, tuning you in to another area in need of transformation.

Finance and Success
There's a dynamic push-pull between your creative life and your life in public. Organizational and group responsibilities call you and take time away from your focus on personal affairs. Patient, steady effort will see you through a short but stressful time.

Rewarding Days
1, 5, 6, 9, 10, 17, 18, 19, 22, 23, 24, 27, 28, 29

Challenging Days
7, 8, 13, 14, 20, 21

Virgo/February

Planetary Hotspots

Jupiter highlights your personal finances and spending patterns starting on February 1 for four months, while at the same time a new Neptune cycle makes you aware of new imaginative approaches to work and health. Chiron adds its voice to Neptune's song on February 16 when it enters Aquarius, opening the door to a deep healing process. The icing on the cake comes on February 25, when Uranus starts its new annual cycle, charging up events in your Seventh House of relationships.

Wellness and Keeping Fit

Although you've been working on strengthening your health and well-being in a particular way since 1998, the need to do so becomes more urgent now as new symptoms emerge. With both Chiron and Neptune in your Sixth House of health, you will probably benefit from holistic and subtle healing approaches, but don't eliminate the help of regular medical professionals. Causes of imbalance may be related to long-term, insidious sources that undermine health by slowly dissolving it, such as stress, lack of exercise or proper diet, or toxic exposure.

Love and Life Connections

You're continuing your efforts to develop a relationship based on equality and individuality rather than the all-too-frequent power struggle. On February 25 you will experience clues to what you can do over the next year to accomplish the next stage in your quest.

Finance and Success

New projects and plans involve making extra expenditures, and February 1 is the turning point for taking these on. You will spend the next four months developing and completing your project, assimilating the money as you go.

Rewarding Days

1, 2, 5, 6, 14, 15, 18, 19, 20, 23, 24, 25, 28

Challenging Days

3, 4, 9, 10, 16, 17

Virgo/March

Planetary Hotspots

Mercury, Saturn, and Pluto are spotlighted this month as all three change direction, entering a new phase of their cycles; they signal concentrations of energy in their respective locations that result in peak events. Mercury starts its first retrograde of the year on March 19, causing you to rethink some of the ways you manage your financial relationships with others. On March 21, Saturn enters the last stage of its cycle—the sign that your focused efforts of the past five months in organizations and groups can now be completed.

Wellness and Keeping Fit

After March 19 you may be called upon to give more attention to your health. By staying grounded, letting go of anxieties, and doing one thing at a time during this period, you'll minimize the effects. You can take advantage of this time by scheduling health treatments. Acupuncture is a way to use the Mars energy that prevails now.

Love and Life Connections

Pluto's ongoing placement in your solar Fourth House is highlighted around March 26. Renovations and improvements associated with Pluto may go beyond your physical surroundings and into your personal experience of past and family ties. Your approach to life and emotional responses are especially influenced by what you learned in your early life. By exploring your personal past, you will be able to make conscious choices about how you experience the present, and gain greater fulfillment.

Finance and Success

All month you'll be working on getting your finances in order, and around March 19, a situation arises that requires added time and attention. What happens then will take about three weeks to complete or resolve.

Rewarding Days

1, 2, 5, 6, 13, 14, 18, 19, 23, 24, 28, 29

Challenging Days

3, 4, 9, 10, 15, 16, 17, 30, 31

Virgo/April

Planetary Hotspots

Efforts at clearing issues in your financial affairs come to a peak on April 3, as Jupiter is highlighted in your Second House. A solar eclipse on April 8 adds further emphasis to the opportunities and challenges you face here, introducing new factors that you will assimilate into your life over the next six months. Once Mercury's retrograde period ends on April 12, the situation begins to clear. A lunar eclipse on April 24 gives you a final chance to work through anything else that needs ironing out.

Wellness and Keeping Fit

Take extra care around April 13, when Mars makes contact with Neptune. You may be accident-prone due to distraction or confusion. Your head may feel clouded, but that will pass in a day or so. Although you're pressed for time, you'll benefit tremendously if you can take a little time away from your current intense level of activity. You're more likely to be able to find the time to do it once Venus enters your Ninth House on April 13. Until Mars leaves your health house, additional health treatments will continue to benefit you.

Love and Life Connections

Extended family ties may be more strongly featured this month as your Third House is triggered by the lunar eclipse on April 24. Chances are that this is part of a continuing saga within your family system. If so, this is the last chapter for a while, to be played out over the coming six months.

Finance and Success

Although you're giving extra time to money matters right now, there are other factors to your continued success: work, career plans, education. Don't ignore these areas completely, even if they need to go on the back burner.

Rewarding Days

1, 2, 3, 10, 11, 15, 16, 20, 21, 24, 25, 28, 29

Challenging Days

6, 7, 12, 13, 14, 26, 27

Virgo/May

Planetary Hotspots

Health and work matters are emphasized again this month as Chiron takes center stage in your Sixth House on May 8, and Neptune on May 19. Mars in your Seventh House of relationships reactivates Uranus on May 15, enlivening your interactions with others.

Wellness and Keeping Fit

As both Chiron and Neptune turn retrograde this month, you'll see exactly how much still needs to be done to bring your health up to the standards you've set for it. Key events will come around May 8 and 19 that reveal more about your situation. You can increase the benefits you receive by using this time to consult with health professionals and getting your questions answered.

Love and Life Connections

If your life with your partner is difficult now, this month is a good time to put your disagreements on the back burner, as Mars moves through your Seventh House. Your partner may be more confrontational, especially on the May 15. Use this time to build trust, dwell on the good things, and seek help if anger is a problem. If you and your partner have a healthy way of working out conflict, this may not be a bad time to clear the air.

Finance and Success

Good communications clear the air in your business or career after May 9. Others support you, and will help you if you need it. Work, however, is another matter: you may feel overwhelmed, in disarray. If you get organized and make a plan, you'll be able to break the work down into doable chunks and better manage your anxieties—perhaps even delegate some of the work to others.

Rewarding Days

7, 8, 11, 12, 13, 16, 17, 18, 21, 22, 26, 27, 30, 31

Challenging Days

2, 3, 4, 9, 10, 23, 24, 25

Virgo/June

Planetary Hotspots

Your efforts at taking advantage of financial opportunities since September last year enter their final stages on June 5 as Jupiter's cycle begins to wind to a close. Although you will continue to grow in this area, you've set the stage for the next five years of growth. The next few months will allow you to more firmly establish this foundation. On June 13, your activities in your home, family, and private life will peak as Pluto's cycle culminates. Uranus turns retrograde on June 14, opening the five-month period of developing the fullest potential of your relationship life.

Wellness and Keeping Fit

The best thing you can do for your health now is to give yourself a break. Get out and enjoy yourself in whatever way you want. Be spontaneous, and don't try to accomplish anything while you're at play.

Love and Life Connections

You've been trying out a new plan for developing your relationship life for a couple of months, but now is the time when push comes to shove. You may have the opportunity to deal with some of the distasteful sides of the situation if there are any problems that need to come to the surface. Now the work begins, no matter what situation you find yourself in.

Finance and Success

This is a good month to make new social contacts through group gatherings and organizations that can lead to business and career opportunities, as Venus and Mercury travel through your Eleventh House. Things are going well in your career life, giving you a welcome break from the dramas at home. In fact, you may feel pulled in both directions around June 13, but that doesn't mean it will be in a bad way.

Rewarding Days

3, 4, 8, 9, 13, 14, 18, 19, 22, 23, 30

Challenging Days

5, 6, 7, 20, 21, 24, 25

Virgo/July

Planetary Hotspots

Dynamic events fill July, reflecting the high level of planetary activity. Your work, health, and daily routines will be most affected as Saturn and Chiron tread related patches of the sky, and then are triggered by Mars. Key dates are July 22 through 28. Mercury retrograde starting July 22 heightens the inconvenience level of the situation but makes it easier to understand the problem.

Wellness and Keeping Fit

When Saturn enters your solar Twelfth House, you'll enter a three-year period where some of your energy will go toward inner development. Some of this may come through events that are beyond your control, or a situation that makes you feel trapped—including illness. This is a good time to generally stay on top of your health: continue treatments that support health balance, such as chiropractic, massage, and acupuncture; engage in self-help measures, from good nutrition to eliminating bad habits. If it comes out through your health, you can at least minimize the effects.

Love and Life Connections

Your charm factor runs high this month after July 22, when Venus enters your sign. This continues to be a good time for social contact, but now for personal as well as professional reasons.

Finance and Success

If your workload is beyond belief this month, it's time for a change in the circumstances that created it. Others see your capabilities and want to give tasks to you because of your skills and reliability. Once they realize that they are undermining your ability to deliver, they will be willing to back off.

Rewarding Days

1, 2, 5, 6, 7, 10, 11, 12, 15, 16, 19, 20, 21, 28, 29

Challenging Days

3, 4, 17, 18, 24, 25, 30, 31

Virgo/August

Planetary Hotspots

The high activity level of last month levels off, but there are still issues to clear up as Neptune reaches the halfway point in its cycle on August 8. There may be confusion to clear and boundaries to establish in order to balance your workload. On August 15, Mercury's retrograde ends, marking a decrease in workload and an increase in freedom. The culmination of Uranus's cycle on August 31 will draw more attention to relationships, exposing an issue that has created misunderstanding.

Wellness and Keeping Fit

Get to know yourself again by taking a vacation now, as the planets give you a break this and next month. Take friends or family with you if you want, but make sure you do things you want to do, or it will be yet another obligation you must face.

Love and Life Connections

Partnerships, whether personal or business, reach an important milestone at the end of the month, which may come as no surprise but will still be difficult. Someone may need more freedom or not be as available as you would like. It's best not to grasp too tightly, as that will create hard feelings and make it more difficult to maintain the relationship.

Finance and Success

This is a good month for you financially as Venus brings balance to your Second House. The area that needs the most attention is your work, as Neptune is highlighted on August 8. There will be confusing information that must be clarified to come to an agreement or understanding. If there is a conflict, it is related to bad information, not the person who brings the conflict to you. Key dates are August 8 and 28.

Rewarding Days

1, 2, 3, 6, 7, 8, 11, 12, 13, 16, 17, 24, 25, 29, 30

Challenging Days

14, 15, 20, 21, 26, 27, 28

Virgo/September

Planetary Hotspots

As Pluto transitions into the completion phase of its yearly cycle on September 2, this year's home-improvement projects are nearly complete. There are plenty of finishing touches to be made, but the bulk of the work is done. The calm that follows can be deceptive—more like the calm before the gathering storm, as Mars begins to slow in preparation for its eleven-week retrograde, which starts on October 1. In your Ninth House, the retrograde will draw your attention to travel, foreign cultures and languages, study, or publishing.

Wellness and Keeping Fit

You're feeling stronger now because you're in the most vigorous part of your yearly cycle. By pacing yourself, you can help this vitality extend throughout the year rather than burning out quickly because you want to use it before it's gone.

Love and Life Connections

You want to connect with others after September 4. It feels like life is starting over again, and now you have some time to circulate socially. It's a good time to enjoy others whose company you truly value—to let them know you care and want to nourish them when you can.

Finance and Success

As Mars begins to slow down, your energy will be focused increasingly on your goals and what you want to achieve in life on a deep level. You have always believed in fulfilling a pragmatic path—one that is visible in your world and produces some financial gain, or at least is not completely without compensation. Now you're looking at a deeper level, because you're not content with your life as it is now. This is a good time to explore other options, and what you decide will affect you for years to come. Travel may be a part of the plan.

Rewarding Days
3, 4, 8, 9, 12, 13, 20, 21, 25, 26, 30

Challenging Days
10, 11, 16, 17, 22, 23, 24

Virgo/October

Planetary Hotspots
Your life picks up again at the month's start as Mars begins its retrograde on October 1, highlighting your activities in unfamiliar lands and studies. Two eclipses, on October 3 and 17, punctuate the month and open another chapter of growth in your resources and the way you handle them. On October 22, a new Jupiter cycle begins, this one to bring a blossoming in your Third House of communications and commerce. Neptune enters the final phase of its cycle on October 26, allowing you to see the progress you've made in improving your health and work conditions.

Wellness and Keeping Fit
Getting in touch with your sense of purpose this month is the most significant contribution you can make to your health. When we feel truly purposeful, we can withstand almost any pressure and surmount any obstacle.

Love and Life Connections
With action all over the heavens this month, you can choose nearly any type of activity you want, but try to include your loved ones. This will help overcome feelings of separation that can breed distrust, undermine mutual support, and stifle open communication. As the month wears on, you'll be drawn more to staying at home.

Finance and Success
Once Jupiter enters Scorpio on October 25 you'll feel the awakening begin in your world of learning. Your curiosity will be piqued in several directions, and your attitude toward life in general is due for an overhaul as Jupiter infects you with its optimism. You may decide to take up a new study, start a writing project, or teach. This will be a harmonious period full of the things you enjoy the most—as long as you don't overdo it.

Rewarding Days
1, 5, 6, 9, 10, 18, 19, 22, 23, 24, 27, 28, 29

Challenging Days
7, 8, 14, 15, 20, 21

Virgo/November

Planetary Hotspots

Uranus enters the last phase of its year-long cycle on November 15, ending its five-month retrograde, while two others, Mercury and Saturn, join Mars in treading the heavens in backward motion. With Uranus in your Seventh House, you've had been busy working out relationship issues; now the tension relaxes and you can think about moving forward again. However, Saturn turns retrograde on November 22, and you'll discover an important responsibility to assume at that time.

Wellness and Keeping Fit

Making sacrifices for others is part of who you are, but you have to feel deeply committed to them in order for it not to be a draining experience. You can prevent serious health problems from occurring if you minimize the stresses that result when you take on a major task that you don't heartily support. If you must make such a sacrifice, find a way to make it meaningful and fulfilling for you.

Love and Life Connections

Mercury draws your focus to the homefront, perhaps through a special activity or event that you must plan and execute. As with any new or unusual endeavor, problems arise, but that does not mean they can't be surmounted. You are capable of handling whatever gets thrown at you at this time.

Finance and Success

The responsibilities you take on this month may be job related. You may be asked to fulfill tasks that you can do alone or behind the scenes, which often make them easier to do because you can work without interruption. There will be a peak of activity from November 18 to 22, giving you an indication of just what's involved.

Rewarding Days

1, 2, 6, 7, 14, 15, 19, 20, 23, 24, 25, 28, 29, 30

Challenging Days

3, 4, 5, 10, 11, 16, 17, 18

Virgo/December

Planetary Hotspots

Communications and travel agendas are completed by December 9, freeing you to take care of other obligations, as both Mercury and Mars return to forward motion. Pluto's new annual cycle starts on December 15, showing you what's in store for the coming year in your home, family, and private life. The year finishes off with Venus turning retrograde for its six-week sojourn backward, this time in your Sixth House of work and health, returning to your Fifth House of fun, children, and romance.

Wellness and Keeping Fit

Now that the planetary pressures are decreasing, you could lose your vigilance and catch the virus you've been trying so hard to avoid. However, as long as you take care of your body's basic needs, your body will support you in your activities.

Love and Life Connections

As the end of the year approaches, you'll find yourself examining your partnerships and agreements with others. Regardless of the type of relationship, all of them will go through a re-examination process by all who are involved. Agreements, both conscious and unconscious, will be renegotiated as you find ways in which the bonds need to be updated to continue to be relevant. Although this process will take the coming eighteen months to complete, the renegotiation will be in place by the end of January.

Finance and Success

Don't let a heavy workload upset your holidays. Let your personal life be the top priority for a while. It's more than acceptable to have a life outside work—in fact, it's vitally important. When you have an identity independent of your career role, you have more confidence and work more effectively.

Rewarding Days

3, 4, 11, 12, 13, 16, 17, 21, 22, 26, 27, 30, 31

Challenging Days

1, 2, 7, 8, 14, 15, 28, 29

VIRGO ACTION TABLE

These dates reflect the best—but not the only—times for success and ease in these activities, according to your Sun sign.

	JAN	FEB	MAR	APR	MAY	JUN	JUL	AUG	SEPT	OCT	NOV	DEC
Move	1-9									31	1-13	13-31
Start a class										8-30		
Join a club						11-28	6, 7					
Ask for a raise						3-28	5-7, 25-31	1-17	3-5			
Look for work	30, 31	1-28	1-5									
Get pro advice	13, 14	9, 10	9, 10	5, 6	2-4, 30-31	26, 27	23, 24	20, 21	16, 17	14, 15	10, 11	7, 8
Get a loan	15, 16	11-13	11, 12	7, 8	5, 6	1, 2, 28, 29	25-27	22, 23	18, 19	16, 17	12, 13	9, 10
See a doctor	30, 31	1-28	1-5			28-30	1-22	16-31	1-20			
Start a diet	30, 31	1-16			28-31	1-11						
End relationship									3, 4			
Buy clothes	10-31	1, 2									5-30	1-14
Get a makeover							25-31	1-17	3-20			
New romance	10-31	1, 2									5-30	1-14
Vacation	17-19	14, 15	13, 14	9-11, 15-30	1-10, 12-28	3, 4, 30	1, 2, 28, 29	24, 25	20, 21	18, 19	14, 15	11-13

LIBRA

The Balance
September 22 to October 23

Element:	Air
Quality:	Cardinal
Polarity:	Yang/Masculine
Planetary Ruler:	Venus
Meditation:	I balance conflicting desires.
Gemstone:	Opal
Power Stones:	Tourmaline, kunzite, blue lace agate
Key Phrase:	I balance
Glyph:	Scales of justice, setting sun
Anatomy:	Kidneys, lower back, appendix
Color:	Blue, pink
Animal:	Brightly plumed birds
Myths/Legends:	Venus, Cinderella, Hera
House:	Seventh
Opposite Sign:	Aries
Flower:	Rose
Key Word:	Harmony

Your Ego's Strengths and Shortcomings

Libra, you are a gentle breeze blowing across the landscape of human affairs, soothing frazzled nerves and encouraging community between individuals. You are an air sign, the second of the zodiac, sharing space with Gemini and Aquarius. Like the other air signs, you seek to connect. Just as the wind loosens seed from pod and brings it in contact with the nourishing earth where it can grow, you are a matchmaker, bringing the right ideas to people, linking two harmonious concepts in mathematics, or finding your perfect companion—whether it be in love, your favorite hobby, or your work environment. You seek harmonic resonance, the exact vibrational balance between all you see. Whether it is a painting, a relationship, a melody, or the objects on your desk, you seek balance and flow.

Your sense of justice is another facet of your nature. Your natural penchant is to see both sides of any issue. You weigh and assess, consider and adjust, and others signal their awareness of your impartiality by asking you to moderate during a dispute. You recognize the delicacy and importance of decision-making, and you're more willing than most to judge a situation carefully before taking action.

For the same reason, you often have difficulty making decisions. You may also be famous for your inability to act, or for deferring decision-making to someone else instead of taking the risk of offering your own opinion. At times you may be scattered, disorganized, and ungrounded, or be out of touch with your feelings. You may also become too dependent on others—especially your partner—to the point of losing your personality to another person. It is just as important to develop your own self-awareness as it is to give your much-loved companions and family a break.

Shining Your Love Light

You may feel like relationships are your whole world, Libra, but you need to become whole and fulfill your uniqueness in order to be a good partner. You are generous, acquiescing, and peace loving, and you enjoy making others happy. You understand the importance of compromise and cooperation, and your diplomatic skills are highly developed. Being an expert negotiator is the key to introducing your own needs into your personal ties with others, and it is a valuable tool in your outer-world life as well. Otherwise, you may find that you tend to cave in to your significant other most of the time, or manipulate him or her into giving you your way without an outright acknowledgment.

Aries is your opposite—and a fine example of how to be true to yourself, while you provide the reminder that it is also important to walk a mile in another's shoes. You'll find a fellow appreciator of beauty in a Taurus, who is also ruled by your governing planet, Venus. Gemini shares your need to make connections as a fellow air sign, and you'll enjoy talking, learning, and growing together. Your airy style may be hard for Cancer to understand, and likewise this sign's watery world for you, but by stretching to know each other's worlds, you'll each develop parts of yourself you never knew existed. With Leo, the two of you can be lazy together, or you can spur each other to explore the world of arts and entertainment, since you both enjoy the bright lights. You'll appreciate the sincerity and dedication of Virgo, while your impartial observations of life and its dilemmas are a breath of fresh air in this sign's often anxious outlook. Another Libra understands you perfectly, but it may be difficult to find someone who will take the lead due to your mutual efforts to acquiesce to each other. You may be mystified by Scorpio's tendency to internalize feelings, but as this sign grows to trust you, you'll see warmth and compassion. Sagittarius will excite your sense of adventure and lead you to explore your world and experience the wonder of its diversity, while you'll help him with his diplomatic skills. Capricorn brings a breadth of vision and statesmanlike quality that you admire, but you may feel intimidated until you realize that she needs love just like you do. You'll find strength and natural understanding in a relationship with an Aquarius, another air sign, with whom you'll share the desire to understand human nature better. Pisces will find her shy, sensitive approach to life relieved by your objectivity, while you'll appreciate her attunement to your needs.

Making Your Place in the World

With your ability to bring balance into people's lives in so many ways, you can find your place in nearly any career path. You are especially well suited to situations that take advantage of your negotiating skills, such as mediation, moderation, hosting and reception, entertainment, and events. Your adeptness at making others feel comfortable is a key quality here, as well as you ability to judge a situation impartially. You can also use these skills in the fields of customer relations, diplomatic service, strike negotiations, and counseling. The weakest link in your nature is your occasional temptation to capitulate to others because you dislike conflict. If you are not willing to allow conflict to surface as a part of the process of healing it, your ability to display your qualities at their finest will be undercut. Your sense of beauty and harmony may also be expressed through the arts, whether you choose to be a fine artist, musician, museum curator, or interior designer.

Putting Your Best Foot Forward

It's good to think and care about others, but it becomes a weakness when we place others before ourselves to the point that we've given ourselves away. This is a danger that you face, Libra, and to put your best foot forward, you must learn to think of yourself as much as you do others. An important component of this is locus of control—where your center of control lies. Is it inside or outside your being? To make sure that your locus of control is in you as it should be, pay attention, in the moment, to how intensely you care about another person's opinion of you. The more you care, the more you are likely to seek his approval more than your own. A high level of approval-seeking puts the locus of control in the other person. If you value your own self-approval at least as much as that of others, you will stay in balance. It also helps if you accept the fact that sometimes you have to risk a relationship in order to improve it. When you bring up an area of conflict, there's always a chance that the relationship will not survive the challenge. However, if the relationship isn't strong enough to make it through, was it worth preserving to begin with?

Tools for Change

Your life revolves around relationships, whether with humans, animals, or concepts. Bringing about harmony in these realms is vitally important to you, but it won't happen without bringing about balance within yourself. It is universally true that when we are at peace inside, we create peace outside. So, by cultivating your own inner balance and awareness, you will find it easier to find and maintain healthy and happy relationships around you. Key to achieving this goal is to develop yourself. You can't act on your own behalf without knowing who you are and what you want. This requires spending time alone—without other people to add their input. It requires exploring your own talents and weaknesses and learning how to use them and how far you can go. Practice asserting yourself with others, letting them know how you feel about the prevailing situation or issue. It also helps if you engage in competitive sports, where you are required to be proactive on your own or your team's behalf. Sports and exercise will also help you develop the physical strength, which provides a subtle support for your psychological courage. Staying in your center—keeping your balance—is also part of this. To get and stay centered, you can meditate focusing on your *hara* (chi) centers or primary chakras, do yoga balancing poses and breathing practices, and engage in creative pursuits like singing, instrumental performance, painting, and writing. The use of the I Ching (Chinese Book of Changes) may also help bring you to your center. Constructive journaling and reflection can also provide support, helping you to mirror your thoughts and feelings—which is vital when you are making a decision. In particular, you will benefit this year from learning to deal better with authority figures in your life or learning to take on the role of a leader and authority yourself. With others, it helps to think of them as humans who make mistakes and have good and bad days, just like you. It may then be easier to talk to them adult to adult. If you are the one in that role, you must take responsibility for those under you, including the unpleasant task of being honest about poor performance or conflict. Knowing that it's for the best and then listening to their perspective as a part of the resolution process will bring the most positive result.

Affirmation of the Year

I listen to my heart to choose my path.

The Year Ahead for Libra

With lots of support from the planets, you'll be pouring your energy into achieving your long-term goals in 2005. You've been building your dreams for a long time, and both Jupiter and Saturn give you wings. Jupiter is in your own sign until October 25—plenty of time to get in touch with all the ideas that excite you at the deepest level. You're in a "Midas Touch" period until then, when opportunities seem to sprout like spring flowers. You're full of energy, hope, and optimism, and life seems endlessly fortunate. This feeling may not last beyond Jupiter's visit in your sign, but you can draw upon it at any time by recalling the inspiration you felt and carrying it in your heart. Once it enters Scorpio and your solar Second House you can get down to the business of laying a foundation for the plans you've made. It's the ideal time to gather resources: skills, money, materials, and time. Creating a schedule is very "Second House" and a great way to begin turning your ideas into reality.

Saturn is in Cancer and your solar Tenth House until July 16, when it enters Leo and your Eleventh House. You've worked hard on building your career over the past two years, and as that period draws to an end you can see the first results of your efforts. It may have been a difficult time if you have shirked responsibilities in the past—and not put in the consistent, diligent effort required for long-term success. Once Saturn enters Leo you'll have the opportunity to continue to achieve—but perhaps not the drive. While social activity for pleasure is important to your happiness and well-being, neglecting your long-term plans will tend to undercut your deepest intentions.

Chiron has been in Capricorn, your solar Fourth House, for three years, and you've had the chance to address deeply buried issues, whether from family or just generally from your past. Certainly you've become better acquainted with your emotional nature, even as that nature has matured through the process. On February 21 you get your first taste of Chiron in Aquarius, your Fifth House. This will feel more comfortable as you discover ways to infuse your life with fun and creativity. You may find that you're no longer content to be bored. You want more excitement, more spontaneity—and that means more challenge and risk. Chiron will give you the chance to find a level of comfort that leaves boredom behind.

Uranus once again finds itself in your Sixth House from the Sun, reminding you that your health is important. Past indiscretions may be coming up as health challenges, requiring stricter, perhaps even galling, limitations to your eating patterns and exercise choices. Surgery may be necessary. More happily, this could signal a time when you find it possible to accomplish some of the health and lifestyle goals that you never quite had the discipline to fulfill in the past. Now that potential difficulties are nipping at your heels, you are more strongly motivated.

As Neptune meanders through Aquarius and your Fifth House, you are experiencing a subtle but unmistakable shift in how you want to express yourself creatively. This is because your primary means of self-expression and social identification—perhaps your idea about what your life is at its very core—is being transformed. If you have children, you may experience changes related to their influence on your life—perhaps spiritual ones.

Pluto remains in Sagittarius and your solar Third House, turning over your sense of your immediate surroundings, which could include your extended family, sibling ties, neighborhood, and the ways you think about your life and your world. Perspective is everything under this transit, and you may suddenly be interested in observing the world with closer scrutiny than before. You may be reading more in an attempt to gain a deeper understanding of science and human nature.

The Aries–Libra eclipses of 2005 place an emphasis in your solar First and Seventh Houses, activating your relationship life. If you are currently in a partnership, it may be time for some changes so that the form of the relationship evolves with your individuality. If you are currently between relationships, you may find new activity in this area of your life.

If you were born from September 22 to October 4, Saturn's transit in early Leo will contact your chart starting July 16. Your solar Eleventh House will be affected in a relatively harmonious way. After your efforts of the last three years, you may be the recipient of particular rewards or recognitions (including financial) related to those efforts. Your reputation and standing in the world has changed, and now you will reap the benefits. If the last three years have been rocky, you may not have taken as much responsible, meaningful, and persistent action as you could have. This may curtail your rewards, but it is never too late to start on the road of diligence. Since this area of your chart also rules social contacts and, in a broader sense, group karma and obligations, you may find yourself reviewing your associations with others—particularly those conducted in a group setting. This includes organizations, your social "set," and your business associates or colleagues—your entire network of acquaintances. You may decide to pare down or restructure this area of your life. Exerting discipline here, perhaps by eliminating contact with people who engage in unhealthy or uninteresting activities, will benefit you. Important dates for you are January 13, July 16 through 23, and November 22.

If you were born from September 25 to October 3, Uranus is making contact with your Sun from your solar Sixth House. Uranus is a disrupter, but only when we have strayed from the "best" path in a spiritual sense. It guides us through shocking events back to our own center only if we have strayed. It also forces us to think in unconventional ways in order to clear obstacles that arise. Consequently, you may find that your health is your guide to growth more than usual this year. It will give you access to all your spiritual lessons—a microcosm of your own macrocosm. You may have unusual or hard-to-diagnose health imbalances that are best addressed through alternative or holistic approaches. You will be sensitive to subtle approaches, and, if your imbalances are not acute or critical, the subtle approaches may be the ideal curative. However, past neglect of your well-being will come to the surface, and a thorough health examination will go far toward avoiding difficulties. Surgery for a long-term problem may be needed. This transit could also denote challenges in your work environment. You may find a disruptive influence there—an element of chaos—either in the form of a person or your workload. Organization may be difficult both at work and at home. Watch for significant events on or around February 25, June 14, August 31, and November 15.

If you were born from October 5 to 11, Neptune's energies will reach your Sun from your solar Fifth House, fueling your creativity. Its transformation is the slow, dissolving process of water upon rocks, eating it away by molecules. Old ways of identifying yourself socially, in terms of your value to a group, may be disappearing in favor of new contributions. If you engage in the arts, your style may change, or you may choose to focus on a new audience. The concepts you bring through may be more universal and broadly appealing as you explore Neptune's boundless depths. Children and their spiritual purity may take on greater significance for you, and you may have a different type of contact with young people than before. Best of all, you may feel inspired to embark on a new facet of your life's path, honing a new identity for yourself through self-exploration. You may translate those ideals into new pursuits that satisfy your need for pleasure and meaning. Neptune often seems to demand an element of surrender or sacrifice, and you may willingly participate in activities that involve this because you experience deeper fulfillment on a hidden level through those pursuits. While this may cause others to react with consternation, it is important to follow your heart. Events that tie into this theme will occur on or near February 2, May 19, August 8, and October 26.

If you were born from October 12 to 23, you'll feel the energy of Saturn in Cancer from your solar Tenth House. As Saturn completes its transit of Cancer, you have a few more months to finish the major efforts you've undertaken to make your life more meaningful and rewarding. However, your results did not grow overnight. Whatever fruits you've earned in the past two years—and they could be considerable—have come because of the last twenty-one years of effort and the seeds planted ten years ago. Now you're planting seeds for the results you'll reap ten years hence, so plan well and be prepared to engage in persistent effort to achieve your goals. It takes years for Saturn's full rewards to come our way; there's no instant gratification here. You may have taken on work that seems to come with no compensation or appears to place an impossible burden on you. It could also be a time of elevation of your position amongst others, and you may even gain renown as Saturn crosses the top of your solar chart. If your reputation is built on a shaky foundation you may be knocked off your pedestal, but this will inevitably result in a stronger base in the long run. Your Saturn theme will show through in events on or around January 13 and March 21, to be resolved by July 16.

If you were born from October 15 to 18, Pluto is on your doorstep this year from its position in your solar Third House. You're experiencing a quiet revolution—perhaps symbolically or in your mind. You may be encountering concepts that take you to deeper levels of awareness or understanding of universal truths. You may be in a probing educational process or period of study that leads you to particularly meaningful insights. These can be used to fuel your own creative process, and you may find yourself writing or communicating about obscure or hidden concepts to those who are less aware—perhaps through a book, articles, or lectures. Your immediate surroundings may be going through changes; this could be anything from a new mall going up in your neighborhood to a renaissance of the arts. Your extended family may be transforming: there may be one or more deaths that have an impact on you but are not unexpected. Your brothers and sisters may be engaged in improving, or perhaps destroying, their lives. In every respect, the thoughts you think and communicate take on more impact and depth, and others come to you for your wisdom and insight. Pluto's energy will be strong around March 26, June 13, September 2, and December 15.

Libra/January

Planetary Hotspots

Like the bang of a starter pistol, the new year has you off the blocks with a sprint. With so much to do in both home and career before the end of the month, you can't afford to hesitate. This is Saturn's doing, as it reaches its mid-cycle peak on January 13. For added spice, Chiron's new cycle starts on January 16, highlighting your home life and pointing out an imbalance in the way you deal with your private and public lives.

Wellness and Keeping Fit

Your life is full enough now that you may be limited in your ability to get out, bobbing between home and work. Work your fitness routine around these requirements. You can work out at home with a videotape just as well as at the gym.

Love and Life Connections

The action is really all about your home life now. Demand is high, whether because of projects you have on the table or because of the needs of those in your family. Whatever the source, you can't ignore what's happening, or the situation will only get worse. The key is to relax some of your expectations of yourself as far as external achievement is concerned. Communications and situations with your siblings or extended family could be surprising around January 28.

Finance and Success

Even though demands are quite heavy now, and you want to succeed, if only to please your superiors and colleagues, there are other things going on in your life that you must make room for. By being up front about what's going on, delegating tasks, and negotiating deadlines, you'll be at your best.

Rewarding Days

2, 3, 4, 7, 8, 11, 12, 20, 21, 25, 26, 30, 31

Challenging Days

9, 10, 15, 16, 22, 23, 24

Libra/February

Planetary Hotspots

With Jupiter in your sign for most of the year, it's a time of fantastic opportunity and expansion. As of February 1, the pattern for what you can accomplish will be set, as Jupiter starts its four-month retrograde period. February 2 sees the start of the new annual Neptune cycle in your Fifth House of creativity and romance, while February 25 brings Uranus's new cycle of growth in your health and lifestyle.

Wellness and Keeping Fit

Uranus has been pointing out the need for reform in your health, work, and daily routines. What we do on a moment-by-moment basis—eating, sleeping, thinking, emotions, attitude—forms the foundation of our health and well-being, and improving your choices in this area will provide the most profound change. Potential issues will rise to the surface around February 25.

Love and Life Connections

Your life is blooming in every direction, and this is certainly true in your relationships. Romance is in the air, whether with a current or new partner. Your children are a continuing source of inspiration and rejuvenation, and you feel energized by it all. On February 2, a new cycle starts in these areas, dissolving old energies and replacing them with new, more ideal forms. What you experience then will tell you what seeds to plant and cultivate in the coming year.

Finance and Success

Your work life may be a source of disruption, which could spill over into your health and the way you manage your daily routines. This will be most apparent around February 25, and if you are going to overcome the effects you don't like, you must pay attention this time. At first it may seem overwhelming or unsolvable, but by thinking outside the box, you'll come up with an ingenious solution.

Rewarding Days

3, 4, 7, 8, 16, 17, 21, 22, 26, 27

Challenging Days

5, 6, 11, 12, 13, 18, 19, 20

Libra/March

Planetary Hotspots

Mars activates the planets of success, Jupiter and Saturn, on March 3 through 7, re-energizing the challenges you faced in January. This probably means hard work and pressure, but stress reactions are based on the way you interpret the challenges: if you see them as opportunities, that's just what they'll be. On March 19, Mercury's retrograde starts three weeks of clarifying communication in your relationships, while Saturn finally helps you relax your inner tension when its retrograde ends on March 21. As if that weren't enough, Pluto's retrograde beginning on March 26 will show how you're doing with changes in your attitude and outlook on life.

Wellness and Keeping Fit

Life's continuing intensity suggests that blending health routines into your other activities may be the way to go, especially this month. Park far away and walk; take the stairs; run in the park; play social sports.

Love and Life Connections

You may struggle with communications as March 19 approaches, but that doesn't mean it's your fault. Others are feeling off-kilter, and you don't need to be thrown off your center, too. Calm and patience will allow the truth to emerge in days or weeks, so perhaps the less said the better.

Finance and Success

Outreach is a continuing focus for you. Looking outward is a state of mind, part of living in a world of possibility. Opportunities open up for you the more you put yourself in this state of mind. Your career situation loosens up after March 21, and you'll soon see just how much you've accomplished with all your hard work over the past two years.

Rewarding Days

3, 4, 7, 8, 15, 16, 17, 20, 21, 22, 25, 26, 27, 30, 31

Challenging Days

5, 6, 11, 12, 18, 19

Libra/April

Planetary Hotspots

Your efforts at creating new opportunities for yourself are reaching their culmination as Jupiter gets to its opposition on April 3. This will signal a peak of activity and a sense of urgency to complete your plans over the next two months. You'll be aided by Mercury as it resumes forward motion on April 12, speeding you on your way with clearer communication and support from your partner. Eclipses will also make this month stand out in memory, and some wrinkles in partnership will get ironed out as the solar eclipse on April 8 triggers change in your relationship life as well.

Wellness and Keeping Fit

You could be accident-prone around April 13 as Mars reaches Neptune in your Fifth House, ruling sports and risk-taking activities. You can avoid this by staying focused on one thing at a time for a few days either side of this date. One of the most important things you can do for yourself this month is to play—it is your best health remedy until the end of the month.

Love and Life Connections

Most of the focus this month is on your partnerships, whether in love or business. Verbal agreements should not be made lightly around April 8, because they are likely to be stacked in favor of the other person. It'll be easier to discuss imbalances after April 12.

Finance and Success

You should be especially careful about signing contracts around April 8, because these agreements may bind you into a situation that you will later regret because of inequality in the documents. If you are called upon to sign something, get the opinion of a trusted, impartial person before writing your name on the dotted line.

Rewarding Days

3, 4, 12, 13, 17, 18, 22, 23, 26, 27, 30

Challenging Days

1, 2, 7, 8, 14, 15, 16, 28, 29

Libra/May

Planetary Hotspots

Your Fifth House is highlighted this month by both Chiron and Neptune as they each turn retrograde. You may find the wound in your romantic relationships as Chiron is activated on May 8. Your idealism may be tarnished when Neptune makes its station on May 19. You may also be considering new approaches to children, sports, games, and creative pursuits.

Wellness and Keeping Fit

Inflammations, viral infections, and accidents are more likely this month as Mars travels through your Sixth House of health. The source could be stresses from work, which will peak on May 15. These could distract you and give you a feeling of being scattered. Unlike last month, injury is more likely to occur from non-athletic activities.

Love and Life Connections

Romance is clearly a challenge this month as Chiron and Neptune signal the opportunity to examine your love ties on a deeper level. First, Chiron will reveal the problems in your current bonds—or perhaps the lack thereof. With Neptune, you may become falsely idealistic about someone new, or you may be disillusioned with the potential partners you encounter. A new approach is in order, and, more than anything, this is not a time to give up—only to be aware of deeper truths.

Finance and Success

Don't let unexpected events around May 15 captivate you so thoroughly that you can't break away. After May 9 a vacation may not only be in order, but necessary to maintain your core of inner strength and efficiency. Even if it's on a weekend, it's the way to keep your productivity high.

Rewarding Days

1, 9, 10, 14, 15, 19, 20, 23, 24, 28, 29

Challenging Days

5, 6, 11, 12, 13, 26, 27

Libra/June

Planetary Hotspots

Jupiter puts the reins of forward motion back in your hands on June 5, and now you'll get to see some of the possibilities for the next twelve years of growth. Two peaks commingle mid-month to create new perspectives in how you deal with the needs of others as Houses Three, Six, and Nine are highlighted on June 13 and 14 by Pluto and Uranus.

Wellness and Keeping Fit

You may find that you feel especially stressed out around June 2, 13, 14, and 25, due to the number of tasks you are trying to juggle at one time. Some of these will be work related, but that doesn't mean they are the top priority. Delegating and prioritizing are your keys to well-being this month.

Love and Life Connections

The responsibilities that arise at the end of the month bring up previously explored relationship situations, but they may be opportunities, not arguments. Look for the chance to arrive through common understanding and agreement rather than by you initiating the action.

Finance and Success

The action is in your business and career life now, as the fast-moving planets transit your Tenth House. This is not without its challenges, because you have matters pulling you home, or perhaps even health treatments to fit into your schedule. Events occurring on June 2 create the heat, and the rest of the month is taken up with resolving what arises then. After June 25, your feeling of being pulled in several directions at once will ease.

Rewarding Days

5, 6, 10, 11, 12, 15, 16, 17, 20, 21, 24, 25

Challenging Days

1, 2, 8, 9, 22, 23, 28, 29

Libra/July

Planetary Hotspots

Saturn enters Leo and your solar Eleventh House—a more hospitable place than its location of the past two years. You'll feel that you can take a more constructive approach and get more accomplished now, and you've earned the right to feel that way. Now you can enlarge your opportunities by developing your social contacts. You won't want to waste your time with people whom you consider unworthy of your attention.

Wellness and Keeping Fit

You may feel like retreating this month, and we all need such times periodically to recharge our batteries. There's much to be gained by listening to this inner urge.

Love and Life Connections

The relative lack of health in your romantic life may prompt you to step out more. Just make sure you go places where you will meet people you actually want to spend time with. This is more likely to occur in classes, events, or organizations based on an area of interest than at a bar or night club. This month, you could feel isolated from others as you identify what's wrong with your previous approach. Over the coming three years you'll have ample opportunity to make changes.

Finance and Success

Mercury turns retrograde in your Eleventh House, emphasizing the adjustment factor you will be dealing with when it comes to social activities and events. You may be questioning your affiliations with professional organizations, wondering if there may be value in changing your role with them, perhaps even withdrawing—or joining at a more committed level. Give it careful consideration: there are many possibilities here, and you don't want to be tied to something long term that you are not dedicated to.

Rewarding Days

3, 4, 8, 9, 13, 14, 17, 18, 21, 22, 30, 31

Challenging Days

5, 6, 7, 19, 20, 25, 26, 27

Libra/August

Planetary Hotspots

Planetary events spark developments throughout the month. On August 8, Neptune reaches the peak of its yearly cycle, revealing deeper truths about your social affiliations. Mercury supports this task as well, highlighting this area through August 8. Uranus brings critical awareness to better health and self-management as August 31 approaches, perhaps in startling ways.

Wellness and Keeping Fit

If you are dealing with a health imbalance, it may reach critical mass at the end of the month. It is best to be prepared, but you have already done much to overcome any obstacles that might present themselves at this time. If your health is generally good, this may just be a time of higher stress than usual. Either way, it's a good time to take it easy.

Love and Life Connections

You're still working on ways to manage your social connections with the outer world for pleasure as well as business. You may be ready to give up on romantic contacts early in the month, and while no one can tell you when it's supposed to be over, there's still hope for you and your love life, so hang in there.

Finance and Success

Although finances are generally going smoothly, you'll have an extra outlay of cash this month for a romantic, creative, or family-related activity or event. The need for this influx will peak at the end of the month, and it doesn't mean it's a bad thing—it could be a lot of fun!

Rewarding Days

4, 5, 9, 10, 14, 15, 18, 19, 26, 27, 28, 31

Challenging Days

1, 2, 3, 16, 17, 22, 23, 29, 30

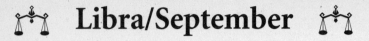

Libra/September

Planetary Hotspots

One lone event marks September, and that means that you'll make plenty of progress this month. Pluto's retrograde period ends on September 2, and then it's full steam ahead. One cautionary word: on October 1, Mars's relatively infrequent retrograde begins, so it's slow this month. Use this time to tune in to what Mars will present to you in the coming three months, as it moves backward through your Eighth House of financial ties with the world. This may make extra attention desirable with regard to your portfolio, expenditures, and income-producing activities. Your work with the inner world—that realm experienced through depth psychology and occult studies—may be especially fruitful during this time if you apply discipline to your path.

Wellness and Keeping Fit

Attitude is everything in health and well-being, and you can strengthen your chi force instantly with optimism and a cultivated sense of peace. Meditate, use affirmations, and try remedies for the emotions such as Bach flowers and homeopathics.

Love and Life Connections

Predicaments with brothers and sisters or extended family may ease up after September 2. Remember that this is part of a long-term process, so the situation may not be completely resolved.

Finance and Success

With Mars activating your solar Eighth House, you'll be keeping a closer eye on your finances than usual as the month wears on. You may decide that you need to renegotiate financial agreements, consolidate debts, or redistribute the current balance of assets in your portfolio. Although you may not be able to get every knot out of the yarn this month, forewarned is forearmed.

Rewarding Days

1, 2, 5, 6, 7, 10, 11, 14, 15, 22, 23, 24, 27, 28, 29

Challenging Days

12, 13, 18, 19, 25, 26

Libra/October

Planetary Hotspots

Mars's retrograde initiates the month, highlighting your monetary ties with others. Two eclipses on October 3 and 17 heighten the drama, which is most likely to be felt in your relationship life. Chiron also returns to forward motion on October 5, relaxing the tensions in your home environment. On October 26, Neptune's retrograde period also ends, and you can move forward with new insights in seeking romance and creativity. But best of all, Jupiter's new cycle begins on October 22, and now it's time to build on the seeds planted this year.

Wellness and Keeping Fit

Your well-being is stable and ever-improving, and the way is clear for you to resume your normal healthy pattern of living. Be sure to sprinkle some fun in with the discipline.

Love and Life Connections

There's an old twist on your relationship balance: the way you handle your shared resources. It's important to be open about this area of your life together, from your values to your budget. Most of all, it is important to have shared goals, for when you agree on this basic level of motivation, everything else falls into place.

Finance and Success

The financial situation you face now may be left over from the conditions you had to deal with two years ago, when the eclipses rocked this area of your life. Although this is not likely to be as powerful as your experiences then, you should respond to it seriously, because you don't want to lose the precious ground you've gained in establishing stability.

Rewarding Days

2, 3, 4, 7, 8, 11, 12, 13, 20, 21, 25, 26, 30, 31

Challenging Days

9, 10, 16, 17, 22, 23, 24

 Libra/November

Planetary Hotspots

Once again, Mercury gives us a chance to grow through greater awareness when it turns retrograde on November 14, and for you this knowledge comes in your attitude toward and perception of the world. Breathe a sigh of relief as Uranus returns to direct motion on November 15 and your health and work life can slip gracefully into the background once again. Get ready to apply yourself in new ways as Saturn commences its retrograde period on November 22, in your Eleventh House, which is the place of organizations and group karma.

Wellness and Keeping Fit

Health matters require markedly less attention after November 15 as Uranus returns to forward motion. Even though this is the finishing off of this round, there are a few more to go as Uranus continues its path through this area of your life.

Love and Life Connections

It's time to buckle down *and* enjoy yourself—or at least, that's what Saturn says. Enjoying social contact is an art, and it contributes monumentally to making us happy. Now is the time when you get to develop this side of your nature. On a deeper level, Saturn reveals to you the deeper aspects of your connections to others—what you carry in common with them by virtue of your shared destiny.

Finance and Success

Mars continues to draw your attention to finances as you iron out the wrinkles there, stabilizing your monetary affairs. Confusion around November 7 gives way to greater clarity, but you have to seek the facts through investigation and willingness to know the truth. Work pressures ease after November 15, and, if you've learned how to manage your workload, never to return with quite the same intensity.

Rewarding Days

3, 4, 5, 8, 9, 16, 17, 18, 21, 22, 23, 26, 27

Challenging Days

6, 7, 12, 13, 19, 20

Libra/December

Planetary Hotspots

Mercury and Mars let you express your internalized tensions on December 3 and 9, when they return to forward motion. They leave you with a more enlightened and realistic approach to your finances and life in general. You are refueled and inspired by the return to "normal," and your appreciation is enhanced by the truths that have been revealed to you. December 15 heralds the initiation of the new Pluto cycle, invigorating your growth process in your Third House of commerce and connection with others. On December 24, Venus begins her retrograde trek through your Fifth House, giving you one more chance to renegotiate your level of romantic commitment.

Wellness and Keeping Fit

With Mars drawing focus to your Eighth House, you may be questioning your motivations for various actions and behaviors. This is a good time to go inside yourself and get in touch with the purpose you feel within.

Love and Life Connections

As December 24 approaches, you'll observe some rough areas in your romantic life. If you are in a committed relationship, you'll want to rekindle the flame of love in some way. If you are romantically involved, you will be looking for a deeper level of commitment or breaking away altogether. All relationships will be renegotiated in both spoken and unspoken ways between now and January.

Finance and Success

Time and monies spent on activities in organizations are not expenditures—they're investments in your future. A substantial project will arise early in the month which will fill your time and require some sacrifice. Although there's no direct benefit now, your efforts will be rewarded once others realize your skills and interests.

Rewarding Days

1, 2, 6, 7, 14, 15, 18, 19, 20, 23, 24, 25, 28, 29

Challenging Days

3, 4, 9, 10, 16, 17, 30, 31

LIBRA ACTION TABLE

These dates reflect the best—but not the only—times for success and ease in these activities, according to your Sun sign.

	JAN	FEB	MAR	APR	MAY	JUN	JUL	AUG	SEPT	OCT	NOV	DEC
Move	10-30											
Start a class	1-9									31	1-13	13-31
Join a club						28-30	1-22	16-31	1-4			
Ask for a raise				12-30	1-12	28-30	1-23	4,5,17-31	1-11	3,4		
Look for work		16-28				11-28						
Get pro advice	15,16	11-13	11,12	7,8	5,6	1,2,28,29	25-27	22,23	18,19	16,17	12,13	9,10
Get a loan	17-19	14,15	13,14	9-11	7,8	3,4,30	1,2,28,29	24,25	20,21	18,19	14,15	11-13
See a doctor		16-28	1-19	12-30	1-12				3-30	1-8		
Start a diet		16-28	1-5									
End relationship										16,17		
Buy clothes	30,31	1-26										
Get a makeover								17-31	1-11,20-30	1-8		
New romance		2-26										
Vacation	20-22	16-18	15-17	12,13	10-31	1-11	3,4,30,31	26-28	22-24	20,21	16-18	14,15

SCORPIO

The Scorpion
October 23 to November 22

♏

Element:	Water
Quality:	Fixed
Polarity:	Yin/Feminine
Planetary Ruler:	Pluto (Mars)
Meditation:	I can surrender my feelings.
Gemstone:	Topaz
Power Stones:	Obsidian, amber, citrine, garnet, pearl
Key Phrase:	I create
Glyph:	Scorpion's tail
Anatomy:	Reproductive system
Color:	Burgundy, black
Animal:	Reptiles, scorpions, birds of prey
Myths/Legends:	The Phoenix, Hades and Persephone, Shiva
House:	Eighth
Opposite Sign:	Taurus
Flower:	Chrysanthemum
Key Word:	Intensity

Your Ego's Strengths and Shortcomings

You live in a world of feelings, impressions, instincts, and insights, Scorpio, because yours is a water sign. You sense the world through the unseen ocean of emotion that we all live in. It's your job to keep us in touch with that part of our nature, as well as your own. You can feel the emotional ambience in a roomful of people—often before you get in the door. Your insights into human nature are astute because you are constantly matching and measuring body language, speech, and feeling to figure out what people are really experiencing. You know that most people don't say what they really feel, and that it's more out of fear or distrust than bad intentions. You are a firm believer in the power of the unconscious realms, and you can put your reality into words by studying Freud, Jung, and psychological astrology. You are more interested in the feelings and motivations of the people in the world around you than you are in those of your close companions or family, although you feel safest in expressing yourself openly with your loved ones. You are a "people-watcher," which often leaves you out of the picture when it comes to participation: you are more likely to be the photographer than in the photograph. This can lead to a curtailing of your ability to connect with others and truly enjoy life. "Careless abandon" is probably a foreign phrase to you. Your comfort level is not increased by the fact that you often reveal to others things that they would rather not know. Because you are immersed in feelings, you represent what many people wish didn't exist, and so you may often find yourself at odds with them if you try to express yourself from your heart. Don't be daunted though, because you know that opening emotional doors is the path to healing.

Shining Your Love Light

Despite that tough exterior, you are warm and sweet inside, but you're hoping nobody will notice it until you want them to. It's your sensitivity that makes you hide yourself away, making it difficult for others to know you as you are. You may be unsure of your assets because you've heard all kinds of things about Scorpio, and you can see the dark places in your own nature. However, those dark places exist in all of us, and it is far worse to be unaware of them than to know what they are, for that is the first step to containing and overcoming them. You are a passionate and tender lover, but rather than being indiscriminate in deciding to whom you show your love, you are very selective and will wait with the patience of Job until you meet the right person and you have built enough trust.

The impetuousness of Aries may shock you, but he'll spur you to take action more easily, while you'll influence him to consider his actions more carefully. Taurus stabilizes you and keeps you in touch with the practical side of life, while you teach her to let go of what she no longer needs. Gemini can lighten your heart and lift your spirits, sharing your curiosity about and need to know the world. Your fellow water sign, Cancer, really gets how sensitive you are and understands the world of feelings you live in, because he lives there too. Lively Leo will challenge you to give more generously to others and connect you more with your social milieu, while you'll bring depth and power to your bond. You'll have much in common with companion sign Virgo, whose loyalty and pragmatism you can rely on. Libra will show you a hidden side of your nature—your need for companionship and harmony with others. No one will know you better than another Scorpio, and if you work on developing trust you can change the world together. Sagittarius will lead you on paths where angels fear to tread, but you will be the stronger for it and enjoy the challenge. Capricorn matches your depth of understanding with breadth of vision for a wise and wonderful blend of capacities. Aquarius may seem like a thorn in your side until you locate your sense of humor and lighten up. Pisces shows what you hide, with an attunement to feelings identical to yours, since you are both of the water element.

Making Your Place in the World

Your adeptness at making your way through the world around you is your greatest strength, Scorpio. Above all, you strive for the ability to manage whatever comes your way, and so you focus on acquiring knowledge about how to handle the mechanics of life. This develops into "savvy"—that worldly wise quality that empowers you to overcome every obstacle that throws itself into your path. You know a little bit about everything, from car mechanics to cake decorating, and with this background you can relax and know that whatever you encounter will be surmountable. This makes you especially good at handling crises when they arise, and you can use these skills in emergency situations, where you maintain a cool head, and in the various helping professions: social work, counseling, medicine, holistic healing, and crisis intervention. You bring a combination of compassion and strength that is as rare as it is precious.

Putting Your Best Foot Forward

Your potential for success and fulfillment will expand astronomically, Scorpio, if you reach out to others more than is your natural penchant. You may tend to work alone and spend time by yourself, but networking is an important part of anyone's life, in both personal and professional pursuits. When you interact with others you get the chance to exchange ideas, even skills. You can plant the seeds of future friendships, partnerships, career positions, and support in times of need. You'll also benefit from learning not to burn your bridges. It is tempting to resolve a conflict by ending it in a way that satisfies your immediate need to win but which destroys the relationship. Even if you think you don't need the relationship in the future and you can afford to lose this person, you may regret that attitude, because you may need to rely on that person—or others they know—again. It is more successful in the long run to develop an awareness of your feelings in the moment and find a way to resolve conflicts as they arise. Learn to express yourself with gentleness and compassion. Sometimes you can't salvage a bad situation, but you can give it your best shot.

Tools for Change

Although you resist change, you understand its necessity, Scorpio. One of the ways you can facilitate change in your life is to explore your world more. You can travel, experiencing new cultures and settings. While you may tend toward the wilderness, the greatest wilderness for you is the sea of people that inhabit the planet. They are at once fascinating because of the mystery of the human psyche and terrifying because of your sensitivity to them, with your watery nature. Making a study of peoples across cultures can be revealing as to what unites us all, but also because of what it shows you about yourself. It's one thing to think that you are insecure around other people, but when you realize that most other people are as well, it turns your reality on its head. Another thing you can do is to learn to let go. This will reduce your intensity and make you more accessible to others. Holding on is emotional, based on fears, and if you learn to overcome your tendency to become attached, you will find others are drawn to you more because they know they won't feel trapped. To accomplish this, you need to develop more objectivity. Study psychology, or even go into therapy. Continue your education if necessary to school your mind. Most spiritual paths teach in part how to master one's emotions and make conscious choices about how to use them. Occult studies teach the means and methods of overcoming our weaknesses as we travel the spiritual path. The study of the tarot in particular reveals the ways that our feelings trip us up and how to overcome those patterns.

Stored emotions and past experiences can cause difficulties as well. Through self-help or therapy you can explore the past and release old memories and feelings. Massage or other body therapies are ideal for this as well. Exercise programs of any sort will help to release stored energies, including memories and emotions.

If you have difficulty relating to other people, there are ways you can improve your social skills. Joining a club or organization where you share the interests of others there gives you something impersonal to talk about, a way to build "social stamina." You can also work with animals, since they teach us to come out of our shell but don't make great demands on us emotionally.

Affirmation of the Year

I live in a world of possibility.

The Year Ahead for Scorpio

It's a year of endings and beginnings, Scorpio, as Jupiter moves you from behind the scenes into a more up-front, expansive role. Jupiter starts the year in Libra, your solar Twelfth House, where it draws you inward to examine your spiritual landscape. You may be studying philosophy, psychology, or things of a spiritual nature. Meditation or spiritual practice may become more important to you, or you could just feel like spending more time on your own—working on a long-term project, hiking in the wilderness, or exploring new areas of study. Your pursuits may feel like a necessary but intermediate step toward new initiatives, and you may feel confined during this time—although we usually are pretty happy with what Jupiter sets before us. After October 24 you'll feel a palpable shift of energy, and your life will expand outward. You'll be noticed more, and even stand out in a crowd. Others will see your unique skills and capabilities and offer new opportunities to you. Even more satisfying, you will be inspired to start some projects of your own, and your efforts will generally be greeted with favor. This "Midas touch" period will last one year and give you a view of the next twelve years (the length of time until Jupiter comes back to your Sun again).

Saturn is in Cancer and your solar Ninth House for the first half of the year. You've been able to coast on this energy, and with your diligence you make many constructive gains in moving toward some of your life's goals. You may have restructured your sense of life direction and tweaked or even transformed your path in preparation for the coming three years, when you will reach a pinnacle in your efforts at achievement in the outer world. When Saturn enters Leo on July 16 you'll enter that phase. It will require harder work, and challenge you to move out of your comfort zone to take on a role of greater public visibility, standing, and responsibility.

Chiron changes signs this year from Capricorn, your solar Third House, to Aquarius and your Fourth House. While it is in Capricorn (until February 21 and again from July 31 to December 5), you will continue the processes of mental development that you began three years ago. This may involve training or prep courses, higher education, continuing education, or your own personal studies. You may be learning new ways of communicating as well. Once Chiron is in Aquarius and your solar Fourth House, your efforts at self-improvement will move into your home environment and private life. You may discover unhealed emotional wounds from which you can now become free.

Uranus remains in Pisces this year, which is the fifth sign from your Sun. You have been feeling its maverick nature in your experiences with children and in your creative, leisure, and risk-taking activities. You may be willing to take greater risks now. Your romantic life will certainly take on intrigue as you discover and enjoy relationships with people who are distinctly different from you in culture, lifestyle, or temperament.

Neptune washes into your life from its familiar position in Aquarius and your Fourth House. Its watery depths are dissolving away old memories and feelings from the past—especially your childhood and family experiences. You may also benefit from taking care that the water on your property is securely held in its place—that pipes, drains, faucets, and heaters are functioning properly.

Pluto in Sagittarius is digging up buried issues in your solar Second House. Your spending patterns could be a time bomb waiting to go off. You may discover (or have already discovered) that you have too much debt, and start working toward rectifying matters. No matter what, you want to empower yourself through your resources, and you may be seeking new skills, more time, and more money with which to run your life.

The eclipses are in Taurus and Scorpio for the most part, directing your attention toward putting your relationships with others on the right footing. You may need to open up more and let others know how you feel.

If you were born from October 23 to November 4, Saturn in Leo will be in contact with your Sun after July 15. Your workload will ramp up as this occurs, but if you accept the challenge that lies before you, you will reap great rewards over the next ten years. Your standing in the community will take on greater importance, and you may be called upon to take a position of high profile or leadership—one that involves real work where you must prove yourself. You may be tempted to ignore other areas of your life in your efforts to achieve, but losing your balance in this way will result in ill health and impoverished relationships further down the road. With your drive and determination, you will surely be able to succeed at all you take on. In fact, this time can be a pinnacle of achievement, when promotion and recognition come your way. Sometimes, however, especially if you did not put the right effort in the best direction, Saturn traveling here can signal a downfall; if so, it is only guiding you toward a new path that is better suited to your true nature. Key dates for this year are January 13, July 16 through 23, and November 22.

If you were born from October 26 to November 4, Uranus in Pisces is contacting your Sun from your solar Fifth House. This is a time of rejuvenation, when you will want to enjoy pursuits from sky-diving to Balinese dance. You'll enjoy romantic contacts more if they are an adventure in some way—something really exotic or distinctive. You may enjoy your partners more if they are from another culture or behave in some unpredictable way. If you are involved in any creative pursuits, your expressive style will certainly change in some significant way. You will introduce elements of freedom and chaos, letting go of old patterns of structure and restraint. If creativity is a more casual activity, you may feel inspired to engage in new, unusual pastimes. If you have children, they will be sources of surprise—even shock—and awakening. They may delight you with their ingenuity or they may jolt you with their forms of rebellion. Injury is also possible, as Uranus rules sudden events and unexpected jolts. Joining that new football league may lead to a misstep and a twisted ankle. Key dates for your Uranus experience include February 25, June 14, August 31, and November 15.

If you were born from November 5 to 11, Neptune in Aquarius will be aspecting your Sun from your solar Fourth House. Neptune can have an undermining influence in this position, so it's important to make sure that the foundations are solid in your home, your emotional make-up, and your life. You may experience difficulties with water—either from plumbing or in situations where standing water exists, such as a swimming pool or jacuzzi. On a more symbolic level, you may feel caught in a quagmire of someone else's emotions, especially someone at home. However, it could be some-one with whom you share a long history, such as your mother or father, even if you don't live with them. Whatever circumstances exist, Neptune shows us where we need to spiritualize our lives, and perhaps make a sacrifice for the greater good. We may feel called upon to neglect one area of our life in order to feed our Neptune area, or vice versa. This is a good time to heal old emotional wounds, such as those left over from childhood (especially the ages of five to seven). We may draw works of imagination and creativity from our healing process, and the act of creating will support the healing as well. Important dates for your Neptune experience are February 2, May 19, August 8, and October 26.

If you were born from November 12 to 22, your experience this year will be colored by Saturn, which is in Cancer and is con-tacting your Sun from your solar Ninth House until July 16. You've been anticipating its arrival for some time, and the first contact was made during 2004, so you already know what's on your plate for the next six months. You've been restructuring your life path, carving out a new sense of who you are as you go, because our path is always a reflection of how we define ourselves. You may choose to take up new studies, or even begin or resume work toward a college degree. You're asking questions, thinking about life in a broader way, expanding your consciousness. This is especially satisfying for you because it gives you answers and quenches your natural curiosity while it increases your objectivity. You may decide to travel this year, whether for work or as a part of your learning process. It will be especially useful if your sojourns take you to foreign lands or unfa-miliar cultures. Either way, contact with other cultures will further support the wider perspective that Saturn's transit fosters. Milestone dates in this process include January 13 and March 21.

If you were born from November 15 to 18, Pluto is transform-ing your life from your solar Second House, which is the place of resources and includes money, skills, and time. This is a sea change that has been a long time coming, and now that it is here you prob-ably know what it involves. However, that may not make it any eas-ier, because Pluto will eliminate things from your life that you still consider essential. This may involve a change in your source(s) of income, which involves risk. Embracing Pluto's changes requires a willingness to take a risk—often a big one. You'll have to weigh the possibilities that you see before you and prepare yourself as best you can. Pluto will push you through the doorway of the "new" whether you are ready and willing or kicking and screaming. It is best to use your energies to empower yourself during the transformation rather than in fighting it. You may choose to acquire new skills or find new sources of financial support. Most importantly, you will need to see yourself and your capabilities in a new, more potent way. Critical dates for your Pluto experience this year include March 26, June 13, September 2, and December 15.

Scorpio/January

Planetary Hotspots

Education is an important part of your life right from the start of the month as Saturn is highlighted in your solar Ninth House. This may involve travel or contact with foreign thoughts and ideas as January 13 approaches. January 16 sees the beginning of another Chiron cycle, emphasizing your Third House of community contact and commerce, bringing out areas of weakness in your ability to connect.

Wellness and Keeping Fit

You'll feel more like taking in a museum exhibit than heading for the hills on a hike this month, but it's good to keep your balance and do both. Don't let busy-ness prevent you from doing what's important for your physical well-being.

Love and Life Connections

Brothers, sisters, and your local community will be a source of comfort and pleasure for you starting January 9. If you can extend a helping hand, it will be welcomed—and most needed around January 16.

Finance and Success

Over the past three years, you've been discovering how your attitude wounds you when it comes to success. You've been learning the value of optimism and replacing negative thoughts with uplifting ones. You've got one more year to perfect the process, starting January 16. If you've been responding to your perceptions, you're already seeing improvements in your outer-world results. You have the opportunity to spend wisely around January 28 in a way that will increase your potential this year and for many more to come, if you make the right choices.

Rewarding Days

1, 5, 6, 9, 10, 13, 14, 22, 23, 24, 27, 28, 29

Challenging Days

11, 12, 17, 18, 25, 26

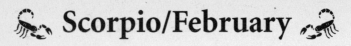 Scorpio/February

Planetary Hotspots

Jupiter begins its four-month retrograde period on February 1, bringing out a need to retreat in order to get some important inner work done. Choosing to fulfill this need will refuel you in ways that will benefit you for the next twelve years. Neptune commences its new yearly cycle on February 2, leading you through another year of emphasis on spiritualizing your home and family life. When Chiron enters Aquarius on February 21, you'll start to see the challenges that still exist in your private life, perhaps stemming from your upbringing. February 25 heralds the initiation of yet another cycle, as Uranus brings you another year of innovation and awakening in your creative pursuits and the lives of your children.

Wellness and Keeping Fit

A health matter may arise around February 1 which requires your attention over the coming four months. If so, your usual level of mobility may be curtailed during that time. However, it is more likely that you will be drawn to explore your inner world more and develop your well-being from a more spiritual level. You may be inspired to serve others in a way that makes you feel more fulfilled—an essential component of good health.

Love and Life Connections

Even though you're already making sacrifices in your home and family life, you may be called upon to make new ones starting this month. Although it's not a permanent condition, what arises reveals a larger issue that must be healed in order to regain your independence.

Finance and Success

You may be inspired around February 1 to dedicate yourself to a cause that means a great deal to you. You may be drawn to serve others in a quiet way, whether through work or volunteer activities.

Rewarding Days

1, 2, 5, 6, 9, 10, 18, 19, 20, 23, 24, 25, 28

Challenging Days

7, 8, 14, 15, 21, 22

Scorpio/March

Planetary Hotspots
The early part of the month is active as you prepare for the challenges of the three-week retrograde period of Mercury. You may feel overwhelmed by detail—like you're going nowhere fast—with increasing intensity until Mercury reaches its turn-around point on March 19. Saturn adds its voice to the chorus on March 21, and you feel an even greater sense of urgency to complete projects that resonate to the rhythm of Saturn's cycle—those which bring you a broader view of the world. Pluto outlines a path of change by once again revealing weaknesses in the ways your handle resources around March 26.

Wellness and Keeping Fit
Between March 5 and 19 is a good time to get advice and support for your health and fitness routines, as Mercury moves through your solar Sixth House starting March 5. If you don't do it before March 19, you may get some misleading information or lab results. Overdoing your exercise plan can result in injury after that, and you may be slightly more prone to viruses as your workload increases the stress you are under.

Love and Life Connections
With most of your energy going to work and service to others, it could be easy to withdraw from loved ones, if only because you're tired. At least let them know what's going on and ask for their understanding.

Finance and Success
It's work, work, work all month long. The pressures are high right now, but that doesn't mean you have to respond to them as if there is a crisis. Peaks will occur on March 3, 7, 19, and 23, with a release on March 21. Forewarned is forearmed. Financial decisions must be made around March 26.

Rewarding Days
1, 2, 5, 6, 9, 10, 18, 19, 23, 24, 28, 29

Challenging Days
7, 8, 13, 14, 20, 21, 22

Scorpio/April

Planetary Hotspots

On April 3 you're two months into Jupiter's focus period, and you can see how your chosen work and health improvement activities will pan out for you. The eclipses on April 8 and 24 underscore the importance of these initiatives and give you a tantalizing choice to make that will affect your life for years to come. You regain an increasing sense of calm and accomplishment as April 12 approaches—the day Mercury returns to forward motion after its retrograde. It has put the spotlight on work and health in a way that has clarified your sense of direction.

Wellness and Keeping Fit

Your inwardly directed activities—meditation, recovery from illness, inner development—reach a turning point on April 3, with two months to go before they become less significant in your life. There could be a learning curve here that you finish during this time. This is generally a gratifying experience with benefits down the road. When Mercury returns to direct travel on April 12, your routines return to normal as well.

Love and Life Connections

Past relationship issues resurface on April 24, even though you thought you'd put them successfully to rest. This could mean that you've relaxed your guard on a commitment you've made; if so, it's time to make course corrections.

Finance and Success

You feel pressure to work just as hard this month as last, but the pressure abates mid-month. In the meantime you have the support of others, but you may have to ask for it.

Rewarding Days

1, 2, 5, 6, 14, 15, 16, 19, 20, 21, 24, 25, 28, 29

Challenging Days

3, 4, 9, 10, 11, 17, 18, 30

Scorpio/May

Planetary Hotspots

Chiron, although still in the early part of Aquarius, has had ample opportunity to reveal the areas in which you need to grow in your private life. As it turns retrograde on May 8 you'll get a sense of what needs change the most urgently—a process that you will work on over the next nine months. You may feel confused or disillusioned around May 19, especially with respect to your home life, as Neptune's retrograde period starts. This is just the preamble, however, to greater clarity that will come from a new level of awareness that is developing within you.

Wellness and Keeping Fit

Your health may be fine, but someone in your family needs extra care, especially around May 8. This could be a long-term issue that will require you being on your toes about taking care of yourself if you are to make it through with your own well-being intact. There is a period when you could be accident-prone during exercise and sports, however—for two days before and after May 15.

Love and Life Connections

Your ongoing sacrifices for someone in your family reach a critical point on May 19 as a new dilemma emerges which must be worked out in the coming five months. Romantic connections will be highlighted from the beginning of the month, with a possible surprise encounter or romantic getaway around May 15.

Finance and Success

After the last two months' hard work, you need a break. This is a good time to take a few days off, or even take a vacation. Even if you can only manage a weekend, you'll benefit greatly.

Rewarding Days

3, 4, 12, 13, 17, 18, 22, 23, 26, 27, 30, 31

Challenging Days

1, 2, 7, 8, 9, 14, 15, 16, 28, 29

Scorpio/June

Planetary Hotspots

Although there are substantial distractions on June 2, don't let them blind you to the shift that takes place on June 5, when you are able to put to rest enterprises you began last September. June 13 heralds the peak of an escalating financial issue, after which you will be more successful in resolving associated dilemmas. New challenges may seem to come out of left field at the same time, as Uranus's retrograde period begins. You'll have five months to work out what's going on and develop a solution.

Wellness and Keeping Fit

The quiet, inwardly directed world you've inhabited over the past four months will soon be a thing of the past as Jupiter returns to forward motion. Although you've still got five months to continue your current trajectory, you've turned a corner in accomplishing your goals.

Love and Life Connections

The ongoing challenge of finding the right romantic partner becomes more important to you as June 14 arrives. You'll be looking for new solutions to the issues you associate with that challenge. A revelation or insight may spur you into action, which could range from realizing that your current partner is not suitable to finding out that someone you've known for a long time is right for you.

Finance and Success

The effects of the financial course that you set for yourself earlier this year will become more noticeable around June 13 as Pluto reaches the culmination of its yearly cycle in your Second House. You've got until September 2 to pour your heart into your new endeavors; then you'll see how well you've done in your steady road toward self-empowerment.

Rewarding Days

2, 3, 4, 11, 12, 13, 16, 17, 18, 21, 22, 26, 27, 30

Challenging Days

1, 7, 8, 14, 15, 28, 29

Scorpio/July

Planetary Hotspots

Saturn and Chiron interact with each other July 16 through 30, as Saturn enters Leo. This brings a dynamic new process of restructuring into your career and how you balance it with your home and private life. The issues will be brought into stark relief through communications and paperwork, as Mercury begins another of its frequent retrogrades on July 22, this time in your Tenth House of career and public life. The Sun adds fuel to the fire as it contacts both Saturn and Chiron on July 23, contributing to a feeling of crescendo at that time.

Wellness and Keeping Fit

During this month full of events, a few minutes spent in athletic activities will support your strength and stability, both physically and mentally. You may be attracted to team sports. Take advantage of it.

Love and Life Connections

You've got a lot on your plate now, and projects at home and work will compete for your time, especially after July 15. The dilemmas that arise now can linger for the coming eight months, but communicating about what's happening in both your personal and career life will smooth your path.

Finance and Success

Career demands make you feel overwhelmed, especially after July 15. They'll peak on July 31, but you won't be completely free of them until the end of the year. Through persistent effort you will accomplish several things of real value in your life regardless of what it took to get there.

Rewarding Days

8, 9, 13, 14, 18, 19, 22, 23, 26, 27

Challenging Days

3, 4, 10, 11, 12, 24, 25, 30

Scorpio/August

Planetary Hotspots

On August 8, Neptune's yearly cycle reaches its culmination, bringing a moment of clarity and inspiration to the challenges you face in your home and family environment. The tightly bound-up feeling of conflict between home and business life relaxes when Mercury returns to forward motion on August 15, but tension builds in your social world as Uranus reaches toward the culmination of its cycle on August 31.

Wellness and Keeping Fit

It's hard to see how you can manage all the obligations that you've committed yourself to, but that makes it all the more important to take each day, each moment, one at a time. This will allow you to focus effectively and complete each task efficiently with low stress. It's not what happens—it's how we perceive it.

Love and Life Connections

This is a month to tread lightly and receptively in relationships, as Mars begins a long transit in your Seventh House of partnerships on August 28. You may notice that people are more aggressive toward you—a good time to observe how you may be contributing to their frustration, perhaps through stoic unresponsiveness. Letting people know how you are feeling, staying in touch even in the midst of distractions, will go far toward overriding the challenges of the rest of the year.

Finance and Success

By August 15 you'll at least have your work organized, and this will give you that all-essential feeling of control over your circumstances. Don't let feelings of chaos mask the progress you're making on August 8 and 31.

Rewarding Days

5, 6, 7, 10, 11, 12, 15, 16, 19, 20, 23, 24

Challenging Days

1, 2, 8, 9, 21, 22, 28, 29

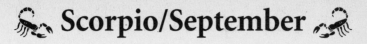 **Scorpio/September**

Planetary Hotspots

Since 1995, you've been working on empowering yourself in new ways through judicious use of your resources, including time, money, and skills. This year has brought you yet another layer of restriction to overcome as you develop new ways to manage those resources. Critical events occurred around March 26 and June 13. As of September 2, you will have accomplished all you can for now, as far as extra effort is concerned. You've discovered some new techniques for negotiating your way through the situation. With several more years to go in resolving it, relaxing your vigilance will cause you to lose ground. Still, as you turn yet another corner now, you can see visible progress.

Wellness and Keeping Fit

Now that you're getting a relative breather from all your responsibilities, take the time to pamper yourself. Visit a day spa, take a vacation, treat yourself to a few new items of clothing, get a makeover—whatever suits you to a "T."

Love and Life Connections

A sense of increasing pressure may reign in your relationship life as the month wears on. This is related to Mars's sojourn in your Seventh House, where it is slowing down to make its biennial retrograde on October 1. You may find yourself feeling the urge to take precipitous action as you anticipate some event or circumstance that you fear or find distasteful. Being patient and mindfully observing how events unfold will be more helpful.

Finance and Success

Blessedly, no new issues arise at work, and your success at handling your resources in a new way is now beginning to show. Keep up the good work!

Rewarding Days

1, 2, 3, 6, 7, 8, 11, 12, 13, 16, 17, 20, 21, 29, 30

Challenging Days

4, 5, 18, 19, 24, 25

Scorpio/October

Planetary Hotspots

October 1 may bring simmering situations to a head as Mars enters its three-month retrograde period in your Seventh House of relationships. There are eclipses on October 3 and 17 to bring an unexpected plot twist to your work and health picture. Chiron returns to forward motion on October 5, allowing your personal emotional and spiritual healing process to move toward completion. Neptune does the same with your home and family on October 26. Best of all, though, is Jupiter's new beginning on October 22, starting your own Midas-touch period when Jupiter is in your sign for the coming year.

Wellness and Keeping Fit

With the eclipses in your Sixth and Twelfth Houses, your health is once again in the spotlight, where it will be for another year. This is a good time to take preventive and holistic measures to head off difficulties, even if you can detect nothing out of the ordinary now.

Love and Life Connections

You may find that others want to challenge you or feel competitive toward you in some way, especially at the beginning of the month. You may be ruminating on how you contribute to your relationships, feeling an imbalance that needs to be corrected. Given your nature, this probably means being more expressive and reaching out more to those you care about. Others may act aggressively toward you through the end of the year, but it's about them more than you.

Finance and Success

As Jupiter enters your sign and solar First House, the world's your oyster. You'll have the Midas touch for the coming year, starting October 25, so think about what you want to create over the next twelve years. That's how long you get to play out the cards you deal for yourself now.

Rewarding Days
1, 5, 6, 9, 10, 14, 15, 22, 23, 24, 27, 28, 29

Challenging Days
11, 12, 13, 18, 19, 25, 26

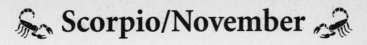 Scorpio/November

Planetary Hotspots

Mercury makes its third and final retrograde of the year starting on November 14, putting added focus on your finances during the holiday season. When Uranus returns to forward motion on November 15 you'll feel your own motion toward your goals shift into gear. You'll be able to rapidly resolve issues that have arisen in your creative and romantic life, as well as with your children. On the other hand, Saturn sets up a new obstacle course for you in your career or business, signaling that it's time to knuckle down and make the needed changes through persistent effort, if not plain old hard work. Chances are, you'll feel like working double time to accomplish your goals, which will be realized over the coming three years.

Wellness and Keeping Fit

As activities heat up again in your career, you must continue your vigilance in reforming your daily habits and health routines. You're feeling energetic at least until November 15.

Love and Life Connections

Around November 7 you are called upon to surrender to a situation at home. This time, it may feel especially tiresome, because you've seen it all before. Maybe it's time to find a new way to deal with it.

Finance and Success

With Mercury in retrograde in your Second House of personal resources, you may find that you have overspent in recent months. If so, this is not the time for an extravagant holiday season, but one of inwardly significant and meaningful celebration—a sure way to create a values adjustment at this often materialistic time. The financial issues aren't likely to leave tread marks on your life unless you ignore the situation.

Rewarding Days

1, 2, 6, 7, 10, 11, 19, 20, 24, 25, 28, 29, 30

Challenging Days

8, 9, 14, 15, 21, 22, 23

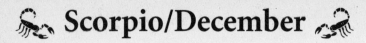 Scorpio/December

Planetary Hotspots

It's understandable if you feel like you've bitten off more than you can chew as the month starts. This feeling will peak on December 5, but you may not feel any palpable relief until after December 9. Pluto makes life exciting around December 15 as its contact with the Sun signals the start of its new yearly cycle. This will bring additional changes in your resources that help you live the life you really want. On December 24, Venus begins its six-week retrograde, opening the door to renegotiating your family relationships.

Wellness and Keeping Fit

Even though your life is filled with obligations, it's important to take some time for yourself. You may not feel like leaving home, and you may not be able to, but you can at least close the door to the world and replenish yourself by doing something you really enjoy.

Love and Life Connections

It's time to renegotiate the commitments and the distribution of energy and effort in your home life. You've been feeling this for some time, but the issues will really come to the forefront around December 24, when Venus turns retrograde in your solar Fourth House. If the situation is truly beyond anyone's control, it may be necessary to get some support from outside the family. If this is the case, be upfront about it and then give others time to get used to the idea.

Finance and Success

As Pluto's new annual cycle begins on December 15 you get the opportunity to set your tasks for the coming year in regard to your finances and self-empowerment through better resource management. Whether this means finding a new way to make money or redistributing your portfolio, you'll feel instinctively where to go around this date.

Rewarding Days

3, 4, 7, 8, 16, 17, 21, 22, 26, 27, 30, 31

Challenging Days

5, 6, 11, 12, 13, 18, 19, 20

SCORPIO ACTION TABLE

These dates reflect the best—but not the only—times for success and ease in these activities, according to your Sun sign.

	JAN	FEB	MAR	APR	MAY	JUN	JUL	AUG	SEPT	OCT	NOV	DEC
Move	30, 31	1-16										
Start a class	10-30											
Join a club									3-20			
Ask for a raise							25-31	1-17	3-5, 11-30	1-8	1, 2	
Look for work			5-19	12-30	1-28	28-30	1-22	16-31	1-4			
Get pro advice	17-19	14, 15	13, 14	9-11	7, 8	3, 4, 30	1, 2, 28, 29	24, 25	20, 21	18, 19	14, 15	11-13
Get a loan	20-22	16-18	15-17	12, 13	10, 11	5-7	3, 4, 30, 31	26-28	22-24	20, 21	16-18	14, 15
See a doctor			5-19	12-30	1-28				20-30	1-30		
Start a diet			5-19, 25-27	12-30	1-12							
End relationship											14, 15	
Buy clothes		16-28	1-22									
Get a makeover									8-30	1-8	1, 2	
New romance		26-28	1-22									
Vacation	22-24	18, 19	18, 19	14-16	3-28	8, 9	5-7	1-3, 29, 30	25, 26	22-24	19, 20	16, 17

The Archer
November 22 to December 21

Element:	Fire
Quality:	Mutable
Polarity:	Yang/Masculine
Planetary Ruler:	Jupiter
Meditation:	I can take time to explore my soul.
Gemstone:	Turquoise
Power Stones:	Lapis lazuli, azurite, sodalite
Key Phrase:	I understand
Glyph:	Archer's arrow
Anatomy:	Hips, thighs, sciatic nerve
Color:	Royal blue, purple
Animal:	Fleet-footed animals
Myths/Legends:	Athena, Chiron
House:	Ninth
Opposite Sign:	Gemini
Flower:	Narcissus
Key Word:	Optimism

Your Ego's Strengths and Shortcomings

As the final fire sign in the sequence, yours is the spark that ignites the flame of the soul, Sagittarius! Your brilliance may be fleeting, but it creates the sustaining fires that bring light into darkness and warm the heart. You're always on the move, for you are ever aware of the possibilities in the next situation, over the next hurdle. You may work way ahead of yourself, even leaving chaos in your wake, so intent are you on reaching toward your next goal. Like your element, your direction is upward, aspiring for the heights of human experience, to prove that we are godlike in our true nature. You seek transcendence, to rise above the limitations of the physical world and perceive the universe as it truly is—and others may see zeal, even fanaticism, in your fervor. Just as your fire follows the path of its fuel as it burns, you are tied to your source of inspiration. You are dependent on others for your sustenance, and without them your flame would soon die. You cover ground rapidly, consuming the ideas and experiences you encounter, absorbing them into your nature and making them part of your unified awareness. You may move quickly through situations and relationships because of your quest for greater knowledge and the fulfillment of your path. You can accept this "traveler" part of your nature or access other parts of who you are to create more lasting, stable bonds. If these qualities are taken to extremes, you may consume experiences too rapidly to gain the full benefit of them: you may get lost in your lofty idealism and lose touch with the "real" world. By keeping one foot on the ground—from managing your finances to listening to others—you will be able to keep your fires of inspiration burning.

Shining Your Love Light

You are loving, generous, open, and honest, Sagittarius—some of the best qualities to bring to a relationship. You carry your natural excitement, inspiration, and energy to any bond, and you want a partner who can keep up with you, respond to your ideas with enthusiasm, swoon to your romantic gestures, and follow you through all challenges on your adventures. This is a way to maintain a relationship for the longer term: if you are always growing together, you won't have time to grow apart, or to leave one or the other behind.

Aries will match you step for step on every adventure, although he's more attuned to action than the "head trips" of philosophy and study. Taurus brings sense and stability into your life, while your vigor energizes Taurus and gets her moving. Gemini is your natural reflection—a complement whose curiosity brings to light new truths for you to add to your understanding of life. You'll develop your compassionate side when in contact with Cancer's caring ways and spark this sign's interest in things beyond the comfort zone. You and Leo are kindred spirits, your fiery energies reaching for the sky together, inspiring each other to new achievements. Virgo will help you become more efficient and organized, while you help her step beyond her insecurities and try new things. You'll find a warm companion in Libra, who will seek balance and harmony in your relationship rather than the extremes of passion you express at times. Scorpio will remind you of the deep, intense energies of the emotions that lie within, while you'll spark his sense of humor. A fellow Sagittarius may keep pace with you in your explorations, or want some of her own as she pursues her own path. Capricorn shares your interest in the greater good, wanting to use your shared wisdom in practical ways to benefit all. Aquarius craves independence as you do, and won't tie you down. Pisces has a passion for exploring the inner realms, just as you have, and will bring a delicate sensitivity to your bond, while you assist this sign in rising above emotions.

Making Your Place in the World

With your drive to explore and stay on the move, you are better off finding a career that values that as a strength rather than considering it a weakness. An office job is not for you, unless it is only a temporary way-station for your activities outside its confines. You also need a position that keeps you inspired and challenged: routine tasks will have you looking in the want ads in no time. Positions with travel may have the thrill you crave—from travel photography to lecture circuits to simply driving a truck for a mail delivery service. If working for someone else feels too restrictive, then working under contract (in sales for instance) or starting a business of your own in an area you feel strongly about will overcome those limitations. If you want to share your inspiration for life with others, there is no better profession than teaching—a time-honored Sagittarian pursuit.

Putting Your Best Foot Forward

Your sense of direction is so strong sometimes, Sagittarius, that you lose sight of the rest of the universe as you travel your path. For this reason, it's important to consciously cultivate an awareness of the other aspects of your life and keep everything in the picture. This means that you need to "ground" every so often and take care of those "adult responsibilities": cleaning the house (or hiring someone to do it), paying the bills, feeding the dog or ourselves. Just as importantly, it's vital to realize that your path may need to change from time to time. As you learn more through experience or added information, you may discover that your old viewpoint is not correct—that the truth is not now as you understood it then. Take care not to wear blinders to the need to adjust, or you could be accused of fanaticism. Tied to this is the need to maintain receptivity toward others. In doing so, you will not have to work so hard to get new information because others will be happy to give it to you. By constantly honing your version of the truth, you will remain in step with your world.

Tools for Change

Since you are always learning, Sagittarius, you are always changing. However, you cannot make as much progress if you do not apply discipline. If you are persistent in your efforts, you will achieve much more. The foundation of discipline is in strength of mind. To begin with, you can benefit from developing principles to guide your behavior. The study of philosophy, ethics, or comparative religious studies will lead you on paths of inquiry toward this development. Another step you can take is to learn to face a situation when it confronts you. While it is sometimes beneficial to back away or avoid difficult issues, eventually you must take appropriate responsibility for your role and make necessary amends. Doing so bolsters your self-esteem and your mental strength. Rely on your characteristic honesty to see you through, rather than moving on to escape. You will also strengthen your mind by broadening your perspective. You can do this through travel—immersing yourself in a new cultural mind set—and through international or cross-cultural studies. Your mind will become more disciplined through meditation as well, since the development of mental discipline is the first step, and perhaps the primary focus, in all meditation practices. As you become more focused and learn to root out undermining thoughts and attitudes, you will become more objective in your assessment of the conditions around you, and steadfastness will naturally flow from this. Next, you will accomplish more if you learn how to make the concepts that you believe in work in the world around you. This means learning more about how that world works, whether through the studies of human nature (such as psychology or astrology), or through learning the ways of the world (such as the realms of finance and accounting or administration and management). Developing your deductive reasoning skills will also support your growth in these areas, perhaps through the study of logic or mathematics. Finally, cultivating the receptive side of your nature will keep you in tune with others. Working on your listening skills, perhaps through training in active listening or compassionate communication, will put the capstone on the pyramid of your mental development.

Affirmation of the Year

Through all transformations, I am only strengthened.

The Year Ahead for Sagittarius

You're in for a year of one of your favorite things, Sagittarius: self-development. The world's your oyster as you get to pick and choose your own path, initiatives, and associates. Jupiter in Libra supports this process from your solar Eleventh House, where it will be until October 25. Awards, honors, and accolades are coming your way—due to you after years of hard work. This may include a raise or honorary promotion, or you may be expected to take the lead in a group effort. Your emphasis will be on group activities during this time, and this is the best place to put your expansive energies in order to create continued success and prosperity, as well as to ensure your future. Maximize your efforts by choosing which groups you wish to associate with, because there will be many to select from this year. Once Jupiter moves to Scorpio, the next sign, you'll feel more like withdrawing, and there may be projects or activities that draw you inward. It can be a productive time as well as a period of great insights as you look at the previous eleven years and see how much you've grown.

Saturn begins the year in Cancer and your Eighth House, but it moves into Leo, a more harmonious placement for you, on July 16. While Saturn is in Cancer you'll still be dealing with the shadow of past financial challenges, perhaps making those last few payments or hanging in there until your salary increase comes through. Think of it as empowering you to accomplish what you really want once your obligations take up less of your energy and resources. Once Saturn enters Leo you'll have more freedom, but you'll be inclined to find ways to express it more meaningfully, as Saturn makes you more serious about achieving your goals.

Chiron also changes signs this year, moving from Capricorn into Aquarius on February 21, then back to Capricorn again from July 31 to December 5. Capricorn is your solar Second House, where you've had additional reinforcement for discipline in your financial affairs. Once Chiron enters Aquarius, you'll be more interested in correcting weaknesses in your ways of thinking and communicating, perhaps finding that you now want to open up areas of life that you previously avoided.

Uranus stimulates further awakening from its position in Pisces, the Fourth House from your Sun. You may experience some unexpected and unsettling events, which nevertheless free you from old restraints. Insights will emerge that deepen your understanding of what drives you. Neptune remains in Aquarius and your solar Third House, inspiring you to gain new insights into the truth. You want to sweep away the cobwebs from your mind and see things as they really are, although your confusion and disorientation may increase temporarily. Pluto makes its slow way through your own sign, transforming your identity, personality, and appearance. You have the opportunity to change yourself into an unrecognizably better manifestation of your true self; in fact, Pluto demands this. You will gain personal power to the extent that you are able to develop your ability to stay centered and in control of your self-expression.

The eclipses move into harmonious places for you this year: your solar Fifth and Eleventh Houses. You will discover new ways to have fun and be creative. You may discover a new group of friends to hang out with, or a new professional organization to help you empower your career.

If you were born from November 22 to December 4, Saturn in Leo will suggest new structures and directions for your life goals once it enters Leo and your solar Ninth House on July 16. A new teacher may appear who will have a strong influence on you and how you grow. Or you may feel challenged by other stimuli to explore new areas of interest. You could take on a teaching role yourself, and, if so, it is a role that is more honorary and spiritual than identified by job title or outer recognition. You may also feel inspired to travel into unfamiliar territory—a foreign land or exotic culture. What you do now will feed future career choices and opportunities—especially in two years, when Saturn moves into your solar Tenth House of career and calling. Saturn located here also affects your sense of spiritual and religious direction, and you may feel that your quest for the truth becomes more important to you during this time. You could become more involved in church leadership, or you could even change the faith you follow. Significant dates related to Saturn's role in your life include July 16 to 23 and November 22.

If you were born from November 25 to December 3, Uranus in Pisces will directly affect your Sun from your solar Fourth House. After all you've been through since 1995, you may feel as though you can't take any more, but this contact will open doorways for you like no other can. Uranus will awaken you to new possibilities that lead you to greater emotional freedom and happiness, if you dare to go where its inspiration takes you. Disruptions and seeming catastrophes are often the vehicles by which Uranus's insights reach us. They may spur you to make a change that you've long been considering, or you may have a sudden epiphany about how to solve a long-standing problem. Family issues may get out of hand, or you may realize that you're inducing chaos in your own life because of your own unsettling childhood. You could decide to move, to renovate your existing home, or to free yourself of obligations in that area in some way. Whatever you choose to create, you'll be seeking greater emotional fulfillment and a deeper sense of connection. Events significant to this thread of your life story are likely to occur around February 25, June 14, August 31, and November 15.

If you were born from December 5 to 11, Neptune's ethereal energy will reach your Sun from your solar Third House. New inspiration will infuse your mental processes and fill you with verbal creativity. You will develop new aspects to your message this year because you are forming new ways of seeing the world. This is an excellent time to attempt attitudinal changes, since your mind will be particularly malleable. You may at times feel confused or disoriented as you let go of old ideas and embrace new ones—changing from the comfortable to the unfamiliar removes our old props and strategies. These changes may be prompted by the realization that the world doesn't work quite the way you had learned it does. Early childhood impressions may have led you to the wrong conclusions, and now you can see quite clearly that the approaches you've taken based on that version of reality don't work. Although you may feel disenfranchised while you make this change, in the long run you'll be more effective and exhibit greater clarity in the decisions you make and in the ways you communicate with others. Turning points in this process will occur around February 2, May 19, August 8, and October 26.

If you were born from December 12 to 21, Saturn in Cancer will be aspecting your Sun from your solar Eighth House, governing the ways you fulfill your obligations to society. Taxes, loans, and other types of indebtedness will assume more importance during this time, and you may find it necessary to devote more of your income to such obligations until around the time that Saturn leaves Cancer on July 16. If your burdens continue beyond that time, you'll have them sufficiently under control so that you can put them on the back burner as you work on other areas of your life. This is not the time to shirk responsibility in these areas, particularly with taxes or regularly scheduled payments. In fact, it is best to take extra care with such matters, and to review your insurance portfolio to ensure that your needs will be met in any eventuality. The ways that your partner handles joint resources may assume greater significance now as well, as he or she perhaps spends more than the two of you can comfortably manage. You may also use this time to engage in studies of the occult, such as tarot or magic, and the discipline involved in these studies may be especially important to you. Events connected with this cycle are likely to occur around January 13 and March 21.

If you were born from December 14 to 18, Pluto will be focusing its transformative energies directly on your Sun. This will have a powerful impact on your identity and the way you present yourself to the world. You are likely to make some major changes this year in everything from the way you dress and look to the path you follow in life. Everything is up for grabs: you could change your job or career, your relationships, your ways of associating with family. All of this will extend from what you discover in yourself as you go through a profound self-examination process. Anything that doesn't match the person you find when you look inside will have to go—if not now, then eventually. You won't be able to make all the changes you want to enact right away; it takes time to incorporate them into our nature and make them an organic part of how we express ourselves in all situations. You have felt these changes coming for some time, and yet you haven't felt prepared to make the alterations until now because you didn't feel you were at your wit's end yet. Now that time has come, and you'll be walking down the path to the new you as fast as you can manage. After this year has passed there may be more to accomplish, but you'll know what that is and how to achieve it. Critical dates in your Pluto process include March 26, June 13, September 2, and December 15.

🏹 Sagittarius/January 🏹

Planetary Hotspots

A situation arises around January 13 and 16 that has a financial impact. Because it involves Saturn and Chiron, what happens now will recur in a slightly different form in July and then from October to December. You'll want to take note of events and think about their potential repercussions when making decisions about how to handle them, for their effects will be far-reaching.

Wellness and Keeping Fit

With Mars in your sign all month, you'll be full of energy and ready to go. You can pour some of this into your fitness program, but if you overdo it, you will have nothing left when Mars moves on. Your high energy could get the best of you if you express it with careless abandon: accidents or injuries could ensue. The potential for this is especially high on January 28.

Love and Life Connections

You may be more aware of your anger this month, and it may be difficult not to take it out on others. Seeing things from their point of view as much as you can will help to neutralize this tendency. Interactions will be especially explosive on January 28.

Finance and Success

You've been restructuring and improving your financial profile for a couple of years now, and your current stage in the process reaches a critical point at mid-month. You'll uncover some new information that you will need to incorporate into your financial plan in some way, but communication and coordination with others will make it easier to implement.

Rewarding Days

2, 3, 4, 7, 8, 11, 12, 15, 16, 25, 26, 30, 31

Challenging Days

1, 9, 10, 23, 24, 20, 21, 27, 28, 29

Sagittarius/February

Planetary Hotspots

Starting February 1 you'll begin a winnowing out process, sorting through the possible futures that lie before you and committing yourself through your own efforts to create the ones you want. February 2 brings the start of a new Neptune cycle of inner development in your perceptions and approach to life—the domain of your Third House. When Chiron enters Aquarius on February 21 you'll have added incentive to improve the way you see the world and how you connect with it. On February 25 you'll begin a new wave of innovation in your home life.

Wellness and Keeping Fit

A trip to the mountains may be exactly what you need to fight off the winter doldrums. Whether it's to ski or hike or sit in a hot tub, getting away from the complexities of your daily life will be as healing as any fitness routine.

Love and Life Connections

The needs of others are an important part of your experience this month, all the more significant because the situations that arise will establish a pattern or dilemma that will be worked through over the coming year. You may be called upon to make sacrifices for brothers and sisters, extended family, or neighbors. Key dates are February 2 and 21. An unexpected event arises in your home or family—perhaps a jolt from the past—around February 25, at the start of Uranus's cycle. This means that you will be working with the situations that arise here for a year as well.

Finance and Success

Connecting with others—through print communication, public outreach, and commerce—is key to your success all month long. It doesn't hurt to advertise.

Rewarding Days

3, 4, 7, 8, 11, 12, 13, 21, 22, 26, 27

Challenging Days

9, 10, 16, 17, 23, 24, 25

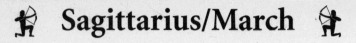 Sagittarius/March

Planetary Hotspots

With Mars activating your chart, a crush of paperwork arrives in the early days of the month, and then again around March 19 as Mercury turns retrograde. On March 26, your continuing pursuit of self-transformation is once again highlighted, with Pluto starting its four-month retrograde period as well. However, you're completing a long-term project at the same time, as Saturn ends its retrograde on March 21, and this relieves some of the pressure.

Wellness and Keeping Fit

You can counteract a tendency to overindulge when dining out this month by staying focused on your health goals. If you set your intentions beforehand about how you are going to eat when you go out—even deciding what you'll have—you will be more likely to maintain your discipline. With Mercury going retrograde in your Fifth House this month, you could be injury-prone when playing sports or games.

Love and Life Connections

You'll discover what you need to develop in your own character in more explicit terms around March 26, when Pluto turns backward in your First House. You're finding out that your experience of relationships is largely contingent on how you act toward others: if you treat them with respect and attention, you get the same.

Finance and Success

With Mars so active and Mercury turning retrograde, disorganization could prove more than inconvenient. Bills should be kept in a safe place and debts paid on time. Don't be afraid to spend money on social events. This is a good investment in your future because people are the lifeblood of opportunity, especially for you this year.

Rewarding Days

3, 4, 7, 8, 11, 12, 20, 21, 22, 25, 26, 27, 30

Challenging Days

9, 10, 15, 16, 17, 23, 24

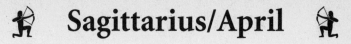 Sagittarius/April

Planetary Hotspots

April 3 brings a crescendo of activity associated with your social networks, organizational duties, and cultural contacts. The solar eclipse on April 8 further highlights the importance of these events and the connections made through them, since it impacts the same area of your chart. A lunar eclipse on April 24 points to a final aspect of your health and work situations that needs attention.

Wellness and Keeping Fit

The eclipse in your health houses on April 24 points out the ways in which your health routine needs fine-tuning for you to reach your goals. You may decide to change your exercise regimen, diet, or simply get more sleep. Over the coming five months you'll be able to realize the results you want.

Love and Life Connections

Although there may be fits and starts to the process, romance is a bigger part of your life this month. The situation is complicated, but things smooth out after April 21 and fully resolve next month. Take care of your belongings when in a crowd around April 13.

Finance and Success

Your creative spark is set off by your experiences this month. Although there is a certain amount of struggle involved in finding your muse, you will settle in as the end of the month approaches and find a truly new way to express your talents. Last month's financial challenges may lead to a need to curtail your usual level of social activity. You may want to participate in a particular event around April 3 that would put you over the top where money is concerned, so weigh all your options before plunging in.

Rewarding Days

3, 4, 7, 8, 17, 18, 22, 23, 26, 27, 30

Challenging Days

5, 6, 12, 13, 19, 20, 21

Sagittarius/May

Planetary Hotspots

Issues arise around May 8 with the way you manage commerce, education, and written communications, as Chiron enters its five-month retrograde period. This is further highlighted by Neptune, when its retrograde starts on May 14. You may feel confused, or discover a need to find a deeper meaning as you attempt to fulfill your life path, which you will work on accomplishing over the coming nine months.

Wellness and Keeping Fit

Preventive health treatments will be especially useful this month as Mercury makes its way through your Sixth House of health support. You may want to get a holistic check-up and then treat what arises with natural means, from herbs and homeopathics to acupuncture and chiropractic.

Love and Life Connections

Situations with siblings, neighbors, and extended family become more complicated, with events occurring around May 8 and 19. You're caught by surprise with a family situation on May 15 as well. Communication is the key—there's support for you from your closest relationships if you talk about your needs.

Finance and Success

Writing projects may confound you now as you enter a phase of less mental sharpness. This will feel like a distraction around May 8, but it will change to feelings of confusion or uncertainty as May 19 passes. You can't push the river. Use this "downtime" (which really isn't) to take of other matters, or just enjoy the view.

Rewarding Days

1, 5, 6, 14, 15, 19, 20, 23, 24, 25, 28, 29

Challenging Days

2, 3, 4, 9, 10, 16, 17, 18, 30, 31

Sagittarius/June

Planetary Hotspots

Powerful events occur on June 2, 13, 14, and 25 to make this a stand-out month. Changes you've been making in your own life have an impact on your home, family, and relationships. On June 5 your intensified efforts within organizations and social groups begin to relax. You'll see the potential for reward over the next six months, now that Jupiter is moving forward again.

Wellness and Keeping Fit

The feverish pace of events this month may leave you feeling tired, and you may be tempted to ignore your regular fitness routine. Instead of avoiding it altogether, you can modify it to boost your emotional strength, since this is where you are being undermined. For instance, take a walk in a pretty neighborhood, lunch on a secluded hillside, or play Frisbee on the beach.

Love and Life Connections

Your social life becomes more active again after June 5, if you can manage to squeeze out the time. Your partner will have something important to say about your new approach to your relationship around June 13. By facing the music and taking responsibility for your actions, you'll be able to recover quickly from any mistakes you have made. Remember, no one has to be perfect, and you may also be able to make suggestions to your partner that will help you both.

Finance and Success

If anyone owes you money, this is a good month to ask for repayment. Debts may be recovered after June 3. Activities in organizations pick up early in the month as you strive to complete tasks you've committed to. Although this keeps you busier than you thought and occupies you through the entire month, there are rewards ahead.

Rewarding Days

1, 2, 10, 11, 12, 15, 16, 17, 20, 21, 24, 25, 29, 30

Challenging Days

5, 6, 7, 13, 14, 26, 27, 28

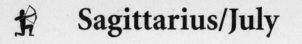

Sagittarius/July

Planetary Hotspots

Issues that arose in January come back with a new twist as Saturn and Chiron interact once again. Starting July 16 and lasting until July 31, there is a choice you can make in interpreting the events that you experience. Your interpretation of what occurs is critical to the outcome. In addition, contacts you make through written communication will be vital. If you are in school, the events will play out in that environment. Paperwork is emphasized during this entire time, but especially around July 19, when Mercury turns retrograde.

Wellness and Keeping Fit

Although you like to take a vacation about this time every year, it may seem as though you'll be cheated of that opportunity by all the activities you're involved in right now. However, a time of high activity makes it all the more vital to get away periodically. If your schedule does not permit any more, at least take a couple of long weekends away, and plan a longer vacation for when the work slacks off. It will be easier to get time away before July 16.

Love and Life Connections

Your relatives are the source of your most interesting social interactions this month. The situations you started dealing with in February are now coming to full expression. This could be nothing more than an extended visit, but it could also be a crisis event. If so, others will find your input extremely valuable.

Finance and Success

You're busy. There is a lot of paperwork, perhaps busywork, as you try to manage all the situations that must be ironed out in your life right now. This is especially true after July 16. Your extra efforts at work this month will be rewarded.

Rewarding Days

8, 9, 13, 14, 17, 18, 21, 22, 25, 26, 27

Challenging Days

3, 4, 10, 11, 12, 23, 24, 30, 31

Sagittarius/August

Planetary Hotspots

Last month's challenges in commerce, perspective, and education spill over into this month, reaching a high point on August 8, when Neptune's cycle peaks to augment feelings of confusion. Crises will move toward resolution rapidly after that, however, as Mercury returns to forward motion on August 15. The end of the month brings a big bang in your home and business life as Uranus reaches the culmination of its annual cycle.

Wellness and Keeping Fit

If you ignore your emotional need for a break, you may end up with an inflammatory illness, such as the common cold, around August 28. This will enforce the slow-down process that your body needs. Perhaps it is better to take a break when you're feeling good so you can enjoy it, rather than to wait until you're feeling bad to be forced into it.

Love and Life Connections

Your extended family situation continues to be an important focus through August 15, with a smaller, related event occurring on August 28. However, your home life assumes greater significance at the end of the month—a culmination of the situation that arose around February 25.

Finance and Success

It may seem as though your paperwork and writing projects are threatening to overwhelm you the first half of the month, and you can't seem to make much progress. This is another one of those times when your brain needs a break to renew its creativity. It will help to engage in kinetic (e.g., physical) and visual activities to enhance the rejuvenation process.

Rewarding Days

4, 5, 9, 10, 14, 15, 18, 19, 22, 23, 31

Challenging Days

6, 7, 8, 20, 21, 26, 27, 28

♐ Sagittarius/September ♐

Planetary Hotspots

September is "planets lite," as Pluto brings us the only major celestial event of the month. Since it's in your solar First House, Pluto's energy can be felt everywhere, and you may choose any arena of life in which to increase your self-empowerment. The last four months have taken you through a trial period with respect to those changes, and now you know better which approaches will work for you and which ones to discard or modify. This will have a tremendous impact on your relationships as others experience the impact of the new you.

Wellness and Keeping Fit

The pressure releases after September 2, and you can see how well your latest steps toward self-improvement are turning out. This may include anything from a personal make-over, weight-loss program, or new fitness regimen to psychotherapy or a commitment to a spiritual path. Use this time to look over what mistakes you've made and determine what to adjust in order to continue your long-term project of personal development and empowerment.

Love and Life Connections

You've got more insight into how your interactions with others contribute to the quality of the exchange. This is in part due to the feedback you've gotten from others, but is due also to your own self-examination.

Finance and Success

After September 4 your dominant focus will be career and business activities. Watch what you commit yourself to this month, because it will come back to bite you over the next three months. Delegate what you can't complete yourself.

Rewarding Days

1, 2, 5, 6, 7, 10, 11, 14, 15, 18, 19, 27, 28, 29

Challenging Days

3, 4, 16, 17, 22, 23, 24, 30

🏹 Sagittarius/October 🏹

Planetary Hotspots

The month opens to Mars assuming center stage as it begins its three-month retrograde period in your Sixth House. This will bring out latent issues in your health and workplace, and it may suggest accidents, inflammations, or surgeries. The eclipses on October 3 and 17 divert your attention to social events and activities, pulling you toward new venues and projects. With Chiron retrograde ending on October 5 after five months, financial complications clear up. Neptune's return to forward motion on October 26 gives you a growing sense of clarity about ways to approach mental activities more efficiently. Perhaps best of all, though, is the start of Jupiter's new annual cycle, giving your inner life a boost as it moves into your solar Twelfth House.

Wellness and Keeping Fit

With Mars retrograde in your Sixth House, your health could be compromised by any added pressure through the end of the year. It is an excellent time, therefore, to take better care of yourself.

Love and Life Connections

You'll feel more like retreating from the world than participating socially so that you can get all your work done. However, events will sweep you away, and you'll find yourself in plenty of social situations throughout the month. You'll have even more opportunity for that in the coming months.

Finance and Success

With Jupiter entering your Twelfth House for a year, there's a project you'd like to undertake away from judging eyes. Now's the time to make room in your life for this replenishing internal adventure.

Rewarding Days

2, 3, 4, 7, 8, 11, 12, 13, 16, 17, 25, 26, 30, 31

Challenging Days

1, 14, 15, 20, 21, 27, 28, 29

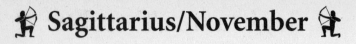 Sagittarius/November

Planetary Hotspots

Mars continues to ferret out areas of weakness in your health and work world so that they can be repaired, especially around November 7. Mercury's last retrograde of the year starts on November 14, emphasizing the growth and transformation you've been working so hard to accommodate in your self-expression. Saturn begins its retrograde period on November 22, increasing your awareness of a renewed search for meaning in your life. Meanwhile, factors at home assume a higher profile when Uranus returns to forward motion on November 15, but this is a relaxation of tension as its cycle moves toward completion.

Wellness and Keeping Fit

Health is a particular focus this month as you struggle to keep up with all the stimuli that are coming at you from all directions. In particular, you'll be more vulnerable to viral infection around November 7, 14, and 18, so take care to sleep and eat well.

Love and Life Connections

Family matters that you've been dealing with since February now begin to normalize as Uranus returns to forward motion on November 15. It's been an awakening process for you as well as those with whom you share your private life. As part of an ongoing process of growth that began in 2003, you can expect more development in the next four years as Uranus completes its stay in your Fourth House.

Finance and Success

Chances are good that you are discovering what parts of your life don't work for you. You may see pockets of dissatisfaction or boredom that you need to restructure. Whatever your situation and the decisions that result, this is the month to begin your action plan. It will take time to accomplish, but you'll be better off for it.

Rewarding Days

3, 4, 5, 8, 9, 12, 13, 21, 22, 23, 26, 27

Challenging Days

10, 11, 16, 17, 18, 24, 25

🏹 Sagittarius/December 🏹

Planetary Hotspots

The planets lighten up early in the month as Mercury and Mars return to forward motion on the December 3 and 9. Hidden obstacles that have been revealed over the past two months can now be more easily overcome. On December 24, Venus begins its six-week retrograde, suggesting new agreements and commitments with brothers and sisters, as well as decisions that affect your educational pursuits. A writing project may be in the offing.

Wellness and Keeping Fit

As Pluto's new cycle begins on December 15, this is a good time to contemplate the developmental processes you want to encourage in yourself in the coming year. This will involve purging old ideas and forms of expression and replacing them with more meaningful ways of expressing yourself.

Love and Life Connections

Relationships with extended family once again become a point of challenge as Venus turns retrograde in your Third House on December 24. Over the next six weeks you'll have the opportunity to rework the commitments you have with others and make sure they fit the emerging situation.

Finance and Success

It is possible that, with Mars backing up in your Sixth House, your job is on the line. You may have discovered that it's time to move on to something new of your own accord, or you may have been laid off. If so, you'll find the job market more receptive to you after December 9. If continuing in your current job, your extra responsibilities are completed soon after December 9, although another peak is indicated around December 27.

Rewarding Days

1, 2, 5, 6, 9, 10, 18, 19, 20, 23, 24, 25, 28, 29

Challenging Days

7, 8, 14, 15, 21, 22

SAGITTARIUS ACTION TABLE

These dates reflect the best—but not the only—times for success and ease in these activities, according to your Sun sign.

	JAN	FEB	MAR	APR	MAY	JUN	JUL	AUG	SEPT	OCT	NOV	DEC
Move		16-28	1-5, 9, 10									
Start a class	30, 31	1-16										
Join a club									20-30	1-8		
Ask for a raise								17-31	1-11	3, 4, 8-31	1-5	1, 2
Look for work					12-31	1-11			3-20			
Get pro advice	20-22	16-18	15-17	12, 13	10, 11	5-7	3, 4, 30, 31	26-28	22-24	20, 21	16-18	14, 15
Get a loan	22-24	18, 19	18, 19	14-16	11-13	8, 9	5-7	1-3, 29, 30	25, 26	22-24	19, 20	16, 17
See a doctor	1-9				12-31	1-11			3-20	31	1-13	13-31
Start a diet					12-28							
End relationship												14, 15
Buy clothes			5-19, 22-31	1-30	1-12							
Get a makeover	1-9									8-31	1-13	1, 2, 13-31
New romance			22-31	1-15								
Vacation	25, 26	21, 22	20-22	17, 18	14, 15	10-12	1-23	4, 5, 16-31	1-4, 28, 29	25, 26	21, 22	18-20

CAPRICORN

The Goat
December 21 to January 19

♑

Element:	Earth
Quality:	Cardinal
Polarity:	Yin/Feminine
Planetary Ruler:	Saturn
Meditation:	I know the strength of my soul.
Gemstone:	Garnet
Power Stones:	Peridot, diamond, quartz, black obsidian, onyx
Key Phrase:	I use
Glyph:	Head of goat
Anatomy:	Skeleton, knees, skin
Color:	Black, forest green
Animal:	Goats, thick-shelled animals
Myths/Legends:	Chronos, Vesta, Pan
House:	Tenth
Opposite Sign:	Cancer
Flower:	Carnation
Key Word:	Ambitious

Your Ego's Strengths and Shortcomings

You are the salt of the earth, Capricorn—and as necessary to the proper functioning of human civilization as salt is to the body. You share the earth element with Taurus and Virgo, but you look at things from the grandest of levels. You observe the broad sweep of history, the rise and fall of civilizations, and the feats and foibles of humanity. Like your element, your movement is downward, establishing on solid ground the institutions that will make humanity safe and culture long-lasting. You strive to enhance the enjoyment of life by setting up structures—rules, laws, protocols—that others can live by when normal relations break down and tension builds. You want to preserve life at its highest level. This makes you cautious, for you have seen the results of hasty action. You learn from others' experiences without having to go down the road to ruin. As you learn, you begin to extrapolate to new circumstances, and this makes you a good leader. You are able to set your emotions aside and think of the good of all, but you must desire to do so: if you are not alert to your potential for seeking personal gain instead, your greatest intentions will be betrayed. You fear failure, because for you the stakes appear too high. You would rather do it right the first time rather than make a mistake and have to start over or ruin your standing in the eyes of others. Although you desire to further the good of others, you also want to be successful for your own well-being, and this can make you ambitious. As long as you adhere to the morals and ethics you hold dear, you will be able to achieve both. You may, in your drive to set the outer world in order, ignore your need for personal relationships, especially intimate bonds. It is important to be able to open up completely, to be vulnerable, to those you hold nearest and dearest.

Shining Your Love Light

Although others may perceive you as reserved or even unloving, you know that a tender heart lies under your smooth veneer. As in all other things, you act carefully in love. You see no reason to rush into a relationship in which you already see fatal flaws, so you build a relationship slowly and, once committed, you stick with it through thick and thin. It's important to focus on opening up and staying open with your partner. You can't get so involved in work that you neglect your love, growing remote. Your partner needs to be part of the action too.

Aries injects a lively, action-oriented energy that will help you take bolder action, while you help Aries think before leaping ahead. You'll find a true helpmate in Taurus—one who will work side by side with you and share your need to deliberate over matters with caution. Gemini wants you to talk (a very good habit to cultivate), while you help this sign develop focus and structure. Cancer brings out your heart and nourishes you with kindness, while you help Cancer step back from emotions and make choices based on both head and heart. Leo also likes being at the head of the pack, adding motivation and passion to your structured, responsible approach. You'll be pleased with Virgo's organized efficiency as you share your earthy, sensual side with each other. Libra will remind you of the importance of balance in all you do, and you'll enjoy the finest of culture and the arts together. You can create truly lasting solutions to human dilemmas with Scorpio's understanding of the unconscious machinations of humanity. Sagittarius's musings result in the core beliefs that are the source for your structures and policies; exchanges between you will enlighten and enhance the insights of each. Another Capricorn sees the world in broad brush strokes as you do, but you must remember to reach out to each other emotionally to keep your love alive. Aquarius might be a thorn in your side, but your structures need shaking up to be relevant, and that's precisely what this sign will do. Pisces values your enfolding protection and stability, while this sign's sensitive side introduces you to a whole new wonderful world of connectedness.

Making Your Place in the World

You have the qualities that make a good leader, Capricorn, but making it to the top the right way can be difficult for you. You are not as comfortable in a subordinate position as in one where you can call the shots. You may be frustrated by the shortcomings of those with greater authority or responsibility, and even see their mistakes in the making. However, if you strive to assert yourself under these circumstances you will be perceived as controlling, and you will not advance. An open environment, where your input is valued as part of a team, is the best place to start. Then, as you gain experience and prove yourself, you can move into positions that are more suited to your natural abilities—without forgetting the value of the team effort. You are an ideal candidate for positions where you can set structure and policy and offer guidance to others with an eye to the big picture.

Putting Your Best Foot Forward

You are the king of discipline, the queen of leadership, but that's not all there is to life, Capricorn. If you want your life to be fulfilling as well as successful, there's another side of your nature that must be developed. That's the feeling side, the part you tend to keep inside and hide even from those you are supposed to be close to. To put your best foot forward, you need to let this part of you come out. You need to learn to tap your own sense of compassion and empathy for others in order to soften your hard edges and make you more accessible. What locks you up is your fear. Fear often appears in your awareness as worry, anxiety, or just a retreat to hide your insecurity. Frequently, your fears stem from fear of pain. You may fear emotional hurt and avoid getting close, or withdraw from your friends and family when you need them most. To overcome your fears, you need to gain more knowledge and wisdom about the things you fear, and then be willing to take risks by making yourself vulnerable— but in a way based on your enlightened perspective. This will shrink the areas of fear in your life, and your feeling, compassionate side, which was there all the time, will shine through.

Tools for Change

This year, developing your soft side is the most important task before you. You need to let others know (at least those who are close to you) how you feel, and that you care about them. You need to learn the language of emotions and how to speak it fluently. This may be daunting, even terrifying to you, but if you break it down into small steps and structured objectives—your forte—you'll be able to step from the world of digitized thoughts to analog feelings.

First, you must learn to play. Play is spontaneous action—anything done on the spur of the moment with a sense of joy and abandon. Play should be disruptive of routine and involve elements of the unexpected, whether it is a turn down an unexplored mountain trail or a sudden decision to ditch the customary beach run in favor of a game of Frisbee. You also need to develop the fine art of wasting time if you express the usual Capricorn tendency to overwork. This means sitting around doing nothing gainful. It could be watching TV (unless you're in the industry), chatting idly with friends or family—or just sitting. Activities that stimulate the right brain and slow you down are also vital to your health and well-being: yoga, dance, playing a musical instrument, attending a concert or cultural event, or participating in a team sport may fill the bill. Focusing on social events that do not generate more business contacts or further your outer-world success will also connect you with others by giving you more in common with them. If you have a life outside work, your loved ones will be able to relate to you better because they will understand you more. Even if you're bad at them, painting, drawing, sculpting, ceramics, textiles—any of the fine arts—are a great place to find your softer side. In fact, it may work better if you're not good at them! When it comes to developing your emotional vocabulary, practice with those you care about the most. However, if you find it hard to break down the old walls, you can practice first with animals. Even if you have to go to the zoo or talk to someone else's pets, you'll find you're speaking the language of love before you know it.

Affirmation of the Year

My ability to open to others is my strength.

The Year Ahead for Capricorn

This is a year for achievement and recognition, Capricorn, plus a whole lot more! Jupiter is making its way through your solar Tenth House from its position in Libra until October 25. You'll be challenged to express your management and leadership skills in new areas and applications. You'll probably spend even more time at work than usual—although the challenge will be to maintain a healthy, well-rounded life. The emphasis will be on your expertise in relating to others: you may be called upon to negotiate or arbitrate a dispute, or you may be the right person to grease the wheels of progress and gain others' willing cooperation. While there's no doubt that there are plenty of opportunities this year, you can overdo it by taking them all on. It's best to pick the ones that seem the most fruitful; if other tasks are pressed on you, realize it's because you're so capable and then find a diplomatic way of saying "no" or delegating. Once Jupiter enters Scorpio the pressure to perform will abate, and you will be drawn into more organizational activities and events—for pleasure and entertainment as well as business. Be as selective in these pursuits as before, and you'll come out a winner.

Saturn moves from Cancer to Leo on July 16, traveling from your Seventh to your Eighth House. For the first half of the year, you will be tying up loose ends in your relationship life, renegotiating agreements, and setting important limits. This may involve not just personal partnerships but business agreements as well. When Saturn moves into Leo the emphasis is still on the way you relate to others, but once the change is made you will focus on shared resources—whether between you and your partner, a bank, or the government. While you understand the wisdom of social and fiscal responsibility, you may still need to redirect your use of resources in some ways. Chiron makes its way into Aquarius on February 21, but it returns to Capricorn from July 31 to December 5. While Chiron is in your sign, you'll be finishing up with some personal growth issues—last holdouts in the new pattern of healthy self-development you've been working on for the last three years. Once Chiron changes signs, the emphasis will shift to the way you handle your resources and possessions. You may find weaknesses there, from your financial portfolio to your generosity, that you can now see and are ready to alter. Uranus continues in Pisces and your solar Third House, where it is creating ripples in your attitudes and perspectives. Your experiences may teach you that your understanding of how the world works is ripe for revamping. Freeing your mind to think independently of outside influences is as critical to personal fulfillment as it is to outer-world success. Neptune remains in Aquarius and the solar Second House. It has been leading you to question your values: are money and property as vital to happiness as they seemed before? You may feel more like boycotting those businesses that do not support the values you now want to uphold. Pluto's slow movement through Sagittarius and your solar Twelfth House is not over, so your inner world and spiritual life are still undergoing dramatic changes. These are often deeply personal and hidden from view, but others will see their effects in a subtle softening of your demeanor.

The eclipses are in the activating signs of Aries and Libra for most of the year, challenging you to redefine the balance between home and work. Your public and private lives may be in conflict, or you may discover that you are not content with a lopsided emphasis on one or the other. This is the time to rectify that.

If you were born from December 21 to January 4, Saturn will restructure your solar energy from its position in Leo and your Eighth House. This house deals with things in life that we cannot control, such as our partner's value system and spending patterns. Sometimes extra expenses arise through something we can't manage or avoid—an unexpected surgery, a plumbing failure, or a child's college expenses. Chances are good that you will have to take on new obligations to society and its institutions (banks, insurance companies, etc.) after Saturn enters Leo on July 16. These obligations come to you because of your deep associations with and commitments to others, not out of anything you have done or can control. They may be coincidental to the process and purpose of your association, or unexpected, but you do have to fulfill them. The hardest part of this is how little influence you have on the situation. You may also find that you are drawn to a study of arcane subjects—those that teach us about how society and its members operate. This can come through psychology, astrology, tarot, magic, numerology—any of those subjects that go beneath the surface to see what's really going on. Key dates for your Saturn process include July 16 to 23 and November 22.

If you were born from December 25 to January 3, Uranus in Pisces will be shaking up your world from your solar Third House. You have recently felt inspired by the words of others, and you may have decided to reopen your explorations in the world of learning. Your attitudes have been changing because you have new information giving you a new angle on old issues. You may want to explore the world in other novel ways as well—perhaps through cultural events and exhibits or by taking up a new language or thought-provoking course of study. As you take a fresh look at the world, you may feel as if you are seeing it for the first time, in a more spiritual light. You may even feel compelled to communicate a new message to others. Whether you write a book, issue a new business brochure, or start a new retail business, you are making an effort to reach out to others. You may also be surprised by events and actions in the lives of your siblings or extended family. You may feel called upon to make a sacrifice for others, but only you can decide if it's right to do so. Significant events related to Uranus's process in your life will occur around February 25, June 14, August 31, and November 15.

If you were born from January 5 to 10, your Sun will be contacted by Neptune from Aquarius and your solar Second House. Neptune often feels like it casts a fog wherever it is found, and this may seem to be the case when it comes to your resources and properties. You may feel unsure about whether you've made good investments, even as you have cause to doubt the advice you receive now. Your instincts are correct: others may not be reliable when you are under this transit. Rely instead on others whose advice coincides with your inner sense of truth, even if it takes longer than usual to come to that point of clarity. Where Neptune is found, it is especially important not to act until the way is clear and all confusion has passed. Your values may be going through a shift as well, to more spiritual ideals. You may want to shift your investments to socially responsible companies rather than supporting those who will only give you a good return on your risk. Since intangibles are also part of our resources—time, energy, and inner qualities—you may find that you increasingly place more value on fulfillment, time to relax, volunteer activities, health, and the like. Key dates for Neptune-related events are February 2, May 19, August 8, and October 26.

If you were born from January 11 to 19, Saturn in Cancer supports a restructuring process in your relationships, in the domain of your solar Seventh House. For the past two years you've watched as it came time for you to deal with your relationships in a new way. Since last summer you've been engaged in renegotiating agreements, perhaps not amicably. You may be dealing with divorce or separation, or dissolution of a business partnership. Alternatively, there could be added responsibilities associated with a relationship commitment: a spouse who is ill or working extra hours, or a business partner who isn't pulling his or her weight. Whatever the case, it is your job to make sure that your needs are met and proper boundaries observed. This requires open communication—perhaps more open than you've been comfortable with in the past. You may have to change many of the ways you usually relate to others, as you discover your role in creating the obstacles that exist. Negotiation is a key to resolving those issues—a skill in which you may need more training in order to practice it well. Resist the temptation to make definitive statements that end discussion, or to assert your control over a situation in order to end the uncertainty in it. Important events related to your Saturn experience will occur around January 13 and March 21.

If you were born from January 12 to 15, Pluto is bringing change into your life from your solar Twelfth House, as it has been since 1995. This continues a rhythmic and slow growth process that proceeds by inches each year, coming from long-term self-examination and discipline—perhaps due to the nature of your spiritual path or a devotion you have to an altruistic goal. Your inner landscape is a much more significant arena for change than your outer world, which may change very little. You may feel somewhat entrapped by your circumstances and complain about the suffering they cause in you, even though you could change them if you wanted to. There are hidden benefits to you, if only because of the spiritual development and inner strength that result. This could also be a time of actual confinement—especially when Pluto makes its exact contact to your Sun—perhaps through illness, incarceration, or a difficult job. Whatever you are experiencing, it is difficult to talk about or to explain what it's about; when the time for this commitment is over, you'll have developed your inner worth to a much higher level. Critical dates for events related to this cycle include March 26, June 13, September 2, and December 15.

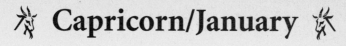 Capricorn/January

Planetary Hotspots

The pressures of the last two months come to a head on January 13, when Saturn reaches the culmination of its yearly cycle. This relates to your ongoing efforts in relationships, restructuring the way you interact with all other people, but particularly applies to your partnerships, both business and personal. This ties in with the start of Chiron's cycle on January 16, which has been supporting your growth in self-esteem.

Wellness and Keeping Fit

Your healing process over the past three years has involved emotional, mental, and spiritual modalities. This is the last year of that journey to better internal balance before Chiron moves out of your sign. In the meantime, take full advantage of the insights it offers. You'll have glimmerings of a workable plan around January 16.

Love and Life Connections

Over the past three years you've been learning about your role in relationships—how to reach out to others rather than wall yourself off. You've also been learning about your own emotional states and sensitivities and, most importantly, how to reveal your vulnerabilities to those you trust and love. Around mid-month you'll be aware of this process once more, as your relationships and interactions with others are more emphasized. You'll find that you need to take responsibility for your own behaviors, while others must do the same—but nothing is anyone's "fault."

Finance and Success

Your future success depends in part on the clarity you can bring to your agreements with others at this time. It's important to be as clear as possible now, so it's wise to start relying on written contracts to handle business deals if you aren't already.

Rewarding Days

1, 5, 6, 9, 10, 13, 14, 17, 18, 19, 27, 28, 29

Challenging Days

2, 3, 4, 15, 16, 22, 23, 24, 30, 31

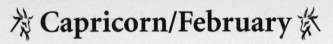 Capricorn/February

Planetary Hotspots

Efforts in career or business reach a high point around February 1 as the opportunities that have emerged over the past four months begin to take on their own life. This relates to the cycle of Jupiter, which began last September 25. Over the next four months you'll have heightened activity in this area to finish the creative process with your new enterprises. Neptune's new annual cycle begins on February 2, fueling your quest for the best way to use your resources (time, money, and skills). February 25 sees the commencement of Uranus's new annual cycle in your Third House, bringing new insights about how you interface with the world around you.

Wellness and Keeping Fit

Your energy will surge after February 5 as Mars enters your sign. This is an excellent time to give a boost to your fitness routine, but it's important not to overdo it.

Love and Life Connections

You could do with a little more enjoyment in your life—why not take in a local museum exhibit or concert? Getting out into your community is just your cup of tea this month. It will give you a way to connect with friends and family, and you'll get the relaxation and change of pace that leisure pursuits bring.

Finance and Success

Neptune does more than cause you to question the way you use your money; it leads you to question your values. Are you spending your money in the best way to support your total well-being? Are you contributing enough to the causes you believe in? When you buy a product, are you supporting businesses with high ethical standards, or do they exploit others? These questions may nag at you a little more as Neptune's new cycle begins.

Rewarding Days

1, 2, 5, 6, 9, 10, 14, 15, 23, 24, 25, 28

Challenging Days

11, 12, 13, 18, 19, 20, 26, 27

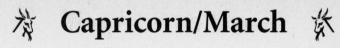 Capricorn/March

Planetary Hotspots

With powerful planetary events highlighting your "action" houses (First, Fourth, Seventh, and Tenth) on March 3, 7, 21, and 23, you'll be spreading yourself thin to fulfill every need that arises. Mercury's first retrograde of the year starts on March 19, underscoring the significance of this time and the way you respond to it. Your home life, career, partnership relationships (business and personal), and identity are under the spotlight, and change is afoot. Hidden factors come out of the woodwork around March 26 as Pluto's five-month retrograde begins—catching you by surprise, but also allowing you to penetrate to the heart of matters so they can be resolved to your satisfaction.

Wellness and Keeping Fit

An excess of success can keep you guessing and disrupt your normal health routine throughout the month. It may be best to try fitness activities that you can do at home, and eat there as well, since this will take less of your time.

Love and Life Connections

Home is the source of your support, and you'll want to spend more time there these days than you're able to. Around March 19 an element of chaos there may make it difficult to feel comfortable. It's important to find the source of the unrest and remedy the problem; it's only a minor glitch if you catch it soon enough.

Finance and Success

What happens this month feeds events in April, the end of June, and the last half of July—all of which will bring peaks of activity into your life. You can temper your experiences at these times by anticipating these crescendos and marshaling the support of others to handle them, both now and then.

Rewarding Days

1, 2, 5, 6, 9, 10, 13, 14, 18, 19, 28, 29

Challenging Days

3, 4, 15, 16, 17, 23, 24

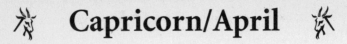

Capricorn/April

Planetary Hotspots

Career and home split your time again this month—especially on April 3, when events may lead to a feeling of urgency. This feeling may be exacerbated on April 8 when a solar eclipse places your home and family life in even higher profile. However, the tension relaxes considerably when Mercury returns to forward motion on April 12. A lunar eclipse on April 24 gives you one more chance to enhance your romantic life and creative self-expression over the coming five months.

Wellness and Keeping Fit

There are plenty of demands placed on you early in the month, and they're a potential source of stress. After April 12, however, you have more of a chance to replenish your batteries and get back on an even keel. Part of your healing should involve finding ways to play. Be open to spontaneous events or activities—anything you consider fun.

Love and Life Connections

Issues with children or romance may arise around April 24, establishing a situation you will be resolving over the coming five months. This will tie in with something you've been dealing with for the past two years.

Finance and Success

Your additional career-related activities peak around April 3 as the learning curve flattens out. You've got it more under control now. This is especially good because events at home are pulling you away from your more public life, particularly around April 8. There is likely to be an unforeseen financial outlay around April 13.

Rewarding Days

1, 2, 5, 6, 9, 10, 11, 19, 20, 21, 24, 25, 28, 29

Challenging Days

7, 8, 14, 15, 16, 22, 23

Capricorn/May

Planetary Hotspots

Chiron starts its retrograde period on May 8, opening the door to intensified growth and healing in your Second House of resources. You've already been working with this area since 1998, through the transit of Neptune, and you've discovered how important it is to draw your income from "spiritually correct" sources. With Chiron also in this area for the coming three years, you'll feel even more inclined to make positive changes. Neptune adds emphasis to this process around May 19, since its retrograde period begins as well.

Wellness and Keeping Fit

You're back in the peak of health again—a successful recovery after a stressful time. This is a good time to go one better and reward yourself with some feel-good health treatments: a trip to the day spa, a massage, even a yoga retreat.

Love and Life Connections

Romance is in the air all month, so go ahead—have a few nights on the town! Go out with your favorite dance partner, or with a group of friends—you'll probably meet someone you want to spend more time with.

Finance and Success

Financial matters require extra attention around May 8 and 19, perhaps leading to an adjustment in your portfolio or management plan. You may be inclined to sign new agreements or enlist the support of new brokers and agents to handle your needs. Such a change is likely to help matters, but you should tread carefully here, relying on the advice of someone you trust instead of your own insights alone. Then be as clear as you can about your expectations. Resist others' efforts to push you to sign papers without forethought around May 15.

Rewarding Days

2, 3, 4, 7, 8, 16, 17, 18, 21, 22, 26, 27, 30, 31

Challenging Days

5, 6, 11, 12, 13, 19, 20

Capricorn/June

Planetary Hotspots

With the end of Jupiter's retrograde on June 5, you turn the corner on the extra effort you've been pouring into your career and business life. Now the time of reward can begin. The coming five months will continue an upward trend that began four years ago, and fuel the successes you experience in the coming six years. June 13 sees the peak of Pluto's cycle, heralding events that highlight background processes of growth. Your dream state may speak to you now, and your spiritual life become more vivid. As Uranus's retrograde starts on June 14 you'll see areas with room for growth in your understanding of the world—enough to make you want to take up a new course of study. You may also receive startling news about siblings and extended family.

Wellness and Keeping Fit

This is a great time to bring your partner into your health and fitness plans. Both your partnership and your health will improve, and you'll get a new perspective that will keep both of you motivated.

Love and Life Connections

You've got time now to spend with your partner, so make it quality time by planning a getaway together. Pick something you'll both enjoy, and not a situation that is lopsided in whom it pleases. The best dates are June 3 through 12 and 15 through 27.

Finance and Success

You've done good over the past eight months, and now your career won't require so much constant attention. You can use your extra time to develop some new secret or sacred initiative that is a personal delight.

Rewarding Days

3, 4, 13, 14, 18, 19, 22, 23, 26, 27, 30

Challenging Days

1, 2, 8, 9, 15, 16, 17, 28, 29

Capricorn/July

Planetary Hotspots

Your focus is drawn to finances, both in terms of your own resources and your access to those of others—from banks to your partner. This area is highlighted during the latter half of the month as Saturn enters Leo, your solar Eighth House, on July 16 and immediately contacts Chiron, already in your Second House. They are in continuous contact during this time, additionally triggered by the Sun and Mars on July 21, 23, 28, and 31 to underscore the significance. Mercury gives you the opportunity for greater understanding of what's happening as it enters its second retrograde of the year on July 22.

Wellness and Keeping Fit

Financial pressures could end up taking their toll on your health, if only because they distract you from your routine. Your most effective weapon against this is to keep events in perspective.

Love and Life Connections

Uncontrolled elements have a foothold in your financial situation, and those elements could be from your children, partner, or romantic life. It's important to realize that others do not have the same attitude toward or understanding of money and assets that you do, and while you can attempt to teach them otherwise, they ultimately will make their own decisions.

Finance and Success

With all the action in your houses of finance, you may be called upon to make new agreements with financial institutions this month. If you can avoid signing documents after July 22 (until August 16), you'll avoid the potential for hidden agendas or factors in the agreements you make. If you must, it's not the end of the world—just make sure you understand everything you can before you sign, even if there's pressure to rush matters.

Rewarding Days

1, 2, 10, 11, 12, 15, 16, 19, 20, 23, 24, 28, 29

Challenging Days

5, 6, 7, 13, 14, 25, 26

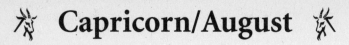 Capricorn/August

Planetary Hotspots

Confusion and illusion clear as Neptune reaches the culmination of its cycle on August 8. A rude awakening may be involved as you assess the situation in your finances. Once Mercury returns to forward motion on August 15, the clouds clear and you feel a sense of stability, albeit on new turf, once again. August 31 firms up a new perspective on life and your connections with others, as the effects of new learning take hold.

Wellness and Keeping Fit

You might think it's impossible to break away from your working life, but this is what the planets emphasize in your chart during the month. You may find it easier to fit in some down time before August 16.

Love and Life Connections

Children need to be permitted to make mistakes, and the ones they make this month are going to cost you, but hopefully not too much. The expenditures that arise may be for unusual but expected purposes, such as attending college for the first time, but they could also be for the first car accident. Whatever the source, taking a long-term perspective will minimize the emotional damage to you and your progeny.

Finance and Success

You're not entirely sure how the dust is going to settle in your finances until after August 12, when Mercury returns to forward motion in your Eighth House. You're still vulnerable, especially to the actions of children or romantic partners, through the end of the month. You may feel as though your long-term plans for the future have been irreparably disrupted, but over the coming two months you'll see how to continue on your path.

Rewarding Days

6, 7, 8, 11, 12, 13, 16, 17, 20, 21, 24, 25

Challenging Days

1, 2, 3, 9, 10, 22, 23, 29, 30

🜊 Capricorn/September 🜊

Planetary Hotspots

After September 2 you'll be more thoroughly freed of limiting and entrapping factors in your life, with Pluto completing its latest retrograde in your Twelfth House. Your sense of inner release may come from months of therapy, psychological self-help, a healing crisis or event, or just a vivid dream. Take note of what happens in your Fifth House affairs of children, romance, pursuits of pleasure, and creative activities. Mars will start its three-month retrograde here October 1, and situations you'll have to deal with then will "set up" this month. You may be able to head off difficulties with a thoughtful word.

Wellness and Keeping Fit

Injuries could occur at this time, and the possibility of that increases as the month wears on. You are most susceptible when engaged in sports or games.

Love and Life Connections

If you carefully observe what is happening with children and romantic partners this month, you'll catch a glimpse of the things to come when Mars turns retrograde in October. You may be able to divert yourself or your loved ones away from sensitive situations or dilemmas, although sometimes it's necessary to learn the lesson firsthand.

Finance and Success

Your creative process may feel particularly stale right now as Mars gets ready to make its retrograde transit through your Fifth House. It behooves you to do whatever you can to stimulate it. This will take about five months to complete. You can get the most bang for your buck by breaking with routine as much as possible: take up a new hobby or pursuit; if you do largely mental work, do something physical or visual; play; allow others to entertain you; travel.

Rewarding Days

3, 4, 8, 9, 12, 13, 16, 17, 20, 21, 30

Challenging Days

5, 6, 7, 18, 19, 25, 26

⚸ Capricorn/October ⚸

Planetary Hotspots

Even though it may seem to go against the grain of what life presents, you need a vacation. You've had your nose to the grindstone all year, and you need some fun. While Mars is retrograde, starting October 1, in your Fifth House of fun and games, it's a good time to reacquaint yourself with the realities of play. You must temper your plans with the facts of your life at this time, but even if you have to stay home and lock the door, you'll benefit from a restorative break in the routines of daily life.

Wellness and Keeping Fit

Saying "yes" to your own needs is the most healing thing you can do for yourself now. You've a tendency to sacrifice for others that is hard on your body, and you have a choice between continuing this unhealthy pattern or changing it and avoiding degenerative diseases in the future. It requires setting boundaries and saying "no" to some opportunities so you can amplify better ones.

Love and Life Connections

Romance, children, and creative pursuits are highlighted now that Mars is traveling backward through your Fifth House. You'll see new ways to manage the situations that have been troubling you. Although solutions will emerge over the next three months and may take two years to fulfill, this is an unequaled opportunity to put this part of your life in order.

Finance and Success

The eclipses on October 3 and 17 speed up activities in your career life once again, but you don't have to bear the brunt of what occurs. You can delegate—and since you need time away, this is the key to getting it.

Rewarding Days

1, 5, 6, 9, 10, 14, 15, 18, 19, 27, 28, 29

Challenging Days

2, 3, 4, 16, 17, 22, 23, 24, 30, 31

♑ Capricorn/November ♑

Planetary Hotspots

Mercury's final retrograde of the year starts on November 14 in your Twelfth House, bringing even greater understanding of entrapping factors in your life. You may not be willing to change anything external based on what you know, but you will feel better about it after this period of revelation is over on December 3. Uranus's retrograde ends on November 15, enhancing feelings of inner independence and revealing ways to incorporate new insights into your daily existence. Your new discipline in financial dealings with others sets in on November 22, and you'll have the coming five months to grow accustomed to it, making it a routine part of your life.

Wellness and Keeping Fit

You're once again vulnerable to illness as Mercury retrogrades in your Twelfth House starting November 14. This could be triggered by mental pressures brought on by intensive studies or extra paperwork. The mid-month is the most critical.

Love and Life Connections

You acquire an ally in the form of Venus when she enters your First House on November 5. This may draw others to you romantically, and it is certain to bring support from people you meet everywhere you go until she completes the cycle on December 16.

Finance and Success

From November 18 through 22 you'll see how the changes you've made in your financial situation are working, and you'll have a chance in the ensuing five months to make adjustments. You're thinking now about the long term, and you'll continue to find ways to restructure your life to increase your financial standing in the outer world—from changing jobs or business emphasis to debt consolidation or refinancing your home.

Rewarding Days

1, 2, 6, 7, 10, 11, 14, 15, 24, 25, 28, 29, 30

Challenging Days

12, 13, 19, 20, 26, 27

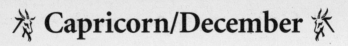 Capricorn/December

Planetary Hotspots

The year completes on a relative note of peace as several planets move to a quieter part of their cyclic pattern. Mercury ends its retrograde on December 3, and your inner life becomes less active. Mars's retrograde is completed on December 9, leaving you wiser and more realistic about your creative pursuits and how you build play into your life. This happens just in time to turn your attention to new frontiers of inner growth and spirituality, as Pluto starts another yearly cycle in your solar Twelfth House. It's also a good time to re-evaluate your budget, as Venus enters its six-week retrograde period on December 24. As the year draws to a close, you'll even be inclined to do a little soul-searching as you reassess your values in light of the events of recent months.

Wellness and Keeping Fit

Continue to celebrate your sense of fun throughout the month, but not by overindulging in alcohol and sweets. You can pour your exuberance into winter sports and then head for the tray of crudités.

Love and Life Connections

This is the time to start working more with your loved ones to build a team approach to finances. By not including them in the past, your financial responsibilities have become an exercise in parental control. With everyone on the team you can develop common goals. You'll be able to develop a working plan by the end of January, but it will take more time to develop the habits that support the plan.

Finance and Success

You're reassessing your values as well as your financial plans as you examine recent events. You're realizing that you need to accommodate others' needs more, as well as communicate with them more about finances.

Rewarding Days
3, 4, 7, 8, 11, 12, 13, 21, 22, 26, 27, 30, 31

Challenging Days
9, 10, 16, 17, 23, 24, 25

CAPRICORN ACTION TABLE

These dates reflect the best—but not the only—times for success and ease in these activities, according to your Sun sign.

	JAN	FEB	MAR	APR	MAY	JUN	JUL	AUG	SEPT	OCT	NOV	DEC
Move			5-19	12-30	1-12							
Start a class		16-28	1-5, 9, 10									
Join a club										8-30		
Ask for a raise	10-31								11-30	1-8	1, 2, 5-30	1-14
Look for work				28-31		1-28			20-30	1-8		
Get pro advice	22-24	18, 19	18, 19	14-16	11-13	8, 9	5-7	1-3, 29, 30	25, 26	22-24	19, 20	16, 17
Get a loan	25, 26	21, 22	10-22	17, 18	14, 15	10-12	8, 9	4, 5, 31	1, 2, 28, 29	25, 26	21, 22	18-20
See a doctor	1-30				18-31	1-28				31	1-13	13-31
Start a diet					28-31	1-11						
End relationship						22, 23	19-21					
Buy clothes					15-30	1-10, 12-28						
Get a makeover		1, 2									5-30	1-14
New romance				15-30	1-10							
Vacation	1, 27-29	23-25	23, 24	19-21	16-18	13, 14	25-31	1-17	3-20, 30	1, 27-29	24, 25	21, 22

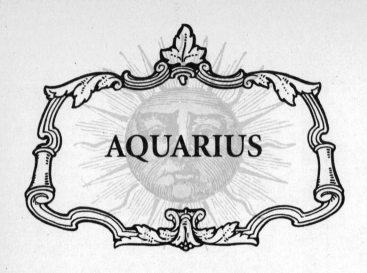

AQUARIUS

The Water Bearer
January 19 to February 18

Element:	Air
Quality:	Fixed
Polarity:	Yang/Masculine
Planetary Ruler:	Uranus
Meditation:	I am a wellspring of creativity.
Gemstone:	Amethyst
Power Stones:	Aquamarine, black pearl, chrysocolla
Key Phrase:	I know
Glyph:	Currents of energy
Anatomy:	Circulatory system, ankles
Color:	Iridescent blues, violet
Animal:	Exotic birds
Myths/Legends:	Ninhursag, John the Baptist, Deucalion
House:	Eleventh
Opposite Sign:	Leo
Flower:	Orchid
Key Word:	Unconventional

Your Ego's Strengths and Shortcomings

Yes, you like to connect to others, Aquarius—it's your airy nature. You just don't want to do it in the "normal" way. Your air is more like an electrical current than a fresh breeze: sometimes you produce more static than flow. However, static has its place, for it stimulates both you and those you contact. You want to startle people awake; you want to get them to think, to rise above the status quo and see what's really going on. Ironically, this binds you to others, even as you may feel repelled by them if they are too limited in their ways of thinking. For this reason, you may "hang out" with a group or organization, but you probably hesitate to join. You may go along with the crowd, but you don't fully immerse yourself in participation. You hold yourself back, remaining aloof perhaps because you don't like the group's politics or you're afraid of losing yourself to their energies. You are sensitive energetically, although you might be loathe to admit it, and truly this does keep you at arm's length. You pick up the "vibes" of a group and know exactly how healthy it is psychologically, especially if you have related training to enhance your awareness.

Like your compadres in the other air signs, Gemini and Libra, you have a quick intellect. You are always analyzing, and if you let your mind relax, flashes of creativity and intuition break through to support the standard logical processes. For this reason, you easily feel stifled when you are forced to engage in routine activities. You have a tendency to ignore the needs of your physical body like food and sleep, and this can leave you feeling ungrounded and scattered. In the worst-case scenario, you can feel split into fragments—but it's easy to avoid if you remember to take care of yourself.

Shining Your Love Light

You love all of humanity, Aquarius, but you have find it harder to share your love with someone close to you than with those you know slightly. Emotions do not come naturally to you, although connecting with others on a mental level does. You enjoy conversing, and this should be a central part of any intimate relationship you form. As you explore your emotions through the relationship it is vital to have something that comes easily to rely on. Your debates and discussions will help clarify your feeling side and deepen your bond.

You'll benefit from Aries's passion for life and total involvement in all that this sign does, while Aries may learn to be more objective from you. Taurus's common sense will add strength your intuitive approach, while you'll lead him to see things from all angles. Fellow air sign Gemini is your social equal—you learn from her versatility, she from your political savvy. Cancer's nurturing will enhance your sense of compassion, while you'll lend him a more objective perspective. Leo will inspire and motivate you to truly engage with others, while you'll induce in Leo a greater sense of equality. You share a delight in things technical with Virgo—she'll help you see their practical uses while you'll support her in thinking out of the box. You'll find comfort and camaraderie with Libra, another air sign, whose cooperative finesse with others smooths your rough edges. Scorpio offers insights into the depths of human consciousness that you find fascinating, while your impartiality is for this sign a breath of fresh air. Sagittarius's focus and enthusiasm gives you a sense of direction, and you can accomplish great things with your shared humanitarianism. Capricorn is as devoted to improving the lot of humanity as you are: your iconoclasm and his regard for tradition make you fine complements to each other. A fellow Aquarian will be similar to you in many ways, offering lively debate, a similar dedication to individualism, and as much drive for independence as you have. Pisces understands your need to travel to the beat of a different drummer, because she also must do so; your common link to the inner world will keep you in sync.

Making Your Place in the World

Because of your above-average intellect, you need a career in which you are constantly learning. More than that, your profession should give you the opportunity to express your mind in creative ways. Research and development in all their facets are excellent avenues for expressing your talents at their best. Your flashes of intuitive insight will be uniquely appreciated there, but out of place in many traditional work environments. Your political savvy, social conscience, and progressive attitude toward life makes you a pragmatist when it comes to institutional change, and you may find a home in a political or social movement. The greatest threat to your success lies in your distaste for routine tasks—a part of every job. The best you can do is to minimize the extent to which you must engage in those types of activities and then get into a disciplined pattern of fulfilling them. To ignore them is to spawn chaos, while taking care of them regularly ensures that they take a minimum of your time.

Putting Your Best Foot Forward

To make the most of your strengths, Aquarius, you need to let go of your tendency toward aloofness and get involved. While objectivity is a great asset, the ability to stand back and observe can be taken to extremes and undermine your ability to connect with others. To overcome this extreme expression, you can go beyond "hanging out" with a group to actually joining in. This certainly means becoming a paying member, but more than that it signifies offering your support as a volunteer or leader—making a commitment and sticking to it. Letting yourself go in this environment is the other side of involvement. If others can see that you are enjoying yourself (and you truly are), more options will open up for you. Another aspect of this is to let go of your natural cynicism, injecting a little faith and openness into your approach to life. When you are cynical you close yourself off to more possibilities than just the one you imagine. If you pass a verdict before a crime has been committed, you sell yourself and others short. While your knowledge of human nature and its tendencies is of untold value, leaving room for hope will not go amiss.

Tools for Change

There are many ways you can enhance your cachet in the social world. The more you understand about human behavior, the better you will be at relating to people and their unique situations. One way to understand people is through the study of psychology, which will show you the reasons underlying their behaviors in terms of childhood experiences and basic human drives. Astrology goes beyond psychology to show the motivations that lie within the purposes the individuals are meant to fulfill as shown by their time of birth. The healing arts help you to see the wounds in yourself and others and facilitate their healing. You may find healing techniques that involve the latest technologies to be particularly appealing, especially those that tap invisible forces and energies, like those associated with tachyons, magnets, and pyramids. Tarot teaches the nature of the spiritual path and the dangers and triumphs of each step. If your emotional IQ needs a boost, you can develop it by providing service to those in need. Volunteering at a retirement or nursing home, at a school, or any place where others need support can help you open your own feelings. Participation in and expression through the arts, from music to visual arts to crafts, will put you in touch with the deeper parts of yourself, beyond the mind. Meditation does the same thing, as it opens the doors to inner vision to reveal all parts of who you are.

As with all air signs, you may tend to be nervous or high-strung. If so, you will be able to keep your efforts consistently directed toward your goals by taking good care of your body, giving your nervous system and mind full support. You can do this by maintaining a good diet: fresh fruits and vegetables, healthy proteins, and unsaturated fats sustain the nervous system the best. Root vegetables help ground you, while protein gives you sustained energy to keep going all day. It's also important to eat regularly rather than skipping meals. It's also important to learn to listen to your heart. Otherwise, your mind works overtime, and your relationships suffer. Your heart will tell you the right choice in many situations, giving the mind a rest. It will also help you understand others more easily and listen to the message behind their words.

Affirmation of the Year

I open myself to a deeper understanding of truth.

The Year Ahead for Aquarius

You're emerging out of the shadows into the light this year, Aquarius, as three planets change signs into prominence-inducing parts of your chart. Jupiter starts the year in Libra, your solar Ninth House, invigorating your aspirations, higher-mind activities, and travels. You may find yourself inspired to take up studies in philosophy, rhetoric, history, religious traditions, or any subject that broadens your perspective of the world. You may be drawn to a new religious or spiritual path, or feel especially focused on your life's quest. Journeys—in heart, mind, and soul as well as body—assume greater significance now, as your curiosity is piqued by what is foreign. When Jupiter migrates into Scorpio on October 25 your focus shifts to responsibilities closer to home: your career, business, and standing in the community. You may be given a new position of leadership or increased status, which could require the fulfillment of increased responsibilities. There may be several opportunities from which you can choose.

Saturn completes its sojourn in Cancer and your solar Sixth House on July 16, where it has been since June 2003. During this time, you've been restructuring the routines and rhythms of your life, focusing on health and exerting more discipline, perhaps as a result of an unfavorable diagnosis or prognosis. Your work situation may have also been an issue, perhaps due to unpleasant working conditions or an unfair workload. When Saturn enters Leo in July, the emphasis turns to equal relationships: those with people you consider your peers. You may find it necessary or desirable to renegotiate some responsibilities, agreements, and commitments with others. You may change the status of some relationships, and you may be asked to carry more responsibility or even a burden over the next three years. In the give and take of relationships, it is now time for you to give. Chiron visits Aquarius from February 21 to July 31, then enters it for good on December 5. While Chiron is in Capricorn it beams its light from your solar Twelfth House of inner development, supporting a healing process that opens the doors to spiritual transformation. Once Chiron is in Aquarius, your home sign and solar First House, you may identify more closely with its archetype of the wounded healer, who finds his areas of weakness and makes them strengths. Uranus remains in Pisces and your Second House, introducing a wild card element to your finances. If you are already unstable there, you may find that additional instability is more than you can handle, and a crisis results. It is most likely, however, that your income acquires a sporadic element to it—either your income is such that it comes in unexpectedly, or periodic windfall profits are added to your steady source. Neptune is still in your sign, drawing your gaze inward to cultivate your inner being. It may lead you on a spiritual adventure, and your psychic abilities may spontaneously develop—especially as you improve your self-understanding. Pluto sends its energy of power from Sagittarius, your solar Eleventh House, suggesting that you are in contact with a powerful network of people whose energies can benefit you in many ways. You may also be attracted to power positions in groups or organizations, accepting the challenge to use this energy wisely. You will certainly feel the pulse of unconscious energy in your group activities, and the challenge will be for you to respond positively to what you know. The eclipses take on a more harmonious feel as they enter Aries/Libra, invigorating your Third and Ninth Houses. Education, communication, circulation—you'll be focused on these key aspects of life to make yourself more whole over the coming year. You may have the opportunity to travel, publish, teach, write, or broadcast under this emphasis. You may also be drawn to pathways branching off from the familiar road that you are treading in life.

If you were born from January 19 to February 1, you'll encounter Saturn's influence in your relationships after July 15. Your spouse or intimate partner will require more focus than before, perhaps wanting more commitment or a different balance of responsibility in your bond. If you have been neglecting your partnership, or if you've left household duties to your partner, it's time to pick up the reins again and reconnect rather than rebelling against the constraints that are part of your agreement to each other. A healthy bond must be reciprocal if it is to last, and if you choose independence over connection, the relationship will eventually self-destruct. You are in general being asked to give more than you have before, and in the give-and-take of all relationships it is time for you to expend more energy than you receive with the knowledge that the others will carry you when it is needed in the future. It is this natural rhythm of relationship that binds us together and creates true equality in the long run. Relationships in business will also shift this year through the same processes. This is a good time to rely on contracts rather than verbal agreements and to make sure that you live up to your obligations, for your actions will be under the microscope now. Key dates in your Saturn process include July 16–23 and November 22.

If you were born from January 23 to February 1, Uranus in Pisces will rejuvenate the world of your resources from your solar Second House. Your income stream may shift this year from a relatively steady flow to a series of irregular injections. This could signal a change from a "job" where you earn a regular paycheck to a business or more entrepreneurial position where your income is a direct reflection of your success in bringing in contracts. Uranus could also signal a hiatus in income while you search for a new position, take time off for education or a project that will later bear fruit, or recover from an illness. Your expenditures may also be subject to change—unexpected expenses are likely to arise, perhaps involving electrical repairs, and you may feel as though you've lost control in this area of your life. Underneath it all, you want greater financial freedom, and this may lead you to take a more stringent approach to your normal budgetary practices. If you curtail your expenses, pay down debt, and develop a diversified financial portfolio, you'll have the freedom you seek. "Get rich quick" schemes won't work. Uranus-related events will occur around February 25, June 14, August 31, and November 15.

If you were born from February 2 to 7, Neptune's waters are dissolving old fixed patterns from your personality this year. Your identity is in flux, and you may be confused about where you're headed, what you want, or how you want to respond to others around you. You want a new image, yet you're not sure where to start. You are aware of more subtle aspects of your nature that you were blind to in the past; now they are revolutionizing your self-image, and the disorientation you feel will dissipate as the pieces of who you are settle in a new but still recognizable pattern. The process is so subtle, it is almost imperceptible, yet over time you will see a dramatic change. If you can stay with the "ambiguous place" you feel you're in until you reorient yourself, you'll empower this transformation all the more. Allow yourself to be vague, indecisive, and hesitant until a clear path emerges. Spiritual concepts, practices, and meditation may be key to supporting your process. You may find that your body and your emotions are more sensitive. You may want to spend more time alone for this reason, getting to know yourself on this new level. Significant experiences will occur around February 2, May 19, August 8, and October 26.

If you were born from February 8 to 18, Saturn in Cancer is contacting your Sun from your solar Sixth House as it finishes its transit in that sign. You're just about done revamping your personal routines, health, and hygiene practices. You may have decided to exert more discipline in what you eat or how you exercise; consistency is the key. The stimulus for this may be worrying symptoms or the negative findings of a health examination: perhaps you're gaining weight or your blood pressure is up. Saturn's method is slow, persistent effort, which lays the foundation for robust results. By changing fundamental actions—eating and activity—you will achieve the best results. Another factor is your stress level. This is affected as much by how much you sleep as by how much work you do or pressure you feel to perform. You may have been focusing on trimming back the time you put in at work, which is most likely more than the standard forty-hour week. While Saturn is in this house, you may not feel like you can cut back on the amount of work you do, but you can work toward the day, not too far off now, when that cutback will occur. By July 16 you should be able to release yourself from your burden. Key events will occur around January 13 and March 21.

If you were born from February 10 to 13, it's time for Pluto to bring change into your life from Sagittarius and your solar Eleventh House. This is not just the house of social contacts, groups, and organizations: it is where we fulfill our role as a member of a group— a larger sociological movement or goal. You may connect with a social or political ideal this year that motivates you to take action to better the human condition in some broad sense. Your goal, with Pluto involved, will foster the just use of power, perhaps self-empowerment for each individual. You may become conscious of the deep inner drives that urge the masses of humanity to particular behaviors, and you may seek to lead them out of those which are self-defeating. You may become interested in organizational psychology, social history, and their applications. Your own interactions with others in groups will take on more significance, and you may become uncomfortable with the undercurrents of some groups you previously felt in sync with. You may decide to shift loyalties or disown one membership in favor of another as your eyes are opened to this deeper level. You may also come into contact with more powerful and influential people through your group activities. They may be able to help you further your career or profession. You will notice significant events related to Pluto's process around March 26, June 13, September 2, and December 15.

Aquarius/January

Planetary Hotspots

With Saturn at the culmination of its yearly cycle on January 13, you've been experiencing increased activity in your Sixth House of work, health, and lifestyle routines for nearly two years now. January 16 sees the beginning of the newest Chiron cycle, spotlighting an inner healing process you've been working with for three years that may be revealing physical imbalances as well as spiritual ones.

Wellness and Keeping Fit

Health has been an ongoing focus for you for two years, and at mid-month you'll get the chance to see how well you're doing with your program. Since Saturn is active here, consistent discipline is the key. You have about three months to go before results are confirmed and a new pattern set.

Love and Life Connections

A potentially explosive situation or event occurs on January 28 in your extended social circle, from social groups to membership organizations. This is related to ongoing changes that you have observed since 1995, as Pluto has moved through Sagittarius.

Finance and Success

You've been working on a process of stripping away behaviors that don't work for you, as the burden placed on you has seemed unendurable. At this peak, you'll get a chance to see how well you're doing at eliminating busy work and bad habits, because your workload will reach a maximum point. If you don't feel maxed out, you're doing a good job.

Rewarding Days

2, 3, 4, 7, 8, 11, 12, 15, 16, 20, 21, 30, 31

Challenging Days

5, 6, 17, 18, 19, 25, 26

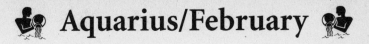 Aquarius/February

Planetary Hotspots

You've been thinking big with Jupiter in your solar Ninth House. You've got new goals in mind, and now, as Jupiter enters its retrograde period on February 1, you're seeing what kind of effort on your part is involved. Take a deep breath and plunge in, because you'll benefit greatly in the long run if you have faith. A new Neptune cycle starts at the same time, reminding you of the ongoing growth process you've been experiencing, revealing the true you. Just to make life more exciting, Uranus's new cycle begins on February 25, continuing changes in the way you manage your resources.

Wellness and Keeping Fit

Inner health and well-being are key this month as the new cycle of Neptune starts on February 2. The importance of this factor in your life is underscored when Chiron enters Aquarius on February 21. For the next four years you'll be able to pinpoint and clear blocks to perfect health with greater accuracy.

Love and Life Connections

You're looking good this month, and this will be reflected in the amount of favorable attention you receive from others as Venus enters your sign on February 2. You can use this time to smooth over past disagreements and avoid potential conflicts, as well as mediate the disputes of others.

Finance and Success

You've been trying to open up your financial frontiers to new sources of income, and as February 25 passes you'll feel new ideas welling up inside that you're excited to try. The scary part is letting go of old, restrictive ways of earning money. That will have to happen, and if you can accept it gracefully, you'll be surprised at how smoothly you flow to the next level.

Rewarding Days
3, 4, 7, 8, 11, 12, 13, 16, 17, 26, 27

Challenging Days
1, 2, 14, 15, 21, 22, 28

Aquarius/March

Planetary Hotspots

There are plenty of issues to resolve this month as the planets acti-vate your problem-solving houses. This is especially emphasized as March 19 approaches, when Mercury enters its three-week retro-grade period—its first of the year. After five months of intense effort in just fulfilling your daily tasks, from work to health regimens, you can breathe a sigh of relief as Saturn takes the pressure off by return-ing to forward motion on March 21. Your attention will be drawn to circumstances in organizations and other types of social affilia-tions—an area where you've experienced considerable growth since 1995—as Pluto's five-month retrograde begins on March 26.

Wellness and Keeping Fit

The pressures of daily life could affect your health this month as a cacophony of events collides with your daily routine. Critical points occur on March 3, 7, 19, and 23.

Love and Life Connections

You're so busy with work, it's hard to fit your loved ones into your plans this month. However, if you communicate with them about what's happening, they'll understand—providing, of course, that this is not part of a larger pattern.

Finance and Success

It may be time to rethink your approach to public relations and out-reach this month in response to Mercury's retrograde transit through your Third House. Watch for miscommunications in writ-ten form around March 19. Your work overload will largely be a thing of the past by March 21, or soon after.

Rewarding Days

3, 4, 7, 8, 11, 12, 15, 16, 17, 25, 26, 27, 30, 31

Challenging Days

1, 2, 13, 14, 20, 21, 22, 28, 29

Aquarius/April

Planetary Hotspots

You're busier than ever at building your dreams when Jupiter reaches the high point of its cycle on April 3. The solar eclipse on April 8 further highlights this area, bringing events to you in rapid fire, enabling you to create your new future. Mercury has also been stimulating the same house, but the crunch is over once it returns to forward motion on April 12. One final event—a lunar eclipse on April 24—draws your focus to Houses Ten and Four, your career and home life. In the coming five months you'll be able to complete a process you've been working with over the past two years.

Wellness and Keeping Fit

Watch for accidents or injuries due to confusion or lack of focus around April 13, as Mars contacts Neptune in your First House. You may have an ungrounded feeling then. You can mitigate this by doing one thing at a time instead of multitasking during this sensitive period. It could happen in any setting, not just while engaged in athletics.

Love and Life Connections

This is not a good time to rush starry-eyed into a relationship, for you'll be likely to take things for granted that may not be true. You may have a great deal of faith where it is not warranted. By giving any relationship time to develop, you keep yourself from overextending emotionally.

Finance and Success

New educational doorways open this month as the eclipses highlight your Third and Ninth Houses. You'll be wanting to expand your horizons in many ways, and you'll get the chance to do so in the coming months, so think about what you want to create and select the best opportunities based on those goals.

Rewarding Days
3, 4, 7, 8, 12, 13, 22, 23, 26, 27, 30

Challenging Days
9, 10, 11, 17, 18, 24, 25

Aquarius/May

Planetary Hotspots

You become acutely aware of areas where you are out of balance as May 8 approaches and Chiron enters its retrograde period. These "wounds" may be emotional, mental, or physical, but there will always be a spiritual aspect to their source, which must be dealt with on the deepest levels if they are to be eradicated. Neptune also starts its retrograde in your First House on May 19, triggering the same areas of your life—your identity, self-concept, and well-being.

Wellness and Keeping Fit

You may experience unusual symptoms around May 8 and 19 that are more easily described in terms of spiritual reality than physical. This doesn't mean that there isn't a physical counterpart that needs to be dealt with by a medical professional, but it may mean that you won't be healing the whole picture without addressing the subtle energy side of your experiences as well.

Love and Life Connections

You are discovering how emotionally healthy or debilitated you are when it comes to sharing yourself in a truly intimate way with those you love and trust. Although you may find that you are adept in this area, it is not a common Aquarian strength, so if you're unsure, err on the side of caution and work on developing your emotional IQ.

Finance and Success

A sudden expenditure is likely to arise around May 15 as Mars stimulates Uranus in your Second House of personal resources. The challenges that arise now foreshadow the ones which will arise next month around June 2 and 14.

Rewarding Days

1, 5, 6, 9, 10, 19, 20, 23, 24, 25, 28, 29

Challenging Days

7, 8, 14, 15, 21, 22

Aquarius/June

Planetary Hotspots

You'll enter a reward and completion period with your goal-fulfillment process when Jupiter returns to forward motion on June 4 in your solar Ninth House. Travel, contact with foreign cultures, and education have been significantly advanced over the past four months. June 13 brings a crunch of activity with social events and organizations, when Pluto reaches the culmination of its cycle in your Eleventh House. This blends imperceptibly with the retrograde of Uranus, which starts on June 14. Its transit through your Second House suggests that a financial challenge will arise at this time.

Wellness and Keeping Fit

An abundance of incidents keeps you hopping through mid-month, and this could dampen your efforts to stay on the straight and narrow path of your recently revamped health regimen. After the dust settles, soon after June 14, you're ripe for a vacation. With all the challenges to come in July and August, this is an excellent time to refuel your energy tank.

Love and Life Connections

Social outings and events are highlighted this month—especially around June 13, when events of particular significance to you will occur. You may have the opportunity to meet someone of special influence or power during this time, which is part of an ongoing process of "amping up" your life through the right connections.

Finance and Success

The broader horizons you've been opening for yourself are now expanding on their own without additional effort from you. Although you will continue to reach for greater heights of understanding and achievement, you've taken the most vital steps—the ones that put you in the picture you want to be a part of.

Rewarding Days

1, 2, 5, 6, 7, 15, 16, 17, 20, 21, 24, 25, 28, 29

Challenging Days

3, 4, 10, 11, 12, 18, 19, 30

Aquarius/July

Planetary Hotspots

Your process of self-transformation becomes less subtle after July 16 when Saturn enters Leo and your Seventh House. You'll see yourself reflected in other people more dramatically, especially when Saturn contacts Chiron for the rest of the month. Key dates are July 19, 23, 28, and 31, as Mars and the Sun trigger them. Mercury adds a sharper understanding of what's going on at the same time when it turns retrograde on July 22.

Wellness and Keeping Fit

You get the chance to see your well-being from a new angle when Saturn enters Leo and your Seventh House of relationships on July 16. You'll get a clearer view of your "interactional" health—how you get along with other people. Now your ability to relate to others, and to make and keep commitments, is under the spotlight, and you'll have the opportunity to heal this part of your life in the coming three years.

Love and Life Connections

You're finding that suddenly it seems like you have to work much harder to maintain the relationships you participated in so casually in the past. You have to prove yourself, show that you deserve what you are given. This is part of a three-year adjustment process where it's time for you to give more than you receive. You'll see just how deep the changes will go in the last half of the month and first two weeks of August.

Finance and Success

Even though you've had financial challenges in the past two months, this month your income balances your expenses. You're still on track to reach your financial goals.

Rewarding Days

3, 4, 13, 14, 17, 18, 21, 22, 25, 26, 27, 30, 31

Challenging Days

1, 2, 8, 9, 15, 16, 28, 29

Aquarius/August

Planetary Hotspots

The situations that arose last month spill over into August as Neptune is highlighted in your solar First House on August 8. Confusion about your situation will be cleared at that time, and you'll know more clearly what to do to respond to the situation. By the time Mercury returns to forward motion again on August 15 you'll be well on your way to mending things. August 31 heralds another crescendo in your financial affairs as Uranus reaches the halfway point of its cycle, highlighting your Second House.

Wellness and Keeping Fit

Your relationship situation may be upsetting enough to throw your nervous system out of balance, and this could mean higher levels of anxiety, with difficulty sleeping and maintaining focus. Try to journal, and talk it out with someone you trust; engage in physical activities that soothe the nerves and pay attention to your dreams.

Love and Life Connections

You can see what's been happening in your relationship life now, and you are beginning to understand what needs to be fixed. Although you're not yet sure what role you played in creating the situation, you'll be clearer about that by mid-month. It is likely that your partner overreacted, but you have to take it seriously. Maybe it took an overreaction to get you to pay attention.

Finance and Success

Financial matters come to a head on or around August 31. At this time you'll get an understanding of just how much reward you're likely to get from this year's enterprises. As part of a continuous process of change, in which you are at the midpoint, the results are not final, but what you know now will inform your decisions about what to adjust for in the next set of plans.

Rewarding Days

9, 10, 14, 15, 18, 19, 22, 23, 26, 27, 28

Challenging Days

4, 5, 11, 12, 13, 24, 25, 31

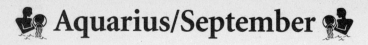 Aquarius/September

Planetary Hotspots

Your social contacts, business associations, and organizational affiliations are once again spotlighted as Pluto begins to move forward on September 2. Now you can see the potential benefits of all your hard work in cultivating those relationships. By continuing your efforts consistently in the next three months, you'll be able to complete the achievement of this step in your long-term goals. It pays to turn your ear toward what is happening in your home and family life now. Mars will start its retrograde transit through your Fourth House on October 1, when your private affairs and personal feelings will be highlighted. A kind word of appreciation with those who share your personal space will support the growth process to come, and it's best not to ignore needed repairs.

Wellness and Keeping Fit

After September 2 there's a long window of opportunity to take a vacation. This is a time when you will pine for freedom and a change of scene more than usual, so take advantage of the break as much as possible for continued well-being.

Love and Life Connections

After the emotional melee of July and August, you're ready for lower-key interactions with your loved ones. Allow your vacation to provide some healing moments together by making only loose plans, rather than creating a lot of structure, which can result in high expectation and tension.

Finance and Success

Everything is calm in your career right now, and you feel supported there. This is good, because you need a foundation from which to make changes in other areas of your life.

Rewarding Days

5, 6, 7, 10, 11, 14, 15, 18, 19, 22, 23, 24

Challenging Days

1, 2, 8, 9, 20, 21, 27, 28, 29

Aquarius/October

Planetary Hotspots

Mars starts its three-month retrograde period on October 1, putting your home and family life in the spotlight. Your home may suddenly need critical repairs due to deferred maintenance or even unexpected problems. A solar eclipse on October 3 and a lunar one on October 17 emphasize educational processes—anything that stretches your awareness beyond the comfortable and customary. When Chiron begins to move forward on October 5 you'll feel more assured about your process of inner growth—a feeling you'll experience again around October 26 when Neptune also returns to direct motion. A new chapter of accomplishment will open on October 22 when Jupiter commences its new annual cycle, this time in your solar Tenth House of career and public recognition.

Wellness and Keeping Fit

Health situations are easier to diagnose and understand after October 14. This may be part of a natural evolution as you have observed your health over the past few months, or it could be the result of working with a health professional.

Love and Life Connections

Family conflicts may need clearing as Mars emphasizes your home life. The areas of disagreement existed before, but newly revealed factors give them more global proportions. This is a time when all are likely to become thoughtful and tread more carefully as they rethink their options. Patience will bring the best possible result.

Finance and Success

New opportunities develop as a result of the ways you've been broadening your path. You can see the potential around October 3 and 17. They come through contacts you make in an educational or foreign setting, possibly through people of an unfamiliar culture.

Rewarding Days

2, 3, 4, 7, 8, 11, 12, 13, 16, 17, 20, 21, 30, 31

Challenging Days

5, 6, 18, 19, 25, 26

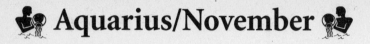 Aquarius/November

Planetary Hotspots

As Mercury turns retrograde on November 14, your activities with colleagues, organizations, and social groups will increase. Misunderstandings may abound, and conflicts arise. Since you are unlikely to be at the heart of the matter, you may be able to provide beneficial mediation to overcome the difficulties. Uranus leaves its retrograde period on November 15, ending a time of relative instability in your income and expenditures and allowing you to pursue plans you've had for gaining greater financial freedom. Saturn enters its retrograde period on November 22, emphasizing the importance of your partnership, where you may be expected to make some concessions to those with whom you share agreements.

Wellness and Keeping Fit

You want to withdraw from the world socially after November 4, and it's not such a bad idea. Although you'll still have to go out of the house for some social activities, they won't prevent you from having this valuable down time.

Love and Life Connections

Even as you're working on improving the atmosphere in your home life, new issues crop up. These could be anything from needed repairs to additional emotional challenges that need to be aired and accommodated. Peak events are likely on November 7 and 18.

Finance and Success

Financial situations requiring extra attention for the last five months resolve quickly after November 15, and you can move on to new pastures of opportunity. It may look like someone who made a business commitment is backing out around November 14. That may be possible, but you won't know for sure until next month. If it is true, it's better that your plans did not move forward any further.

Rewarding Days

3, 4, 5, 8, 9, 12, 13, 16, 17, 18, 26, 27

Challenging Days

1, 2, 14, 15, 21, 22, 23, 28, 29, 30

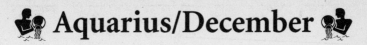 Aquarius/December

Planetary Hotspots

On December 3, Mercury turns forward in its path, with a positive effect on your career and social life. Mars adds to the sense of accomplishment and release when its retrograde ends on December 9. Pluto's new annual cycle starts on December 15, bringing your group and volunteer activities to the forefront. You'll see new enterprises that you'll want to undertake in the coming year to create future success. There's one more plot twist left in the year, which arises around December 24. Venus enters its six-week-long retrograde period then, heralding a self-examination and self-development process.

Wellness and Keeping Fit

Although you're under a lot of pressure now, your health stays on an even keel. It's relaxing to know where you stand, even if it's not as good a standing as you had hoped for. Now that you know what the problem is, you can begin to make amends.

Love and Life Connections

You'll be questioning the way you approach relationships as Venus enters its retrograde period on December 24. Suddenly you're looking at your behavior from the perspective of the other people in your life, and seeing the flaws in your attitude and the level of respect you've been extending their way. This humbling experience can lead to breakthroughs with your loved ones if you are willing to be honest about what you've found and make some changes.

Finance and Success

The tensions between family and career lighten up considerably by December 9 as Mars and Mercury return to their "normal" forward motion. This clears the path for you to consider the way you want to develop your life through social contacts for another year, as Pluto's new cycle starts on December 15.

Rewarding Days

1, 2, 5, 6, 9, 10, 14, 15, 23, 24, 25, 28, 29

Challenging Days

11, 12, 13, 18, 19, 20, 26, 27

Aquarius Action Table

These dates reflect the best —but not the only—times for success and ease in these activities, according to your Sun sign.

	JAN	FEB	MAR	APR	MAY	JUN	JUL	AUG	SEPT	OCT	NOV	DEC
Move					12-28							
Start a class			5-19	12-30	1-12							
Join a club	1-9									31	1-13	13-31
Ask for a raise		2-26								8-31	1-5	1, 2
Look for work						11-30	1-22	16-31	1-4	8-30		
Get pro advice	25, 26	21, 22	20-22	17, 18	14, 15	10-12	8, 9	4, 5, 31	1, 2, 28, 29	25, 26	21, 22	18-20
Get a loan	1, 27-29	23-25	23, 24	19-21	16-18	13, 14	10-12	6-8	3, 4, 30	1, 27, 28	24, 25	21, 22
See a doctor	10-31	1-16				11-30	1-22	16-31	1-4			
Start a diet						11-28	19-21					
End relationship								17, 18				
Buy clothes				15-30	1-10, 28, 31	1-11						
Get a makeover	30, 31	1-26		15-30	1-10							
New romance				15-30	1-10	5-7						
Vacation	2-4, 30, 31	26, 27	25-27	22, 23	19, 20	15-17	13, 14	9, 10, 17-31	1-11, 20-30	1-8, 30, 31	26, 27	23-25

PISCES

The Fish
February 18 to March 20

♓

Element:	Water
Quality:	Mutable
Polarity:	Yin/Feminine
Planetary Ruler:	Neptune
Meditation:	I successfully navigate the seas of my emotions.
Gemstone:	Aquamarine
Power Stones:	Amethyst, bloodstone, tourmaline
Key Phrase:	I believe
Glyph:	Two fish, swimming in opposite directions
Anatomy:	Feet, lymphatic system
Color:	Sea green, violet
Animal:	Fish, sea mammals
Myths/Legends:	Aphrodite, Buddha, Jesus of Nazareth
House:	Twelfth
Opposite Sign:	Virgo
Flower:	Water lily
Key Word:	Transcendence

Your Ego's Strengths and Shortcomings

Just like Cancer and Scorpio, yours is a water sign, Pisces. You are a representative of that unseen, emotional world of which we all partake. You often are the barometer of humanity, measuring the emotional and psychic atmospheric pressure around you. You may even pick up on the energies of others far away from you, for your sensitivity is unbounded by distance. You are aware of your energy field—or you should be, because it is the source of your health more than most signs. It is important for you to manage it, for otherwise you may tend to collect others' thoughts and feelings in your energy web, taking them on as your own. You are naturally psychic, and visual images may be your strongest way of connecting with the inner realms. However, in order for your visions to be clear and untainted by your own projections, you must engage in psychological and spiritual growth to ensure that you are filtering out your own unconscious drives and yearnings. Although water tends to move downward, yours is the tiny droplets of mist more than a solid body of water, carried on the air and lifted easily upward. Your idealism is a reflection of this, and so is your prophetic side. You may dream— whether at night or by day—of a new, more hopeful future, which is the first step in bringing it to pass. Your body may tend to be sensitive to environmental factors, from the latest virus to the negativity others project in an argument. Taking care of your physical body— eating well and regularly for instance—as well as your energy bodies will enable you to minimize such effects. If you become ill, feel unaccountably tired or agitated, or become scattered, it's a sign you need to pull back to your center and find your self again.

Shining Your Love Light

Your sweetness and pliability attract others to you, Pisces, and help the waters of love flow smoothly. Your openness is endearing and you exude an unconscious air of mystery that others find enchanting. However, you may find relationships to be a great challenge because of your tendency to take on others' energies. Although we all tend to adapt to each other in relationships, you have a greater tendency than most to change yourself for your partner. You may feel overwhelmed by them or even submerged in their nature. Developing your personal boundaries and having space to be by yourself each day will help you stay in touch with your inner being. Regular time alone and a healthy level of individual activities are your antidote.

Aries will teach you to strike out on your own, while you will lend this sign a compassionate perspective. Taurus grounds and stabilizes you, while you provide and emotional uplift with your idealism. You be able to lighten up and see a more mental side to other people with Gemini, while he'll learn to appreciate the inner realms you sense. Fellow water-type Cancer completely understands the world you live in, and together you'll enhance each other's creative, healing energies. Leo will inspire you to reach out to others, while you'll teach Leo to think more about the needs of those around them. Virgo helps you sort and organize ideas and things, helping you bridge the gap between physical and metaphysical realities. Libra will think about and support you, and you'll enhance her intuitive awareness of the world. Scorpio enthralls you, takes you more deeply into your feeling side, and then teaches you how to contain it. Sagittarius shares your lofty idealism and helps you focus it into meaningful activity, while you bring out this sign's caring side. You'll greatly appreciate Capricorn's structure and discipline, while you'll help him get in touch with his inner being. Aquarius will teach you to be more socially adventurous and not get so involved in others' emotions, and you'll help her let go of her cynicism. A fellow Pisces will understand you implicitly, but you'll have to make sure not to amplify your common weaknesses, instead choosing to be grounded and disciplined together.

Making Your Place in the World

It is better to take advantage of your sensitivity than to suppress it in order to work in an uncomfortable environment, Pisces. You'll do better in a profession that values your caring, compassionate side. Often, this places you in a service role, such as nursing, social work, or psychology. However, you are better off in roles where you are not overexposed to others' energies. You do better within a situation that naturally limits your stimulation and contains the forces of the outer world to a manageable level. Generally, this means that you should only be receiving one stimulus at a time. A field or position that keeps you from direct contact with the public may work best—even better if you can work alone, at least part of the time. Choosing a career in a creative field, from the arts to research, can give you a deep sense of fulfillment and limit your exposure at the same time.

Putting Your Best Foot Forward

One of the biggest issues you face in life is bringing your visions down to earth. You have such wonderful, lofty dreams, but manifesting them is another story. The delicate process of translating them into matter can be developed in several ways. First, it helps to know as much as you can about the world you want to penetrate. Learn the industry or milieu, its jargon and its methods, that you are targeting. Learn what's important to those who run the show and how to pitch your ideas to them. Perhaps you need to develop pragmatic skills—in business or finance—as well. Don't be afraid to hire others to cover areas in which you are not skilled. You have to know that your ideas can be achieved, but you don't have to dream up every part of the plan or carry it out on your own.

The most important thing is to have confidence in yourself and your ability to carry through to the end. You may not accomplish your goals sometimes because you give up too easily, or you may not persist in pushing your ideas out there, being shy when you should be bolder. If you are clear about what you want and sure you can achieve it, you'll find a way to do it.

Tools for Change

Because you are so sensitive to the energies around you—it is part of your purpose—you will stumble under the weight of all that and lose your clarity unless you develop a routine for staying in good psychic shape. First, it helps to know what you're encountering in the world. Studying the psychic, energetic realms and how they work is essential, which can be learned through spiritual and psychic development courses and training in subtle healing. Once you know how the human energy field works, you can relate it to what you are experiencing on an unseen level. You will become more aware of when others' energies are affecting you, and you will be able to consciously and compassionately deal with them. You will also find that you have a tendency to collect certain types of energies more than others because of your own blind spots. Working to clear those blind spots through self-development will help you clear your inner windows of perception. Bach flowers, which heal the emotions and help balance our own energy field, will support your own healing process, while homeopathics will help with constitutional weaknesses as well as the imbalances that arise in the physical body. Staying grounded and centered are vital as well, since this helps you let go of the energies you encounter by sending them down into the earth, which can cleanse them. Meditation techniques, especially those involving breathing practices, help balance the pranic forces in your aura and keep you from absorbing others' energies so easily. It also helps to be choosy when selecting your friends—those you are close to and readily open up to. You can also let them know how the inner world works for you, so that they understand how deeply you tune in to what they're feeling. Of course, you will need to be around all kinds of people, but be sure to give yourself some time each day where you can retreat into your own space and catch your psychic breath, regaining your clarity. If you are carrying an extra burden of others' vibrations, such as from early childhood conditioning, it will help to journal it out, get some energy healing, or pursue therapy to get in touch with related events.

Affirmation of the Year

I experience all rejuvenating forces gracefully.

The Year Ahead for Pisces

You'll have the opportunity to complete old processes and prepare for upcoming new ones this year, Pisces, as three planets move into the cadent, "completing" houses of your solar chart. Jupiter exemplifies this pattern as it travels in Libra and Scorpio, your Eighth and Ninth Houses. While in Libra, Jupiter gives you an influx of support from others—the society at large as well as those with whom you share closer bonds. New streams of income may develop, and opportunities for building financial power may come your way. This is a good time to re-examine your financial portfolio or source of future security to make sure it keeps up with your growth in wealth. Take care not to become cavalier, because Jupiter can make us overly optimistic about the risks we face. Preserving the primacy of caution over faith will ensure a solid, stable result. When Jupiter enters Scorpio on October 25 it also moves into your Ninth House, and you will start a period of preparation for next year's pinnacle of success. It's an ideal time to expand your horizons in some way—through travel, study, enhancing your spiritual or philosophical acuity, and otherwise broadening your perspective. This puts you in "leadership mode," giving you the vision of how best to use the coming time of increased power and status.

Saturn completes its transit of Cancer to enter Leo on July 16. While in Cancer, it inhabits your Fifth House of children, playful pursuits, and romance. You may have felt burdened in this area, unable to enjoy life's pleasures because of obligations. This may also indicate that you've made a serious pursuit out of a hobby or creative activity—something from which you can earn money. Once Saturn moves into Leo your focus turns to improving your health, work experience, and life routines. It will be important to reduce stress, as the pressures in the workplace may increase along with your workload. Chiron moves into Aquarius on February 21, although it returns to Capricorn for a final lesson in self-responsibility from July 31 to December 5. While Chiron is in Capricorn, you have the opportunity to complete growth and healing in your group relationships. You may find that you have a significant role in resolving a deep-seated and long-standing conflict. Aquarius is your solar Twelfth House, the place of spiritual development and inner connection with universal consciousness and life. You may find that you feel more connected to others when you are alone, and you may seek to enhance that bond through spiritual practice or meditation. Health issues could arise that seem to hold you back in making externally recognizable progress, but on the inner levels you are growing quickly indeed.

Uranus stays in Pisces again this year, your own sign and First House. It continues awakening you to who you really are, inspiring you to courageously bring the true you into expression in the outer world. Neptune is making progress in its journey through Aquarius and your solar Twelfth House. You're making progress as well in exploring your inner landscape. You may be involved in a project or activity that requires considerable sacrifice on your part, which others may not understand. Whether you have their support or go it alone, you know that it's what you must do. Pluto is in a challenging position to your Sun in Sagittarius and your solar Tenth House, where it has been since 1995. It is making you aware of power dynamics in your own life, as well as in the outer world of business, politics, and international affairs. The eclipses are shifting your focus from exploration and education to the functions of your Second and Eighth Houses—those of your resources and the ways you avail yourself of the resources of others. You may need to adjust the ways you earn and spend money, adjust your financial plans, or seek new income streams during this time.

If you were born from February 18 to March 2, Saturn in Leo will begin restructuring your routines and health practices when it enters your Sixth House on July 16. This is a good time to get a thorough health examination so that you can take a structured approach to heading off difficulties before they occur. You will find it helpful to take responsibility for your health condition as it is, and to develop and execute a plan for improving it as soon as possible. Although it will take time to accomplish your goals, the results will be profound. While at first you may chafe at the limitations you must accept, you'll soon grow accustomed to the new strictures on your life and wonder why it took you so long to make the changes. Your work life may become more burdensome, either because you have an increased workload, or because the pressures to perform your regular tasks are greater. You may be promoted, although it will be to a role with greater responsibility rather than authority or compensation. Learning to delegate is vital now, and if you do not have the power to do so because of your position it is important to negotiate ways to make your workload more reasonable—or leave the job behind for one where your genuine needs are honored. Key dates for your Saturn process are July 16 to 23 and November 22.

If you were born from February 22 to March 2, your Sun will be in direct contact with Uranus, since Uranus is in Pisces and your own sign. It may feel like Uranus is introducing you to yourself, giving you a mirror to the events in your daily life. Some of these may seem shocking, and you may be surprising others with the boldness of your new plans, even the way you look, but they are things that you have been preparing for quite consciously for some time. Now, opportunity and inspiration are meshing to give wings to your new identity and path. You may seem to be making sudden changes, but they are part of a powerful progression toward a greater vision of your life that you launched when Pluto was contacting your Sun in 1996–99. As this path unfolds, you are discovering even more possibilities and benefits. Although Uranus can bring us unexpected, shocking events, these are less likely to take us by surprise, or even occur, if we are in alignment with our true self, for this is what Uranus events bring about in our life. Dramatic changes may take place in your body this year as well, and the potential for acute health events is higher than usual. Taking care of your body and making sure that you pay attention to the signals it gives will help you avoid such challenges. Milestone events are likely to occur around February 25, June 14, August 31, and November 15.

If you were born from March 3 to 8, Neptune in Aquarius will dissolve hidden issues and old patterns from its position in your solar Twelfth House. While your life seems placid to others, you know that a lot is happening inside. These changes have been occurring since 1998, but your peak year is 2005; during this time, you can expect greater progress in personal growth and spiritual development than before. You may experience emotional pain as you let go of old ways of being, and you could even become ill; however, these are transitory effects, and the more easily you let go the more quickly the pain will pass. Your level of sacrifice may peak this year as well, as the needs of others put your own on the back burner. You may be required to be the primary caregiver for someone close to you, or you may be involved in a project at work with a large workload and low visibility, or volunteer activities could consume your time and attention. This brings growth to you in another way than through your own direct action, but it is just as powerful. No matter what, your personal story, meditation, spiritual practice, and other ways of taking care of your own needs will see you through this time of comparative isolation. Turning points in your growth process will occur around February 2, May 19, August 8, and October 26.

If you were born from March 9 to 20, Saturn's final months in Cancer will put it in contact with your Sun from your solar Fifth House. This harmonious transit, which started last summer, has been making you more productive—especially if you are involved in creative pursuits in any way. You may find that it influences your style to be more structured and less fluid. You may be taking a more businesslike attitude toward your artistic activities as well. If you are involved in a romance, your relationship may become more serious, or the obstacles to a deeper commitment may be bothering you more than before. You may feel as though it's time to decide where your relationship is going. If you have children, they may require more time and effort from you now, as they enter a phase of their lives that requires more guidance from you. This does not necessarily indicate that there are problems, but there could be issues that need to be resolved before they can move forward in a new area of growth. They may temporarily need stronger limits than before, or they may need to take more control of their own lives, living by rules that you create as a team. Turning points in your Saturn experiences will occur around January 13 and March 21.

If you were born from March 11 to 14, Pluto in Sagittarius is empowering you from your solar Tenth House. This long-term transformation is pushing you toward greater self-fulfillment as well as fulfillment of what you perceive to be your mission in life. You are constantly discovering more depth in what you have to offer: the talents you've cultivated over the course of your life and how they can be used to support others. As you come to see yourself through the eyes of others, you are seeing ways in which you have learned to give away your natural power. Now you are gaining insight into how to take that power back and express it wisely. This is a slow growth process whose peak occurs over three years. As you reach that peak, you may encounter people who are controlling or devious in their interactions with you. You may also be surprised by the strong reactions you get from others. These events underscore the importance of getting in touch with the undercurrent that flows through all relationships based on our natural drives to survive and be loved. As you learn to understand your own unconscious motivations, you will also learn to understand and manage your interactions with others more successfully, because you will cease giving your power to them. Key events will occur around March 26, June 13, September 2, and December 15.

Pisces/January

Planetary Hotspots

Much of your life has revolved around children and creative pursuits over the past two years, and related activities crescendos on January 13 when Saturn is spotlighted in your solar Fifth House. At the same time, Chiron's new cycle is starting in your Eleventh House, and events around this time will spur the process of growth through groups and organizations.

Wellness and Keeping Fit

Don't let career or business events near the end of the month throw you for a loop. Your immune system could take a hit, and you could end up with the latest cold or flu virus. You can achieve some emotional distance—and therefore some physical protection—by identifying yourself independently of your career role.

Love and Life Connections

Your social circle—an area of growth for you over the past two years—is highlighted this month. At mid-month you become more acutely aware of the bonuses and liabilities of the groups to which you belong. You may have additional obligations to organizations or feel burdened by the challenges that group membership can bring. If the trouble is meeting the right people, some helpful introductions may come your way now.

Finance and Success

Introductions around January 13 may prove beneficial to you in the coming months. You've been looking for a source of new information or business, and this may be it. On January 28, explosive events could occur which affect you in your career in some way, if only indirectly. Calm and patience are called for.

Rewarding Days

5, 6, 9, 10, 13, 14, 17, 18, 19, 22, 23, 24

Challenging Days

1, 7, 8, 20, 21, 27, 28, 29

Pisces/February

Planetary Hotspots

You've been having a good fall and winter, financially speaking. Opportunities to gain more income are coming to you from many quarters. As Jupiter enters its four-month retrograde period on February 1, you'll see how well you're managing those pursuits. Your idealism will peak around February 2 as Neptune starts its new cycle in your solar Twelfth House. The most significant event of the month for you, however, is the initiation of Uranus's yearly cycle on February 25, which occurs in your First House. You've been feeling this very deeply each year since it entered your home sign in 2003, as it prods you to deal with personal issues that you've avoided in the past.

Wellness and Keeping Fit

Your body will send you signals around February 25 of health imbalances that still need rectifying. You can make a plan for how to accomplish this, whether on your own or with the help of your favorite health professional. In the coming five months you'll be able to substantially reduce the symptoms, if not completely eradicate them.

Love and Life Connections

Although you'll feel like retreating for most of the month, after February 25 you'll be more receptive to social activity. In fact, others will be drawn to you, and you'll find it hard to resist their proposals. This is a good time for a new hair style or other way of creating a new look, because others will be able to see the beauty in you.

Finance and Success

You've made some plans to develop an increase in income, and now it's time to decide which of several directions you will take. It will take some focused effort for about four months, after which time you'll be able to step back a little and let things manifest.

Rewarding Days

1, 2, 5, 6, 9, 10, 13, 14, 18, 19, 28

Challenging Days

3, 4, 16, 17, 24, 25

Pisces/March

Planetary Hotspots

As the world spins at a faster pace around you, you're trying to maintain your stability. Group events trigger financial opportunities and challenges around March 3, increasing creative activity over the whole month. You'll turn the corner on this on March 21 as Saturn begins to move forward again in your Fifth House. Mercury's first retrograde of the year starts on March 19 in your Second House of personal resources, suggesting a temporary shortfall in cash, time, or tools to complete your work. On March 26 your ongoing career transformation will grab your attention, suggesting a new direction in which to build success.

Wellness and Keeping Fit

You may experience a healing crisis on March 23. This is a good thing—an event that points to exactly what is wrong in the body and how it needs to be healed. Once you get to the core of the matter, treatment is simply a matter of following through.

Love and Life Connections

Your love light shines brightly until the March 22, and others will extend themselves on your behalf. If challenges arise in your relationships with children or your romantic life around March 7 and 21, facing them responsibly will bring the best result. Establishing or maintaining boundaries will be important.

Finance and Success

Your contacts with others stimulate business, and you may receive an offer early in the month. Accepting it will help achieve the income goals you have set for yourself, but you'll have to make short-term sacrifices to bootstrap yourself into this new echelon. These will become evident as March 19 approaches, and you should take the time to make sure you can handle the transition.

Rewarding Days
1, 2, 5, 6, 9, 10, 13, 14, 18, 19, 28, 29

Challenging Days
3, 4, 15, 16, 17, 23, 24

Pisces/April

Planetary Hotspots

The culmination of Jupiter's cycle on April 3 suggests heightened activity in your financial world. More cash may be flowing in, but it's flowing out at least as fast just now, as you climb to a new level of income. The solar eclipse on April 8 presents another opportunity that requires investment of time and money, and, if taken, will keep you very busy over the coming six months—and greatly change your life. Mercury's return to forward motion on April 12 signals the end of the increase in cash flow. You're seeing your recent educational enterprises begin to bear fruit as the lunar eclipse of April 24 lights up your Third and Ninth Houses.

Wellness and Keeping Fit

On April 21 you experience another healing crisis, but this one is more subtle and symbolic, involving spiritual realities. However, it is just as deep, if not more profound, as it gets to the root cause of various ailments or weaknesses your body has displayed over the years.

Love and Life Connections

Keep your communication with your loved ones open when it comes to money. You need to let them know what your plans are so they'll be behind you as you make this big step. You'll enjoy getting out to cultural events and exhibits with your friends and loved ones after April 15.

Finance and Success

You're in the midst of fulfilling your new commitment as the month opens and Jupiter's cycle peaks on April 3. There are two more months of increased activity before you reach your new normal. The eclipse on April 8 suggests that you can benefit greatly in the long run by making some larger-than-usual expenditures over the next six months. Travel may be involved.

Rewarding Days

1, 2, 5, 6, 9, 10, 11, 14, 15, 16, 23, 24, 25, 28, 29

Challenging Days

12, 13, 19, 20, 21, 26, 27

Pisces/May

Planetary Hotspots

Inner development is highlighted when Chiron starts its five-month retrograde period in your Twelfth House on May 8. Events may occur that relate to areas in which you have been making sacrifices for others. This is a part of your spiritual path—the need to serve others—but it's time to let go of pursuits that hold you and the recipient of your services back. Neptune turning retrograde on May 19 further underscores this process and pushes you to let go of old forms. Have faith that new ones will replace them.

Wellness and Keeping Fit

Your energy level is up now, but don't let that lead you to recklessness. Accidents, burns, or injuries could ensue, especially around May 15. Compensate by focusing on staying emotionally balanced and doing only one thing at a time. You could be vulnerable to illness around May 8 and 19.

Love and Life Connections

You are discovering that some of your relationships are difficult because people are not meeting you halfway. This becomes a source of irritation as Mars enters your sign, and you will seek to rectify matters in no uncertain terms. This is not an unkind thing—rather it's necessary in order to take care of yourself. Just understand that you've accepted the situation for a long time without balking, so it's not all their fault.

Finance and Success

You'll be wanting to work in the background now in order to get all your work done, and you may be able to do just that as the planets assist you. You're beginning to see just how much work you set out for yourself. Whereas before you had faith that you could do it, now the reality of completing it is emerging.

Rewarding Days

2, 3, 4, 7, 8, 11, 12, 13, 21, 22, 26, 27, 30, 31

Challenging Days

9, 10, 16, 17, 18, 23, 24, 25

Pisces/June

Planetary Hotspots

Jupiter's return to forward motion on June 5 signals the end of your intensified efforts to increase your income. You'll begin to see the rewards of your work in the days, months, and years to come. The culmination of Pluto's cycle occurs on June 13, coinciding with a peak of activity in career at the same time that your home life calls you. Uranus's retrograde begins on June 14, and the pace of self-development quickens.

Wellness and Keeping Fit

You'll work more efficiently if you take a little time here and there for leisure activities. Pleasure is your healing balm this month. Take advantage of free moments whenever you can.

Love and Life Connections

Life is good and romance is in the air. Although you may be busy, you'll still have time to share with your loved ones. Children will also be a special source of joy. Situations at home pull you away from business or career around June 14. There may be a repair needed, or a family member may need extra support.

Finance and Success

You're hunkered down for intense effort in order to get your work done, but disruptions occur around June 13, 14, and 25. They will probably not take you away from your project for long, however, and your most intense work will be completed by then anyway. You're over the hump financially, and now you can move ahead with Phase Two of your plan. Added expenses may arise around June 25.

Rewarding Days

3, 4, 8, 9, 18, 19, 22, 23, 26, 27, 30

Challenging Days

5, 6, 7, 13, 14, 20, 21

Pisces/July

Planetary Hotspots

The issues surrounding the service work you do for others become more challenging in the latter half of July, as Saturn enters your Sixth House and contacts Chiron starting on July 16. Critical dates are July 21, 22, 23, 28, and 31, as Mars and the Sun add highlights to the process. Mercury enters its three-week retrograde on July 22, further increasing activity in these areas.

Wellness and Keeping Fit

Your health may weaken if you allow the pressures of the work you do for others to get to you. Besides setting boundaries on how much you attempt to do, it's important to make sure you get your full allowance of sleep and eat a high-nutrition diet. Since the main planetary show takes place in your health houses, you could experience a health crisis no matter what you're doing at work. This could be the flare-up of a chronic condition that you are already aware of. If you've been diligent in working toward balance in this area, problems can be avoided. Key dates are July 16, 21 through 23, and 28.

Love and Life Connections

Blessedly, relationships are not a hot spot right now for you. With so much change in other areas, it's good to know that you can rely on those close to you for support.

Finance and Success

Your workload may go ballistic after July 15. This is a signal to ask for support rather than soldiering on alone. You may need to put in extra hours—not a problem if this is not a regular habit. Bringing in temporary help may be the solution.

Rewarding Days

1, 2, 5, 6, 7, 15, 16, 19, 20, 23, 24, 28, 29

Challenging Days

3, 4, 10, 11, 12, 17, 18, 30, 31

Pisces/August

Planetary Hotspots

The chaotic feel of last month carries over to August, peaking on August 8, when Neptune reaches the culmination of its cycle. You'll feel close to being overwhelmed by your responsibilities then, but this feeling will dissipate rapidly as the challenges are overcome soon after August 15. Relationship dynamics become more startling toward the end of the month, when Uranus's cycle peaks in your solar Seventh House.

Wellness and Keeping Fit

You cannot give to others without regard for your own well-being. Your health may still be in "recovery mode" until mid-month. You'll be able to get back to your regular routine then—perhaps with some modifications to accommodate recent challenges.

Love and Life Connections

It's time to renegotiate your agreements with your loved ones. You're discovering how far you can push yourself, and it's not as far as you thought. If you are going to continue to progress on your current path, you'll need more support and understanding from those you love, and it's okay to ask for that, even if it creates a temporary imbalance in your favor.

Finance and Success

Confusion and chaos in your work life may reign around August 8 as Neptune's cycle peaks. It's important now to keep a balance between meeting your own needs and attempting to meet those of others. By August 15 your rhythm of life essentially returns to normal. You may need to renegotiate some agreements and deadlines at the end of the month after the dust settles.

Rewarding Days

1, 2, 3, 11, 12, 13, 16, 17, 20, 21, 24, 25, 29, 30

Challenging Days

6, 7, 8, 14, 15, 26, 27, 28

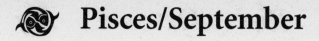

Pisces/September

Planetary Hotspots

Pluto's in the spotlight as its retrograde period ends on September 2. Activity in your career or business intensified as this date passes, but when the dust settles you'll see how much progress you've made through your consistent efforts since 1995. It's wise to stay attuned to commerce and written communications this month, as Mars will begin its retrograde on October 1 in your Third House, lasting three months. Keep in mind that misunderstandings are likely to occur, or that you may overcommit yourself and get overwhelmed by data and paperwork.

Wellness and Keeping Fit

This is a good time to get in the habit of driving close to the speed limit, especially in your own neighborhood. When Mars turns retrograde next month (and even before), you may be more vulnerable to accidents or getting caught for traffic violations. Keep yourself and others safe by giving this a little more thought now, so you're used to your new habits by the end of the month.

Love and Life Connections

Keep your ear to the ground this month, especially when it comes to your connections with extended family, brothers, and sisters. They may need extra assistance in some way in the not-too-distant future. This ties in with Mars, which enters its retrograde October 1.

Finance and Success

Plans for success that you hatched last December are now nearly complete. You can see how well you've done at accomplishing your goals—and whether they were worth accomplishing. As you enter the last phase of Pluto's cycle, you'll be looking back to see how far you've come and what's still missing; then you'll be making new plans in December for the coming year.

Rewarding Days

8, 9, 12, 13, 16, 17, 20, 21, 25, 26

Challenging Days

3, 4, 10, 11, 22, 23, 24, 30

Pisces/October

Planetary Hotspots

Mars's retrograde starts on October 1, and you may take on a writing or commercial project that requires a great deal of extra effort—perhaps too much. The eclipses on October 3 and 17 deepen this effect, but also suggest that the potential benefits will last for a long time—perhaps years—if you can pull it off. When Chiron goes direct on October 5, five months of healing the groups you feel devoted to are over. In the next three months you can tie up loose ends in those efforts. The best part, though, is the start of Jupiter's new cycle on October 22 in your Ninth House of travel and contacts with foreign cultures and ideas.

Wellness and Keeping Fit

As Mars turns retrograde on the October 1, be on your guard when traveling close to home. You may be involved in low-speed car or pedestrian accidents. You are also more likely to be cited for traffic violations over the next three months, so it is a good time to observe the traffic laws very carefully. You're given a clean bill of health as Neptune returns to forward motion on October 26.

Love and Life Connections

This is a great time to take a vacation with your loved ones and invest some time in the relationships that have helped you over many obstacles. You need the replenishment, and so do those you are close to.

Finance and Success

Travel and other ways of reaching beyond your current horizons can be used to increase your prosperity over the coming year as Jupiter enters its new cycle on October 22 in your Ninth House. The eclipses on October 3 and 17 reveal how you're doing with your financial management plan, and a new set of possibilities occurs to you.

Rewarding Days
1, 5, 6, 9, 10, 14, 15, 18, 19, 22, 23, 24

Challenging Days
7, 8, 20, 21, 27, 28, 29

Pisces/November

Planetary Hotspots

Three planetary events occur in mid-month. Mercury enters its last retrograde of the year on November 14, this time in your Tenth House, coinciding with an increase in career or business activity. Uranus's retrograde ends on November 15, and you can see how much progress you've made in your self-development process over the past eight months. Saturn enters its retrograde on November 22, making you aware of responsibilities you can or must take on to complete the next step in the development of your work, both to support your own success and to provide service to others.

Wellness and Keeping Fit

You see a need to exert more discipline in managing your health. Ferret out those therapeutic eating habits and find replacement therapies—a cup of tea or a walk instead of a dish of ice cream. Most importantly, whatever you decide, write it down. It will be easier to remember what to do because it will take more definite form, even if you never look at the paper again.

Love and Life Connections

You're in the mood to get rid of clutter, and you can use this time to eliminate things in your home that you no longer need. Even before Mercury turns retrograde on November 14 you can feel the urge, see the things you can pass on to others, recycle, or discard. A clean house reflects a clear mind.

Finance and Success

Mercury retrograde in your Tenth House heralds a period of intensity in your career, as you catch up on duties that you left incomplete while you were focused on other tasks. It's a great time to get organized, clean out old files, and make way for new ideas. As your career has shifted, so too should the things that support your career.

Rewarding Days
1, 2, 6, 7, 10, 11, 14, 15, 19, 20, 28, 29, 30

Challenging Days
3, 4, 5, 16, 17, 18, 24, 25

Pisces/December

Planetary Hotspots

The planets move into a state of release this month, and the tension in your life relaxes accordingly. Mercury turn forward in its path on December 3, and the fever pitch of career activity cools off. Mars does the same on December 9, and situations concerning your written communications and commercial activities move into the background. Pluto starts its new cycle in your Tenth House on December 15. This allows you to get in touch with new ideas for furthering your career. Venus ups the power on your inner growth process when it starts its retrograde on December 24, lasting six weeks.

Wellness and Keeping Fit

Now you feel like you can celebrate the holidays, although not with the old unhealthy patterns of eating or living. You're wary of the temptations that the holidays bring, but you'll just have to do your best and treat every new day as fresh, with no mistakes in it.

Love and Life Connections

When Venus turns retrograde, as it does on December 24, it ordinarily involves renegotiating agreements with others. This retrograde is about renegotiating with yourself. You will instinctively be drawn to ponder your own love for yourself and how you treat yourself. This will profoundly affect your relationships with others—more so than any external changes that could be brought about.

Finance and Success

If you've felt bound up by paperwork over the past two months, you'll be relieved to know that you'll feel the energy moving again after December 9. You've got some new ideas about how to put forth your message to others, and you can begin to execute them after that time. New career goals emerge in your consciousness around December 15—more from what you don't want than from what you do.

Rewarding Days
3, 4, 7, 8, 11, 12, 13, 16, 17, 26, 27, 30, 31

Challenging Days
1, 2, 14, 15, 21, 22, 28, 29

PISCES ACTION TABLE

These dates reflect the best—but not the only—times for success and ease in these activities, according to your Sun sign.

	JAN	FEB	MAR	APR	MAY	JUN	JUL	AUG	SEPT	OCT	NOV	DEC
Move					28-31	1-11						
Start a class					12-28							
Join a club	10-30											
Ask for a raise	10-31	26-28	1-22								5-30	1-14
Look for work						28-30	1-22	16-31	1-20	31	1-13	13-31
Get pro advice	1, 27-29	23-25	23, 24	19-21	16-18	13, 14	10-12	6-8	3, 4, 30	1, 27, 28	24, 25	21, 22
Get a loan	2-4, 30, 31	26, 27	25-27	22, 23	19, 20	15-17	13, 14	9, 10	5-7	2-4, 30, 31	26, 27	23-25
See a doctor	30, 31	1-28	1-5			28-30	1-22	16-31	1-20			
Start a diet		1-28	1-5			28-30	1-22	16-31	1-4			
End relationship		23-25										
Buy clothes						3-28						
Get a makeover		16-28	1-22									
New romance						3-28	5-7					
Vacation	5, 6	1, 2, 28	1, 2, 28, 29	24, 25	21, 22	18, 19	15, 16	11-13	8, 9, 11-30	1-8	1, 2, 28-30	26, 27

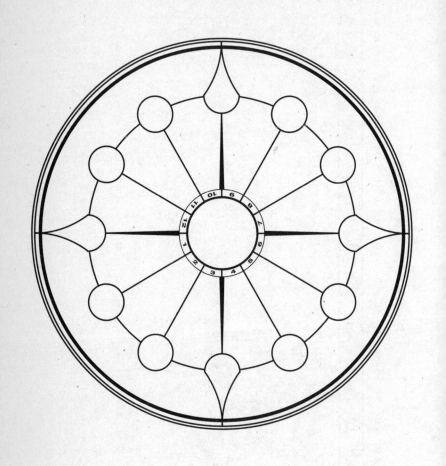

Articles

Contributors

Nina Lee Braden

Stephanie Clement

Alice DeVille

Sasha Fenton

Leeda Alleyn Pacotti

Bruce Scofield

Rowena Wall

Around the Chart
Your Personal Sun

by Sasha Fenton

Even if you know next to nothing about astrology, you will realize that the hour in which you were born has a modifying effect on your character. Indeed, it is a combination of the time, place, and date of birth that sets the position of the Ascendant (also known as the rising sign). You may also be aware that the Ascendant can be responsible for the way that others see you. This is true, of course, but there is another factor that can cause variations in personality, even between people born under same Sun sign, and this is the actual position of the Sun in your chart. Finding the Ascendant requires specialized astrology software or tricky calculations, but finding a reasonable approximation of the Sun's position at your birth is a piece of cake.

Naturally, there are many other astrological factors that help to make up the component parts of your personality, but the position of the Sun in the sky when you were born is in a league of its own. Fortunately, this is extremely easy to work out. I will now show you how to construct a simple little chart that will show just where your

Sun was at your time of birth, and in a moment I will also show you how to interpret this.

Instructions for Making Your Chart

Take a piece of paper and a pencil and draw a large circle. Using a ruler, draw a line down the circle from the top rim to the bottom rim, and then draw another line across the circle from one rim to the other. This gives you a circle with four quadrants. You now need some kind of symbol to represent the Sun. Astrologers use a small circle with a dot in it, so that is as good as anything—but you can use a smiley face or even the word "Sun" if you like.

Now consider your time of birth and place your symbol on the chart according to the following instructions:

- If you were born close to dawn, put your symbol somewhere near the end of the line on the left-hand side of your circle.
- If you were born around sunset, put your symbol near the end of the line on the right-hand side of the circle.
- If you were born close to noon, put it near the top of the circle.
- If you were born close to midnight, put it near the bottom of the circle.
- If you were born between dawn and noon, place your symbol somewhere in the upper left-hand quadrant.
- If you were born between noon and sunset, place your symbol somewhere in the upper right-hand quadrant.
- If you were born between sunset and midnight, place your symbol somewhere in the lower right-hand quadrant.
- If you were born between midnight and dawn, place your symbol somewhere in the lower left-hand quadrant.

If you are really finicky, you might even be able to place your Sun symbol in exactly the right place for your time of birth, but you will need to consider the relative length of the day or night when you were born. For example, the further we get from the equator and the closer we are to either pole, the longer the days in summer and longer the nights in winter. There is a discrepancy for those born during Daylight Saving or British Summer Time because you will need to deduct an hour from your time of birth. However, this is such a simple system that even a rough birth time will suffice.

Now that you have placed your Sun in the right quadrant, read the following to see how this affects your personality.

Sun on the Left Line

If your Sun symbol is to the left of the chart, the Sun was either about to rise or had just risen when you were born. An astrologer would say that your Sun was close to your Ascendant. This gives you an ambitious and self-centered personality. A birth that took place before dawn would make you bubbly and outgoing—and you would be easy to spot at a party or in a crowd. This would be even more evident if you were born under a fire sign, such as Aries, Leo, or Sagittarius. A birth that takes place after sunrise makes for a shyer and more retiring outer manner. Even so, you will still be keen to promote your ideas and to reach out for what you consider to be important. When some signs (Taurus, Leo, Libra, Sagittarius) are combined with a dawn birth, you can make your mark in the fields of music or as an entertainer.

You are self-motivated and, to some extent, also self-centered. You do not wait for others to tell you whether you are worthwhile because you know you how valuable you are. You do not wait for things to happen because you prefer to make them happen. You take responsibility for your own life and you are happy to earn good money and provide a good lifestyle for your loved ones. This is even more evident if you were born under the cardinal signs of Aries, Cancer, Libra, or Capricorn.

Although you are happy to provide for your family in a financial sense, if you were born a little before dawn, you would be disinclined to give up your career and aspirations in order to serve your family. If you were born a little after dawn, you will be shyer and less outgoing, and much more inclined to give time and practical care to others. You may also be intuitive and quite psychic at times. The Sun on this line suggests that you can live alone if necessary, although you may prefer not to.

Sun on the Right Line

If your Sun is on the right-hand line, it is close to your Descendant. This means that you tend to measure your value by some outside means, such as the opinion of others. You may only really feel worthwhile when you receive approval for the work that you produce, or perhaps only when lovers and friends tell you that you are great. It is sometimes hard for you to see how important you are in your own right.

You are a giving person, and this is even more so if you are born under the mutable signs of Gemini, Virgo, Sagittarius, and Pisces. You could be very self-sacrificing if you were born under the water signs of Cancer, Scorpio, and Pisces, and in this case you may expend far too much energy on the needs of others. You could be really driven to please a boss or to be seen as a success if you were born under the signs of Leo, Virgo, or Capricorn. It is unlikely that you would live alone, and you may find yourself with demanding or difficult partners at times. If you have the right partner and the right boss, you will feel better about yourself, but you really need to develop a strong sense of self if you are to avoid being swamped by those who take advantage of your good nature.

Sun on the Top Line

This is an ambitious placement, as your Sun is close to what astrologers call the Midheaven—literally where the Sun was at its highest in the sky on that day. If you were born before noon, you will be especially keen to achieve goals and to reach your aims and aspirations in a worldly sense. You may marry a person who is older than you or who is from the "right side of the tracks." You have an eye for detail, so you may be keen on collecting antiques or knowing about such things as stamps, coins, and hallmarks. If you were born a little after noon, you may be equally keen to expand your knowledge—but this time through higher education, travel, or spiritual studies. You could be drawn to teaching or instructing others, and you may settle in a foreign land for a while or even on a permanent basis.

Your ambition will be greater if you belong to the cardinal group of Aries, Cancer, Libra, and Capricorn. Your desire to expand your mental, physical, and spiritual horizons will be greater if you are born under the mutable signs of Gemini, Virgo, Sagittarius, and Pisces. It is unlikely that you would work from home or even wish to spend too much time indoors, as your rightful place is out in the world. You may take up a career in politics, especially if you were born under the signs of Aries, Taurus, Leo, Aquarius, or Pisces. A parent may be a wonderful role model, and he or she would have encouraged you to make a success of yourself. If born before noon, you may remain close to older members of the family, but if born after noon you would prefer to keep your distance.

Sun on the Bottom Line

If you were born with the Sun close to the nadir, your intuitive powers are strong and you may be quite psychic. You have a powerful urge to understand where people are coming from. Once you have learned to do this, you may become a psychologist, counselor, or a successful astrologer—or perhaps just a really reliable friend. To some extent you seek a spiritual pathway, and you may even end up working in the spiritual or psychic arena. Even if you do not take up spiritual matters, you will always need a spiritual or meaningful element in your life. This is enhanced if you were born under the signs of Cancer, Leo, Virgo, Scorpio, Sagittarius, Aquarius, or Pisces. You may be interested in history and the past. This may be on an academic level or it could lead to an interest in genealogy, antiques, or even a fascination with past lives. This will be even more emphasized if you were born with the Sun in Cancer, Virgo, or Scorpio.

You are probably conscious that your childhood (and perhaps even a past life) had a major influence on your personality and your actions, and the circumstances of this may somehow have robbed you of self-esteem. Even if you were born under an outgoing sign such as Aries, Leo, or Sagittarius, you are quieter and more retiring than others born under those signs. If you were born under a "quiet" sign such as Capricorn, Aquarius, or Pisces, this would be even more marked. Your parents and background exert an inescapable influence. While some of this is helpful, some of their behavior will be demanding, embarrassing, draining, or destructive. You may marry someone who spends a lot of time at work, or they may socialize a great deal or spend hours yakking with people on the phone. Your partner may never understand your need for peace, privacy, and the time and space that you require for reading and thinking. It is possible that you will choose to work from home. People gravitate to your home—and while you do receive invitations to visit others, you somehow prefer it when the world comes to your door. People bring their problems to you. You must place some limits on this if your abode is not to become a free rescue-center, with you acting as an unpaid social worker.

Sun in the Upper-Left Quadrant

Unless you were born very soon after sunrise, you are a friendly soul with plenty of ambition for yourself or for the group of people with whom you associate. The closer to the dawn that you were born, the more likely you are to be self-effacing, self-sacrificing, and apt to hide your feelings from others. The closer your time of birth is to noon, the more ambitious and worldly you will be. Any position in this quadrant gives you a desire to shine and an idealistic streak that pushes you to help other people when you can.

If you were born during mid-morning, there will be a touch of eccentricity and originality about you. You may be unrealistic if the air signs of Gemini, Libra, or Aquarius are your Sun sign. You could become involved in charity work, local government, or committees of various kinds. You will always have many influential friends, and if you were born under the signs of Aries, Taurus, Leo, or Scorpio you could aim to become part of an up-market in-crowd. You will be truly eccentric and less interested in impressing others or having powerful friends if you were born under the signs of Sagittarius, Aquarius, and Pisces. A parent will have exerted a powerful influence on you, encouraging you to reach for the stars—in some cases, the stars of astrology.

Sun in the Upper-Right Quadrant

You can be quite intense, and this intensity can take one of a variety of forms, depending how close to noon or sunset you were born. If your birth time occurred shortly after noon, you are a seeker after the truth, and you may travel or read a great deal in order to garner information, insight and knowledge. A birth time in the middle of the quadrant denotes that your emotions and feelings are extremely intense. You might become outraged by injustice in the wider world, and you are also extremely aware of hurt on a personal level. The Sun here indicates that you can love very deeply, but you can also bear grudges and feel real hatred toward those who have betrayed your trust.

You are intuitive—and this is no bad thing, because your life will always be wrapped up in the concerns of others. The intensity of your feelings will be strongest if you were born under the signs of Cancer, Leo, Scorpio, and Capricorn. However, you could be inclined to keep your feelings under wraps most of the time, unless you are provoked beyond endurance. You may have some quite amazing ups and downs in your finances, mainly due to the actions and behavior of those with whom you connect in a financial sense.

Sun in the Lower-Right Quadrant

If you were born shortly after sunset, you may be too hard working and self-sacrificial for your own good, and you could even make a martyr of yourself. This tendency will be emphasized if you were born under the signs of Leo, Virgo, Scorpio, Capricorn, or Pisces. Anything that relates to health will interest you, and you could become involved with giving or receiving alternative therapies. This is especially so if you were born under the signs of Virgo, Scorpio, or Pisces.

A later birth makes you more fun loving and extremely family oriented, but the love of your life will be your children rather than your lovers and partners. A mid-evening placement will add an entrepreneurial streak, and this is especially so if you were born under the signs of Aries, Gemini, Leo, or Capricorn. It could draw you into the world of music or entertainment if your Sun is in Taurus, Leo, Libra, or Pisces.

The closer to midnight your birth, the more likely you are to work from your home. Many people in the psychic and mystical arenas are born around midnight, so this is likely to be the case for you too. Later birth times suggest that parental figures have had a strong influence in your life, both for good and ill.

Sun in the Lower-Left Quadrant

If you were born shortly after midnight, your greatest need is to communicate and to get around and meet people. This could direct you toward a career as a writer, journalist, teacher, or someone whose work takes you from place to place. A powerful intuition and a keen interest in the nature and behavior of others might take you down a spiritual or psychological pathway. This placement might make you keen to become a good amateur astrologer—and perhaps even a professional one. This is even more the case if you were born under the signs of Gemini, Leo, Sagittarius, or Aquarius. A birth time that is closer to midnight encourages you to become a back-room person or a researcher who writes or gets messages across on the Internet rather than in a face-to-face manner. This would be even more powerful if you were born under the sign of Virgo, Capricorn, or Aquarius.

A birth later in the night makes for quite a different character, because you will be keen on providing financial security for yourself and for your family. While you may still be a good communicator, you are also interested in creating beauty in one of many forms, and you may work with your hands. This may make you keen on decorating, gardening, photography, hair or nail art, or on making clothes or soft furnishings. You may be drawn to work in the fashion industry or the worlds of art, music, or dancing. The drive to create interesting images and things of beauty will be strongest if you were born under the signs of Taurus, Cancer, Leo, Libra, Scorpio, and Pisces. You need your own bank account and your own savings plan. You get jittery when you are dependent upon others, or if the state of your finances fluctuates due to the way that others handle money. You have a powerful drive to ensure that you will be financially secure throughout your life.

If you were born shortly before dawn, you are self-motivated, ambitious, and determined to make your mark in the world. The closer this takes you to the Ascendant (see Sun on the left-hand line) the more powerful the urge to succeed.

For Further Reading

Camilleri, Stephanie. *The House Book: The Influence of the Planets in the Houses*. St. Paul: Llewellyn, 1999.

Breaking It Down
Sun Sign Decans

by Stephanie Clement

Have you ever wondered why you are so different from your friends who have the same Sun sign? They approach life so differently from you, it's as if they were actually born under a different sign. Maybe they were—in a way.

Each sign of the zodiac contains thirty degrees. The Sun moves through the zodiac about one degree each day, so that it moves all the way around the circle in a year. Astrologers divide each sign into increments, called decanates or decans, which means "ten." Each ten-degree segment of a sign has a distinct flavor all its own. The sign influence is there for all thirty degrees, but it is overlaid with a secondary influence that colors its expression. This means that a person born early in the sign will express the energy differently from someone born late in the sign. Let's look at those differences. You may want to make a list of birthdays of your family and friends so you can see deeper into their personalities as you read along. In some cases you may not be sure which decan someone's Sun is in, so read both the previous and following delineations to get the full picture.

Aries

Aries is the sign of enthusiasm, boldness, and courage. Aries people always seem to know exactly what they want, although they can change their minds and go in a new direction without a second thought. Aries individuals are inspired by ideas that have not yet manifested in concrete reality.

First Decan: March 21 to March 31

The raw enthusiasm of Aries charges forward without first scoping out the terrain. There is an intense focus that prevents you from seeing the larger perspective. You may achieve your goals in life, but unless you find a way to broaden your viewpoint, you will also miss a lot. You may even miss the deeper emotional or spiritual meaning in the focused activities you do so well. Take a deep breath: you will smell the roses!

Second Decan: April 1 to April 10

You express the essence and exuberance of youth in everything you do. You are full of passion for life and everything it offers. As you experience life, you begin to elevate your desires from basic hunger and lust to a more discriminating level. Hunger becomes the basis for discriminating tastes. Lust is the forerunner of unselfish love and true compassion.

Third Decan: April 11 to April 20

Your special talent is sharing your enthusiasm with others. You latch on to an idea, use your intuition to see where it will take you, and then inspire others to follow. You denounce lies and corruption wherever you find them. When you follow the clear light of truth, you become a hero of sorts. Other people admire your strength and determination in the face of opposition.

Taurus

Taurus is more stable than Aries. This sign reflects endurance, persistence, and a practical outlook on life. If you can see it and touch it, a thing is real. If not, then you have to consider it on a soul level to determine its value. Taurus seeks financial and material security.

First Decan: April 21 to May 1

You manifest the fertility of springtime in everything you do. You are quick to invest your creative energy in a new activity. You are also quick to leave an overly emotional environment, or one that spells physical danger. You have the power within you to heal yourself and others. This strength grows as you turn away from purely material desires.

Second Decan: May 2 to May 11

The second decanate of Taurus exemplifies the steadfastness of the warrior who fights a righteous battle. You struggle with whatever life sends. You emerge victorious by avoiding problems that are not truly yours, and involving yourself with problems that call upon your consciousness—those you identify as being your true tasks in life. You become a master of your environment.

Third Decan: May 12 to May 21

You take the creative power of the earth sign Taurus and turn it to your will. You learn to control your own desires and direct them in skillful ways. As you guide your powers carefully, you develop the habits of care and attention. The keys to your success are mastery and control.

Gemini

Geminis are versatile and adaptable. They appear to flit from flower to flower like a butterfly, but inside they study their world and grasp new subjects readily. Because they love change, they also enjoy travel. Geminis absorb ideas from different eras and cultures, and form their own belief systems.

First Decan: May 22 to June 1

Whatever work you do, and whatever games you enjoy, you are always seeking the truth. This may not be an outwardly expressed goal. Your mind is always looking for the objective truth in the environment outside yourself. Part of your journey through life includes the wish that you may help others to understand the world around them and to seek their own truth.

Second Decan: June 2 to June 11

You think at light speed. Your ideas cover the fullest range you can possibly manage. You also listen to the inner voice of intuition. Objective reality only comes alive for you when you fuse the facts with the information flowing from deep within your psyche. This marriage within the mind is reflected in human companionship, which is nearly as necessary as food for you.

Third Decan: June 13 to June 21

You are willing to entertain thoughts and feelings that emerge from within your heart and mind. You value truth, but you value understanding even more. Thus you can be a master of dream interpretation, and certainly you pay attention to the nuances of language and symbolism in every communication. You may be adept at learning foreign languages or computer programming languages.

Cancer

Cancers are nurturers. Whether male or female, they know how to care for others. Their mantra could be "stay in the flow," as they enjoy life best when it moves predictably. Change is all right if it can be foreseen and planned. A comfortable home is cultivated, and so is time for contemplation. This sign reflects an emotional nature.

First Decan: June 22 to July 2

Your emotions are like the tides, ebbing and flowing in a predictable, if not regular, manner. If you follow the urges of your emotional extremes, you flounder amid dark or excessive moods and desires. If instead you watch the ebb and flow of feelings, you can maintain forward momentum while accommodating the changing feelings within yourself. You don't drag others along unless you want to.

Second Decan: July 3 to July 12

You seek to accomplish something of significance in your life and work. You want people to remember you for your positive, creative actions, and not for temporary lapses or errors. You must look within yourself to find the path toward significance. In the process, you face your own demons and reclaim the energy they have stolen from you. Then forward progress is swift.

Third Decan: July 13 to July 22

Your life is a constant series of choices among the diverging paths you see in your future. Occasionally you find yourself in a raging flood of emotions, and other times you choose a meandering peaceful interlude. Many times you feel that any path would have led you in the right direction. Occasionally the river takes several channels, and you are challenged to choose without being able to foresee the outcome.

Leo

Leos want to be in charge—of themselves, of you, and of the world. Their creative efforts often show inspiration from unseen sources. They make good leaders when they infuse others with their vibrant energy. They tend to be successful on their own merits. They have lots of good ideas.

First Decan: July 23 to August 2

You have the heat of desire within you. This creative desire is not limited to any one area of your life—it can affect everything you do. You discover that by focusing on admirable desires you make swifter and better progress. Eventually you seek a position of leadership where you can demonstrate what you have learned. Then desire is elevated to the level of aspiration.

Second Decan: August 3 to August 13

Children play a specially significant role in your life, even if you have none of your own. You have a gift for teaching, and sharing this gift brings great joy into your life. The good leader rejoices in the success of his or her followers. You seek to create change around you and you use your energy to assure that these changes are beneficial to everyone involved.

Third Decan: August 14 to August 23

You have the capacity to rule your world. Will you do that by sneaking and stealing? Probably not, because you can do far better by allowing your associates to do their own best work. You seek to satisfy your own desire for love and material comfort by doing your own best work too. Focus your thoughts on the most positive aspects of the present and the future.

Virgo

Virgos like order at the level of details. Their closets and kitchen cupboards are always organized, and so are their minds. They have a sense of propriety, and they like rituals that respect each individual. They can focus too much on details and miss the larger picture and the opportunities it offers.

First Decan: August 24 to September 3

You make the most of life by carefully examining the many opportunities before you. You benefit when you discern the path most likely to achieve success. However, you also remember the past, and can take a step back in order to change direction and move forward toward even greater success. You know more than one way to handle obstacles.

Second Decan: September 4 to September 13

You handle responsibility well when you first assess a task and develop a plan of action. You scope out the details and sort out ideas and methods that work best for you, regardless of what other people are doing. It may not be an accident that Labor Day often falls within this decanate. Focus on your work and avoid needless criticism of others.

Third Decan: September 14 to September 23

You experience tribulations, just as everyone does, and you have the capacity to overcome them and move forward. Your special methods include perseverance through painful situations, knowing there will be an end, and faith that there is a reason for the trials you experience. Out of each experience is born the next golden opportunity, and you keep long-range goals in mind every step of the way.

Libra

Libras seek balance in their thinking and in their approach to the world. They consider harmony to be an essential of life. Each relationship is precious to them. As they relate to others, they are developing a sense of themselves. They seem to give in easily, but in reality they are choosing when and where to give.

First Decan: September 24 to October 4

The Sun here shows you the clear path of balance. You know the perils of selfishness and you know the joys of selflessness. Your relationships are less foolish when you seek harmony, and you know the healing power of love to improve the lives of the people around you. When you attune yourself to your partner, you share thoughts and feelings without any need for words.

Second Decan: October 5 to October 14

You grow in power when you honor both your conscious thought processes and your inner intuitive capacity. Using both aspects of your mind allows you to maintain your position in the world and not succumb to the stresses that inevitably come your way. Each difficulty you face strengthens your resolve to deal fairly with everyone in your life.

Third Decan: October 15 to October 24

You are capable of great good. You are also capable of creating disasters in your life if you exploit other people and act on greedy desires. If you seek to help others as you care for yourself and your family, then your efforts bear fruit. By benefiting others you allow positive energy to flow through everything you do. You don't give in, you simply give.

Scorpio

Scorpios have deep, intense emotions. However, they don't always reveal everything they are thinking or feeling. Sometimes they bury feelings so deep, even they don't know the feelings are there. Scorpios investigate their worlds to understand how and why change occurs. They benefit from meditation and soothing music.

First Decan: October 24 to November 3

You may struggle to find ways to express your creative energy effectively. Sexual activity is not the only avenue available to you. You may want to practice meditation or follow a religious path to find other creative outlets that are just as compelling as sexual activity and childbearing. Try to be open to the creative possibilities all around you.

Second Decan: November 4 to November 13

You are fully capable of understanding the dark side of life. While you probably don't engage in black magic or murder, you understand something of the motivations that lead others to these acts. Because you understand the dark side, you accept the responsibility for transcendence. You sacrifice the animal within you to attain greater spirituality.

Third Decan: November 13 to November 22

You have the capacity to attain the highest level in your career or other creative interests. You experience fear, but you also have the courage to move through fear to a place of accomplishment. Your life is filled when you are helping others not to make tons of money, but to fulfill your own desire to help other people. You understand hidden forces in nature.

Sagittarius

Sagittarians have many interests and can be easily distracted from a task by anything colorful, loud, or emotionally charged. They are always ready for action and love sports. This sign often exhibits two distinctly different personalities: one cheerful and adaptable, the other more thoughtful or even pessimistic.

First Decan: November 23 to December 2

You are most successful when you align yourself harmonically with your surroundings. This means that you must first understand your internal harmony and then find a sympathetic environment. Music may be a big part of your life, even if you are not yourself a musician. In appreciating musical harmony from others, you may discover your own inner tranquility.

Second Decan: December 3 to December 12

Although you are not a Scorpio, you have much of the intensity of that sign. Your best expression of life is one that rises above the ordinary and reaches for the highest spiritual potential. This means that everything you do, from eating to sex to study to action, comes from an inner reservoir of energy and expresses best through clarity of vision and high ideals.

Third Decan: December 13 to December 22

Born near the darkest time of the year, you appreciate the depth of night and the power of the dark. You also understand that the soul passes through the dark and into the light again. You very likely have considered reincarnation or other facets of the afterlife, and you have formulated a working model of the universe that accommodates your sense of life's continuity.

Capricorn

Capricorns climb for the fun of it. They want to be in control of their own lives, even as small children. There is a sense of caution when beginning something new, but the desire to reach the top overcomes their hesitation. This sign appreciates the value of cash and other rewards, and will work hard for advancement in life.

First Decan: December 23 to January 1

Just as the days lengthen around your birth date, your life tends to gain prominence as you get older. Your best plan is to act openly and directly without any deceit. You also find yourself in positions where you can be instrumental in correcting wrongs done by others.

Second Decan: January 2 to January 11

You find that the law of karma works in your life on a day to day basis. The more you understand this, the easier it is for you to avoid actions that cause harm to others. You also feel karmic results much more quickly than some people. You therefore seek to stay on a path going in a positive direction for you and for others around you. It's easier to think first than to repent later.

Third Decan: January 12 to January 21

You have the capacity to understand the interaction of personal selfishness and greater spiritual love. You can be selfish, but you are much happier when you are expressing love for the people and things in your life. Through love you transform all of your emotions into more positive energy. Your best alternative to negativity or pessimism is love.

Aquarius

Aquarians are always observing the people around them and learning new ways to use their tools and toys. They demand the chance to test new possibilities. They seldom follow the beaten path, preferring the adventure of something different. They often benefit through the efforts of others.

First Decan: January 22 to January 31

You have natural horse-sense. You are able to figure out ways to accomplish your goals without having to muscle your way through to the goal. Your intuitive ability can be sharpened through practice and attention. Your life is filled with joy when you experience the unusual. You don't pretend to understand everything about the world and its workings.

Second Decan: February 1 to February 10

Throughout your life you expand your consciousness by first experiencing the objective world, then dreaming great dreams, and finally by manifesting those dreams through action. Even the best dreams need to be rooted in something practical if they are to develop into anything more than dreams. You can benefit from the study of universal symbols.

Third Decan: February 11 to February 19

You have faced discord in your life. Were you able to find a way to get through it? Evidently—you are reading this article! Each difficulty you have faced has led you to the present, and future difficulties will lead you to even greater things. Without some discord we could not experience either equilibrium or satisfaction. Looking at your darker side permits a healthy mental balance.

Pisces

Quiet and somewhat solitary, Pisces people are happy to stand back and observe. They enjoy comfortable surroundings and can become overly insulated from the realities of the world. They perceive other people's feelings and intentions on the psychic level, and may see auras around people and objects.

First Decan: February 20 to February 29

You find that acts of selfishness only lead to dissatisfaction in your life. When you can adopt an expectant attitude, you find that as you give, you not only receive, but you receive ten times. This suggests that giving freely leads to getting all that you could possibly need. You benefit from finding a mark like the Pole Star and using it to guide your life and actions.

Second Decan: March 1 to March 10

A keynote to your understanding of life resides in the fact that all progress involves effort and some conflict. While you don't need to become a doormat for others to walk upon, you can benefit from cultivating the capacity to give freely to others. Be sure, if sacrifice is required, that you sacrifice yourself and not others. They have their own unique problems, and don't need yours.

Third Decan: March 11 to March 20

Born near the Spring Equinox, you experience the nearly equal length of day and night as a metaphor for balance in your life. You have the capacity for healing others when you have learned to balance energies within yourself. There is also a spiritual energy flow that works through you when you have set aside desire for personal aggrandizement and taken up conscious work to benefit others.

For Further Reading

Burk, Kevin. *Astrology: Understanding the Birth Chart*. St. Paul: Llewellyn, 2001.

George, Llewellyn. *Llewellyn's New A–Z Horoscope Maker and Interpreter: A Comprehensive Self-Study Course*. St. Paul: Llewellyn, 2004.

Sun Sign Finance

by Bruce Scofield

I n our age of money (you know—those green tickets we have to use to get things we want) we are often challenged to know exactly what to do with it when needs aren't so immediate. Much of the time, for many of us, money comes in with our paycheck and goes out with the bills, but sometimes there is a surplus. While it may seem reasonable to an Aquarian that such a surplus should be turned around to help those who don't have a surplus, the Scorpions among us may not see it that way. In fact, it is likely that most people who have a surplus want to hold on to their money and make it grow. But how? Herein lies the message of this article—one person's investment strategy may be another person's nightmare. Personality is expressed in everything, including where we put our money. There is no one right answer about how to invest, but there are important correlations between investment strategies and one's Sun sign, as we will see.

The Basics

Before we get to such distinctions, let's just talk about money. There is a wide range of decisions about money that people in our age routinely make. Many choose to not think about an investment strategy at all, and so they leave their money in the local bank and draw under 1 percent interest. As long as they don't know very much about money and investing, they will be happy. While it may seem ridiculously cautious to most aggressive investors, this is still an investment strategy, albeit a very conservative one—and it would have outperformed most other investment strategies in 2000 and 2001 after the tech bubble burst. Most other years, however, it doesn't come close to what other investments return. An even more conservative investment strategy is to put your money in cash in a container and bury it in your backyard. I've known people who have done this, and it does save a lot of paperwork. Like keeping your money in the local bank, it is a way of holding on to your money—one that would have been a reasonably good move just a few years ago when the market dropped.

Most local banks offer certificates of deposit that have higher interest rates than checking and savings accounts. The only catch is that once you put your money in a CD, as they are called, you can't take it out until it reaches maturity. The longer the period of maturity, the higher the interest on the return. So the certificate of deposit is another very conservative investment vehicle that may appeal to those who want to keep their money local, make a few points more on interest, and have plenty of time on their hands.

Money market accounts offered by financial institutions invest in short-term securities and generally offer returns higher than a bank account. They are purchased at one dollar a share and may even come with a checkbook—but you can't cut a check for less than a fixed amount (for instance, five hundred dollars).

On the next rung up the investment ladder are bonds. Bonds are basically IOUs to either the government, your town or city, or a corporation. You give them your money, which they use to run their operations—and then they will give it back to you with some interest. In general, the amount of interest that a bond will pay varies inversely with interest rates. When one goes up, the other goes down. Bonds come in short, intermediate, and long term—a choice you need to make based on whether you are looking to make a little money on the side or are going for a long-term investment. In general, though, bonds are a fairly conservative investment strategy that return an interest rate that ranges from about what you'd get from your local bank to upwards of 10 percent.

Stocks are very popular investments and have, over the long term, earned investors higher return rates than bonds. When you buy a stock, you are buying a piece of a company. As a stockholder, you will receive an annual report from the company and you will be asked to vote on issues brought up by the board of directors. If your company grows, so does the value of your stocks—and if you decide to sell at that point, you will make a profit. But stock investing is very risky and stock prices can fall, or even crash.

There are conservative stocks, called blue chip stocks, that have a long history of steady growth despite economic fluctuations over the years. Many conservative investors will only buy these stocks. They will grow in value modestly most of the time—but they *will* generally grow. Other stocks may be far more risky. Technology stocks have a volatile record. In the late 1990s, many got rich buying and selling the new Internet stocks, which outperformed all other stocks in the market for a few years. But then they crashed—and crashed in a big way. Fortunes quickly made were quickly lost. There are also penny stocks (stocks whose share value amounts to just a few pennies) that some find appealing. A small investment buys a huge number of stocks, but there's always the long shot that the company issuing the stock will be fabulously successful and the penny stock will become a dollar stock.

Mutual funds are collections of stocks that are managed by a professional. When you invest in a mutual fund, you are merely adding your money to the pool of resources that is managed by the fund manager who then buys and sells stocks. Since the fund manager is a professional, you expect them to know what to do in various markets—you trust them to make the right decisions and you pay for their expertise when they scoop off a little from your account. This "fee" is normally around 1 percent, so if they are able to bring in returns of over 3 percent a year, you are still doing better than the bank. Many mutual funds have values that increase well over 10 percent a year in good markets, and for this reason they have become a very popular investment vehicle. But because they are composed of stocks, they can crash too. Mutual funds can be conservative, aggressive, or even socially responsible.

Gold and precious metals were once a popular and secure invest-ment. Today, advances in extracting metals have kept prices down and gold is no longer used as a standard for currency. Jewelry manu-facturing still requires precious metals, however, and jewelry is still a high-priced commodity that holds its value.

Real-estate investments have traditionally proven sound. While there are ups and downs in the real-estate market (many see an eighteen-year cycle), in general, property and buildings have increased in value. In recent times, with the stock market down, real estate has been a good investment.

Art and collectibles are often very good investments, but you have to know your materials. I once met a wealthy man who had put virtually no money in the bank, but instead had bought paint-ings. His judgment was apparently very good because when he began to sell them, the returns were astronomical. I've also known a few people who have done well with antiques, rare books, maps, and magazines.

Sun Sign Investments

Now we come to part two of this article: how the twelve Sun signs prefer to invest their money. As you may have noticed, the various forms of investing listed above come with varying degrees of risk. Some signs are clearly conservative, and asking them to put their money in a high risk investment vehicle is asking them to make themselves feel insecure. In general, the earth and water signs (Tau-rus, Cancer, Virgo, Scorpio, Capricorn, and Pisces) tend to be con-servative. On the other hand, some signs love a risk and would be completely bored with low-risk investments. In general, the fire and air signs (Aries, Gemini, Leo, Libra, Sagittarius, and Aquarius) tend to be risk-tolerant. While the following text describes the signs as if they were Sun signs, the descriptions will also apply to some extent to Moon signs and rising signs. Women take notice—you may find that your Moon sign is better described below. At the end of each section, some investment sectors are mentioned that may be of spe-cial interest to each Sun sign—and therefore make a good invest-ment. The more you know about what you invest in, the better you'll do over the long term.

Aries

People with the Sun in Aries are not natural investors. This is mainly because they generally don't think too far ahead and they like to keep their life simple—so they can turn on a dime when they want to. Some Aries types can be extremely suspicious of anything outside their world, and would prefer to keep their own money in their desk drawer. But if they do invest, they generally have no patience for a long wait and will tend to go for moderate- to high-risk investments—especially stocks and aggressive mutual funds. For some Aries types, money becomes a tool or weapon in the world of investments. They like to change things, moving money from one investment to another, and strive to keep up with the current market conditions. Very often they lose money because they don't want to wait—but more often quick money moves turn out to be exactly the right thing for them to do. Investing in stocks can become a kind of competition (something that Aries likes) or it can be an adventure. Any Aries that is confined to a small space will need an outlet for a risk-taking, adventurous personality, and trading stocks on a computer may meet these needs very well. One mistake often made by Aries investors is to not know when to stop taking risks and move their investments to safer havens during low-market periods. They just can't take the boredom of conservative investment vehicles and will try to put it off for as long as they can. Aries investors may want to look into manufacturing, energy and utilities, and sports-related business as potential areas of investment.

Taurus

This, the sign of money itself, loves to invest and see money grow. But Taurus types don't take big chances like the fire signs do. What Taurus signs like to do is put their money down and then wait. And wait. And wait. It could be thirty years or more, but they will eventually call in the investment—and guess what? They will have made a bundle! I know a Taurus (with Aries rising) who has invested only in utilities for fifty years and has done much better over that span than a Sagittarius I know who has had big wins, but also big losses, in the broader stock market. Still, the stock market can be jarring and upsetting, and many born under the sign of the bull will find themselves more comfortable with other investment strategies—particularly those that are more down to earth. Taurus is well suited to invest in real estate, property, and things of an earthy nature. The patience that real estate demands, and the sheer substance of it all, is very appealing to Taurus. Jewelry, fashion, and art are also good investments for Taurus—a sign that has an instinctive sense of what looks good. Also, agricultural and mining operations are appropriate for this sign, as these industries deal with the earth itself.

Gemini

Gemini is not a conservative sign, nor is it always a big risk-taking sign. What Gemini likes is diversification. The financial portfolio of a Gemini should include a little bit of everything. All kinds of investments are appealing to Geminis: the more they have, the more interesting investing as a process will become for them. But this Sun sign should also pay close attention when it comes to investing. Does the Gemini's financial advisor (who could be someone paid for advice, or maybe just a friend) know what he or she is talking about? Is there logic to what this person is saying? Gemini is easily influenced by others' ideas, and bad advice has sunk many a Gemini's boat. All things being equal, Gemini will do well investing in transportation and communications—this includes airlines, automobile manufacturers, and the media. Computer and software manufacturers may also be areas where Gemini types have some special insight, thus allowing them to develop a successful investment strategy.

Cancer

Like Taurus, Cancer is generally a low-risk investor. Many Cancer types simply hate to part with their money, and may store it in envelopes hidden throughout their homes. If they do invest in the stock market, it will probably be in a money-market fund or a mutual fund that has a reliable reputation. Also like Taurus signs, Cancers will wait for money to mature: they will not take it out if there will be any—even a very small—loss of value. Basically, Cancer types can be cheapskates of the highest order. But after long periods of time, long after everyone else has left a particular market or stock, Cancers will be found holding a little more money then they originally invested. Overall, however, the stock market is not a good place for Cancers. They should be in real estate: homes and property are what this Sun sign is about. They have a sixth sense about such things and will often find a property for sale at a low price, buy it, fix it up, live in it for a while, and then sell it for twice what they paid for it. Cancers may also find financial success in matters pertaining to the past and to history. Investing in antiques, buying a historic home, and collecting items from the past are good investment strategies for this sign.

Leo

While Leo is not a sign normally associated with investing, it usually knows something about the subject and in some cases can be quite involved in the process. Leo is, after all, a fire sign, and is always looking for something exciting and a bit risky. Life should never be dull for a Leo. While it is true that some Leo types may know very little about investing because they have someone else doing it for them, most will have something authoritative to say on the subject. Some of them will be glad to teach you a few things and maybe even sell you on some of their own original investment ideas. For Leo, the stock market is a big casino—a way to gamble legally every day. Investing in gold is another possibility for Leo—which is the sign of the metal gold itself. On another level, investments in the arts are often appealing to Leo types. For example, an investment in a play or film, or an investment in an actual work of art like a painting, are usually good bets for Leos precisely because they have good taste and intuitively know what something is really worth. It's all an extension of their own preoccupation with self-worth issues.

Virgo

Like the other earth signs (Taurus and Capricorn), Virgo is more often than not a sign that avoids major risks. Virgos likes things clean, clear, and under control. Investments in the stock market may give them the jitters: they would prefer a money-market account or a certificate of deposit to any account that moves up and down like a roller coaster. While real estate would probably be a good investment vehicle for these signs, they generally prefer to deal only in new construction and this can be far more costly than investing in existing buildings. I think the reason for avoiding, if possible, "used" buildings has to do with purity: older buildings may have other peoples "cooties" (physical or psychic) in them. One type of investment that Virgos may find of interest is in antique mechanisms of various kinds. These might include watches, cameras, barometers, electronics, scientific instruments, etc. Many Virgo types have a real fascination with precision technology, and this interest can translate into insight and understanding about gadgets—and *that* translates into making good choices about what to acquire now for profits later.

Libra

In nearly every area, Libra types strive to make balanced judgments. This is especially true when it comes to financial matters. Libras will weigh all the alternatives not just once, but several times over. Then they will consult charts and run their ideas by others to achieve a measure of objectivity. Then they'll sleep on it. Finally, after all this, they will plunk their money down. By this time the best opportunities will have already passed, but, since they've probably made a good judgment, they will receive acceptable returns in the long run. As for particular markets, Libras are most often practical, and will invest in the most reliable companies in the stock market (the blue chips), but will also hold some bonds and perhaps keep some money in cash (a standard bank account or a money-market account). This is what is called a balanced portfolio. When one part of the economy goes down—say, stocks plunge—the bonds and the money market hold the investment portfolio up. When interest rates go down and bond values drop, stocks may do better and the investment portfolio remains more or less balanced. The Libra way of investing amounts to good advice for most investors. Libra is a most social sign and may also do well investing with partners in real estate. Libras may also find that joining an investment club is stimulating and helps them make better judgments.

Scorpio

With Scorpio we come to a sign is that is either totally involved with investing or won't even consider it. But for the sake of this article, let's assume that the Scorpio types we are talking about have embraced, or, more accurately, strangled the concepts involved in strategic financial investing. Remembering that in traditional astrology Scorpio is a sign of Mars, the aggressive planet, it makes sense that Scorpio is a sign willing to take risks and try to beat the competition. Stock investing brings them to a state of mind that is very close to who they really are. In this arena, groups of people merge their money (shared resources) to gain some control over a public company. They are essentially betting that this company will outperform the market, thus making money for themselves. What does it take for a company to outperform the market? Certainly the vitality of the sector that the company operates in is key, and certainly the decision-making ability of the board of directors is important. But there are also hidden factors operating—which are the ones that Scorpios need to know. In some cases such hidden information may amount to insider information, and this is illegal. In most cases hidden factors can be determined through a thorough investigation of the company—another task perfectly suited to Scorpio. Besides stocks, Scorpio will also do well in bonds and in real estate—particularly investments that require a rehabilitation of some sort. Not a few Scorpions have created a real estate empire for themselves. Investments in mines, and also in energy, are other possible areas Scorpio may do well in.

Sagittarius

For sure, this is an astrological sign of risk. Sagittarians live for excitement and the thrill of something they haven't done lately. This being said, the stock market, which is basically a form of legalized gambling, is most appealing to this sign. Once in the market, Sagittarians will buy and sell, all the time hoping that there will be, in the final analysis, some kind of profit. Now, there are many Sagittarians who become quite wise about the ways of the market and do quite well in it, but unfortunately this is not always the case. The Sagittarian strategy of throwing dollars to the wind doesn't always work, and many find that when all is said and done they have lost a bundle. One of this sign's biggest weaknesses is that they get so excited about a particular stock that they commit too high of a percentage of their portfolio on it. If the stock goes up they get rich, but if it doesn't—they lose their shirts. So here is the key to Sagittarian success in investing: diversity, diversity, diversity. Some investments appealing to this sign include travel-related industries, foreign or global market investing, and importing and exporting. But again, it's most important to study the subject matter before throwing money at it. For the more conservative Sagittarians, real-estate investments that include rentals may be attractive. The rental income provides a steady stream of cash while the value of the property gradually increases.

Capricorn

This sign does not take any unnecessary risks. Investments in the stock market are not the first choice: money-market accounts, certificates of deposit, or bonds would come first because time is not always a major consideration for this sign. Investments may come and go, but Capricorns will stay with what works—and way down the road they will have more money than you will. This kind of conservatism is almost always successful over long periods of time, but Capricorn brings more to the table. This is a sign that recognizes what is truly valued in society and will put money on those items. This sign does not invest in new ideas, inventions, or radical technologies. Capricorn does not push the envelope of progress forward, but rewards that which has already established itself—and this is indeed the secret of Capricornian investing. Go for the tried and proven businesses in stocks, and balance this with a hefty percentage of your portfolio in cash and bonds. Capricorns who take major risks often lose money, but those who play with care make money. Like Cancers, Capricorns may err on the side of caution, but they make up for it in the long run. Capricorn is a sign of control, and seeks ways to predict the course of economic trends. The serious Capricorn investor will study charts and data—and maybe even use astrology to foresee the direction of the economy. Other areas in which Capricorn may find success in investing are in high-quality antiques, office buildings (real estate), mines, and agriculture.

Aquarius

If Capricorn is the sign that supports the status quo, Aquarius is the sign that supports that which will eventually supplant the status quo. In general, Aquarians aren't particularly interested in financial strategies; they are more interesting supporting an idea. This means that Aquarians had better be very careful about where they invest their money, because they may not live long enough to see a profit. Stocks, bonds, and money markets in general are all mainstream investment vehicles and, as such, aren't particularly appealing to a sign that strives to blaze its own trail. Investing in a company that manufactures a product that will improve life on the planet will be of interest, but as I said, this may be a long shot—and who has fifty years to wait for a big payoff? The one area of investing that may appeal to Aquarius are mutual funds, and in particular socially responsible mutual funds. Like other mutual funds, these funds are collections of stocks managed by a professional money manger. The difference is that the stocks in the fund are screened according to certain standards. In some cases the fund will not include any companies that manufacture weapons or are associated with gambling or alcohol. Most funds will not include companies that pollute or degrade the environment in certain ways, or mistreat their employees. Many will do careful profiles of a company's CEO and will not buy their stock if there are any questions about this leaders' integrity. The long and short of it is that with a socially responsible mutual fund, you are investing in companies that have been carefully selected and are thought to be a positive force in the world. These mutual funds have an excellent record and are actually very good investments. Aquarians always like to know that they are doing something to make the world a better place.

Pisces

The best case scenario for a Pisces investor is that they (1) have some kind of institutional support, and (2) that investment decisions are made by the institution and not them. Many Pisceans do work for institutions and never give a thought to what's really going on with their money. Many Pisceans are true futurists, spending their lives envisioning the future—and this gives them some sense of control as time passes. But the unlucky Pisceans who aren't hooked up to an institution or are paid to dream must confront something they are often not cut out to do: deal with the material world. Investing in the future of material things can be too burdensome a thought for many Pisces signs. The "now" itself is enough to deal with. Because of this potential difficulty, many Pisceans hesitate to make long-term investments. Some of them will put cash in a jar and hide it in their closets. Others will put all their money in a bank only because they like the teller who takes their checks, or perhaps invest all their money in a stock just because they overhead someone say it was a winner. With Pisces we are not always dealing with reality as, say, Capricorn knows it. The highly intangible world of finance, where your money goes somewhere that you never see and then comes back ten years later a little bigger, is just one more abstraction forcing its way onto the Piscean thought stream. What probably works best for Pisces are investments in tangible things like art and antiques, rare books, maps and documents, musical instruments, and gems.

For Further Reading

Abergel, Matthew. *Work Your Stars!: Using Astrology to Navigate Your Career Path, Shine on the Job, and Guide Your Business Decisions.* New York: Fireside, 1999.

Clement, Stephanie. *Charting Your Career: The Horoscope Reveals Your Life Purpose.* St. Paul: Llewellyn, 1999.

Handling Those Difficult Signs

by Nina Lee Braden

Why do I keep attracting Leos into my life? I seem to be surrounded by Libras! Every boyfriend that I've had has been a Capricorn, and every one of them has driven me crazy!

Have you ever noticed a pattern with the Sun signs that you attract into your life? Do the so-called "difficult" people in your life seem to fall mainly into one or two Sun signs?

We all have had experiences with difficult people. As we begin to find out their Sun signs, we may discover that many of them share the same sign. Are the nitpickers who drive you crazy Virgos? Are the crazy-makers in your life Geminis? Are the people you love to hate Scorpios? Any sign can be difficult some of the time, just like any person can be difficult some of the time. We may get along splendidly with a sign most of the time, but under certain circumstances, or when going through a rough patch, we may find that the normally smooth relationship with our friendly Libra develops real problems.

We can't change other people, but we *can* change how we let them affect us and how we react to them. Let us concentrate on our own perceptions and our own reactions to best use our personal power when dealing with difficult signs.

Fire Signs

Fire and Fire

If you are a fire sign (Aries, Leo, and Sagittarius), you may find other fire signs a real problem. Many Sun sign guidelines talk about how compatible the fire signs are with each other. I have not found this to be the case. While it is true that fire signs have much in common with other fire signs, these common qualities do not make for easy relationships. Fire signs tend to be very competitive with each other. They each want to be in charge. They each want respect. They each want to be the brightest flame, albeit in different modes.

With fellow fire signs, you may have frequent and regular explosive battles. You may feel that they don't respect you, don't give you the deference that you deserve. You may feel that they are constantly trying to exert themselves when they should not. You may have trouble understanding why they don't just follow your orders. One way to handle these problems is to recognize that, like you, these people are full of fire. They need (not just want, but need) to shine. They need to have times in the limelight—a lot of time for most of them. You may need to find a way to grant them some showcase time. They also thrive on praise, and when they do not get it they may exhibit extreme behavior in order to get some attention. It is much easier to prevent problems with a fellow fire sign than to stop problems. Fire sign conflicts tend to escalate until there is a mighty explosion. One of you will inevitably say or do something that you will regret. Use the flame of the fire to temper yourself so that you can better work with your fellow fire signs.

Fire and Air

If you as fire sign run into difficulties with an air sign (Libra, Aquarius, or Gemini), it may be because you see the air sign as too passionless, too wishy-washy, too uncommitted. You may want to shout, "Don't you care? Can't you commit?" Be aware that the air signs come from a different place than you do. They do tend to live more in their minds than you do, but this is not necessarily a bad thing. They may be better at seeing the big picture than you are. They may see important details that you miss. They may make connections that you don't see. You need these air signs in your life; they provide a necessary function. However, they may indeed lack passion compared to you. Put your fire on low radiance to warm them up a little. Your fire can be contagious if you don't have it turned up full force. At full strength you may overwhelm an air sign, and he will either burn to a crisp in your flame or vanish in a puff of vapor.

Fire and Water

Fire is hot and dry, but water is cold and wet. Fire and water don't have anything in common with each other. You may find yourself very much attracted to water signs (Cancer, Scorpio, and Pisces), but you may also be clueless as to what is going on inside of them. They may seem unnecessarily complex and mysterious. Why can't they be simple and out in the open (like you)? What's all of this touchy-feely intuitive stuff that they have going on? Why are they so moody? Why are they giving you the cold shoulder? Why do they keep throwing a wet blanket on you? With water, be persistent. Quick flashes on and off will not do. With water, a steady flame is best. You may never understand water, but you can learn to live with water. You may, however, want to remember to be on the alert around water because water can douse your flame.

Fire and Earth

As a fire sign, you may feel like a zooming rocket around earth signs (Capricorn, Taurus, and Virgo). Why are they so slow? Why are they so careful? Why are they always wanting to be so practical? Why are they so attached to their possessions? Well, it's because they're earth signs. They are all about stability. They are all about firmness. They are all about tradition. They are all about reliability. You may resent them. You may become angry with them, but they are the hearthstone for your fire. They do restrain you, yes. But they also allow you to burn safely rather than out of control. They rein in your potential destructiveness. Of course you may find them uncomfortable! Learn to respect them and give them tribute for the very important role that they play in your life. However, learn also to recognize when they are too restraining and too limiting. Do not let them smother your light.

Air

Air and Air

If you are an air sign (Libra, Aquarius, or Gemini), you may love being around fellow air signs and may find them the least difficult of all signs. However, even these most congenial signs can sometimes be difficult for you. Perhaps they want to talk too much, not giving you enough "air time." Perhaps they want to take your ideas and run rampant with them, taking your ideas in directions that you don't want them to go. Perhaps they don't pay sufficient attention to your ideas, being busy discussing their own. Their ideas may seem eccentric or strange, or their thinking may seem unrealistic. Try appreciating their ideas for their novelty value and for the stimulation that they provide for your own thinking. Don't worry about truth or validity; just enjoy the mental ride.

Air and Fire

As an air sign, you may enjoy the company of fire signs (Aries, Leo, Sagittarius). However, you may be frustrated around them because they seem too intense, too zealous, too passionate. They don't understand your need for flexibility and play. They are more interested in action than in talk. They may want to act while you are still thinking and talking, still contemplating and planning. They may also want to take over your ideas and co-opt them as their own. They may see you as the Idea Person and themselves as the Action Person. There is some truth to this perception, but they may go to extremes with it and thereby steal from you your well-deserved accolades. Enjoy the warmth and enthusiasm of the fire signs, but don't let them make your life into a wildfire.

Air and Water

Air signs can learn a lot from water signs (Cancer, Scorpio, and Pisces), but this doesn't mean that there is instant understanding or rapport between the two elements. Air signs tend to be outgoing and social. Water signs tend to be introspective and private. Air signs think; water signs feel. When you find yourself scratching your head around a moody water sign, watch her body language. Water signs often talk the talk of an air sign, but they are really walking the walk of a water sign. Therefore, they may seem like they are on your wavelength, but they are really coming from a different place. They are more sensitive to moods, feelings, and impressions than to words, thoughts, or logic. Their lack of logic may drive you crazy, but try to understand that there is value in intuition and intangible awareness. They may need your help in finding words or language to express what they are feeling. Work patiently with them, and the two of you may come to mutual respect and understanding.

Air and Earth

Air and earth have an interesting relationship to each other. Normally, air and earth would have little in common. Air is masculine, hot, and wet. Earth is feminine, cold, and dry. However, all signs have planetary rulers, and two air signs share planetary rulers with two earth signs, giving the two elements more in common than they would normally have. Specifically, Libra and Taurus are both ruled by Venus, the planet of love, and Gemini and Virgo are both ruled by Mercury, the planet of communication. These two sets of signs may find that they share a lot of interests but that their overall approaches to those interests will be different.

Air is about theory; earth is about practicality. Air takes pleasure in thinking and talking. Earth takes pleasure in doing and relaxing. The air person may find the earth person dull, slow, and boring. Air wants to be flexible, but earth is steadfast. Air may feel that earth is too rigid, and that earth is trying to suffocate or stifle him. The qualities of earth are often just what air most needs, but air cannot see that and tends to resent earth rather than appreciate earth. If you as an air sign are feeling frustrated by an earth sign, stop and study the earth person. See what you can learn from her. See where her strengths are. She may be going overboard with her earthiness, but you may also be over-reacting because you sense your own lack.

Water

Water and Water

Water signs (Cancer, Scorpio, Pisces) seem to generally enjoy being around other water signs. However, there is real danger of too much empathy. If you as a water sign are around a moody or depressed water sign, you may find it all too easy to pick up on her emotional "garbage." You may find that although you felt fine earlier, the longer you are together the more depressed or worried or anxious you become. Conversely, there is sometimes a bit of competition among water signs: "I'm more psychic, more sensitive, more intuitive than you are." There may be a sense of martyrdom: "I feel the pain of the world more than anyone else." You may feel that your fellow water sign is doing rather too much emoting. If this is the case, take a break from fellow water signs and go spend some time with fire, air, or earth.

Water and Fire

As a water sign, you may find yourself drawn to fire signs (Aries, Leo, and Sagittarius), but being attracted to them and understanding them are two different things. One problem is that as a water sign, you probably do have more insight and understanding into a fire sign than a fire sign does to you. However, the fire sign will not see it this way and will even resent you if you attempt to explain to him how he really feels or what his real motivations are. There is a real possibility of becoming rather arrogant and assume that you really do understand everyone. You understand a great deal, so this is an easy mistake to make. Do not make it with a fire sign. You have less in common with fire than with any other sign, and you may need to apply some rational thought and study to the understanding of this sign and not just rely on your intuition and feelings.

Water and Air

When water signs are around air signs (Libra, Aquarius, Gemini), they have to be extremely careful of their speech. Air signs are the masters of words, and often water signs have a tendency to communicate via feelings and impressions and to assume that others will understand their intentions even when their words do not describe exactly what they intend. This is a mistake, and never more so than when around air. Air lives for words, language, thoughts, and ideas. Your sometimes cavalier treatment of their primary focus will irritate them to no end. They may become badgering, asking you ceaseless questions. They may want to argue with you, insisting, "But you said. . . ." You may not remember what you said, only what you felt. The air sign, however, will most definitely remember your words, so choose your words carefully around him.

Water and Earth

Water signs may find that they gravitate toward earth signs (Capricorn, Taurus, and Virgo). Water and earth are natural allies. Unfortunately, even good allies can grate on each other's nerves. Water resonates and responds to deep emotions. Earth signs have emotions, but they tend to keep them under wraps and not display them. Water may take earth's natural reserve for a lack of feeling and accuse earth of having no feelings. If you are a water sign having trouble with an earth sign, stop and realize that there are many different kinds of feeling and many ways of expressing feelings, all valid. Undisplayed feelings are no less valid than displayed ones. Encourage your earth friends to open up to you, but do not criticize them if they fail to do so.

Earth

Earth and Earth

If you are an earth sign (Capricorn, Taurus, and Virgo), you may find other earth signs very comfortable and may prefer to spend a great deal of your time with them. However, there will be times when you find fellow earth signs boring, dull, and stodgy. They may want to relax when you want to work, or they may want to work when you want to relax. You might want to simplify and enjoy life, but they may want to do some serious career-building or file reorganization. Just when you are ready to throw out those old magazines that you've saved up, they may decide that the magazines should be catalogued and archived for future use. You may wonder, "How can someone be so much like me in some ways and yet so different in other ways?" If you can forget about analyzing and just enjoy a mutual activity, you'll probably do best with a fellow earth sign.

Earth and Fire

Earth signs may occasionally enjoy the energy and enthusiasm of fire signs (Aries, Leo, and Sagittarius), but it is very easy for a little bit of fire to go a long way for the typical earth sign. You may find fire signs overbearing, pushy, noisy, and boisterous. They may seem rude, insensitive, and uncouth. You may just want to relax, but all they want to do is to get you up and busy doing whatever it is that they want. If you find yourself getting all heated up by a fire sign, it may not be such a bad thing. Try to enjoy the passion, the spark, and the flame, but know your limits. You may want to call it a day while the fire sign is only getting warmed up.

Earth and Air

Earth and air are opposite elements, but Mercury rules Virgo and Gemini, and Venus rules Taurus and Libra, giving earth signs and air signs (Libra, Aquarius, and Gemini) some common ground. Despite this common ground, earth may have a difficult time with air. To earth, air will often seem flighty and frivolous. Air is too ephemeral, too fleeting. Earth treasures stability and tradition, and air's flexibility and adaptability may seem disrespectful and whimsical. Earth wants air to be serious and profound, but air tends to laugh in earth's serious face. If air laughs in your face, look in the mirror. Maybe you are being too serious. Maybe you would benefit from a little levity. Maybe you should try a small measure of frivolity.

Earth and Water

Earth often feels comfortable with water signs (Cancer, Scorpio, and Pisces). However, when earth and water get together, there can be a tendency toward sluggishness, coldness, and depression. Boredom and stagnation can set in. There can be a sense of heaviness and oppression. Earth may have a feeling of being washed away with the tide. Earth may even feel powerless—and earth doesn't like to feel powerless. The earth sign may feel all "washed out" in the presence of overbearing water. Earth is all about boundaries, but water is all about merging. Sometimes water does not respect the boundaries of others and will try to merge inappropriately. Respect your own boundaries, and do not allow water to infringe upon your privacy. Stand up for your own integrity and give water a lesson in respecting personal space. You and water will both profit from this lesson.

Learning From Difficulty

No matter how much we may want to change someone else, we can't really do it. I can, however, change the way that I see someone else, the way that I think about someone else, the way that I feel about someone else, and the way that I react to someone else. As I begin to make these changes, sometimes there will be ripples that will stimulate change in others as well.

Try to avoid difficult people whenever possible, but when it's not possible, try to learn from them and adapt yourself in order to live in peace and harmony. Life is too short for unnecessary difficulties.

For Further Reading

Davison, Ronald. *Synastry: Understanding Human Relations Through Astrology.* New York: Aurora Press, 1991.

Tierney, Bil. *All Around the Zodiac: Exploring Astrology's Twelve Signs.* St. Paul: Llewellyn, 2001.

Romancing the Signs

by Rowena Wall

Are you struggling to figure out how to get closer to a certain somebody? New relationships can be difficult at best. If, however, you know the person's Sun sign, it can get a lot easier.

At the risk of sounding redundant, I will remind you that a good relationship analysis requires comparing each party's entire chart. There are many things that can affect a relationship and all things should be considered. However, to get a little insight on how to proceed, learning about your potential partner's Sun sign is very helpful indeed. So grab your hat and let's take a look.

Aries
Aries signs are usually a little macho. This is a high-energy sign that wants things to be happening all the time, so it's important that you don't show signs of laziness or slow moving. People under this sign lose interest in you pretty fast if you show resentment at their constant activity. If you are a "slow mover," not inclined to jump to conclusions, you may not be as comfortable as other signs might be.

For an Aries, a great date would be to sit in front of the TV with a professional sport blasting away. You will sit beside your partner, massaging his or her neck or back, and keeping him or her supplied with popcorn and beer. Your heart-tugger also likes surprises, so you need to be Johnny-on-the-spot and keep this sign on its toes. Aries signs are so easily bored that this will be something you have to work out carefully

You may have already noticed that your favorite Aries is pretty sexy. Aries signs attract the opposite sex very readily, so you need to be prepared if you are a jealous or possessive type—an Aries might resent you if you tried to hold him or her back. These signs love that attention they get. Interestingly, you'll wind up deciding that these signs are worth the extra maintenance.

Taurus

It's long been rumored that the male Taurus is one of the greatest lovers in the zodiac. If it's true about the males, then I would hazard an opinion that it's true about the females as well. Presumably, the reason for highly sexed Tauruses is based on their exquisite sense of touch.

These signs are very nurturing, and they care about their "possessions" very strongly. (If you haven't noticed yet, you become a possession with a Taurus when you get into a relationship with one of these signs.) Tauruses can be very possessive and jealous as well. Of course, that sometimes perks up your ego, but problems can arise if they take it too far. Let's face it: no one likes to be smothered.

Usually, Tauruses are good providers. They work hard and they often have an enormous amount of luck in making money. Once they start on a path, they're not likely to give up. Because of this determination, they're very successful in the financial world. Money seems to flow to most Tauruses' hands.

Taurus signs will be slow to get involved in a relationship. They like to take their time and be cautious about how they proceed. Of course, this is the correct way to get into any relationship, but it just seems that a Taurus will drag it out a little more than necessary on many occasions.

Gemini

Most astrologers say that you never know who you're coming home to with a Gemini. This is more accurate than you think: Geminis have hundreds of different personalities and they're interested in almost everything. One could comfortably say they're "nosy" as well, so if you want to know the latest gossip, find a Gemini.

As a lover, Geminis are great. First of all, they're a lot of fun, and so the whole routine becomes entertaining as can be. And of course they have all kinds of techniques to share with you. That alone would be worth the trip!

If you have a Gemini in your sights, it's important that you do things "differently," Don't make the same old overtures that you might with other signs. Bring something creative to the relationship. Be sure to appreciate your Gemini's jokes, and, if you have any gossip, by all means be prepared to share it.

Wear your walking shoes when you go with a Gemini. These signs never sit still at a party (or anywhere else for that matter). If you're going to hang on, you need to be prepared with some fast-moving feet. Break up your normal routine and say and do something unexpected.

In short, Geminis like to stay really busy—and they want their partners to keep up with them. There's not a lot of patience here, so don't look for it. If you can't keep up, you may have to drop out of the race!

Cancer

Cancers are very complex people. They tend to be moody and can change moods rather quickly. They are very sensitive, but, they can also be as hard as a crab's back. They can become immovable, and when they reach that state you may as well forget it for the day, and try again tomorrow. But Cancers can easily understand your deepest thinking. They love for you to confide in them about all the times your heart has been broken, or how misunderstood you've been all your life.

The best way to get next to Cancer signs is to feed them good food. They'll love you forever if you feed them well, so if you're a good cook, consider yourself one rung up on the ladder.

You might also want to remember that these signs will definitely be feeding you back as well. Cancer is a very nurturing sign, and they're great healers, so expect chicken soup if you have a cold or any other malady. Most Cancers have a mother's touch in helping you to get well—in fact, they're often referred to as "mothers of the zodiac." Depending on the circumstances, you could probably get used to such great treatment.

Leo

Most Leos like to be seen *and* heard. They're seldom shy. So if you've spotted one that you would like to have a relationship with, it won't take a lot on your part to accomplish that. Since they have rather strong egos, they tend to believe you're pretty smart when you tell them they're great. What's more, if you didn't have time to say that, then they'll tell *you* how wonderful they are. Of course, they love it when you show the proper amount of appreciation. Always let a Leo know they are appreciated. They thrive on that.

Expect a Leo to be outstanding at a party—Leos are the guys with lampshades on their heads, dancing to weird music. And Leos are great lovers: they literally live and breathe romance, so you have a head start at the very beginning. But this means you need to be romantic too. Bring flowers or other favors expressing your great pleasure with them. Please remember, too, that they are always right, and so it will do you no good to insist otherwise.

If you want to have a lot of fun, meet lots of new people, and go to interesting places, then a Leo is perfect for you. Just kindly remember at all times that you must let the Leo be the boss. That's just the way it is for the king.

Virgo

Virgos are pretty particular in things and people. This means if you are going to make any headway with them, you must accept their rabid desire to have everything absolutely "perfect" at all times. If you're the type that slings your clothes across the room or throws your shoes any which way, then you've got the wrong person. You must be neat—and preferably organized. Of course, Virgos love the challenge of alphabetizing your spice cabinet, so it might be wise to save something for them to do in moments of stress. Just be sure that you're not a slob of some sort, because if you are you'll never get a second look from them.

This is also a sign, like Cancer, that will "doctor" you. (In fact, many great doctors are Virgos.) Suffice it to say that if you need some kind of medication, they most likely have it on their shelves or in their pockets. Virgos are also sensitive and, to a large extent, shy, so don't come on too hot and heavy: you'll scare them away.

You may never suspect it from their prim and proper manner, but these guys can be very good lovers as well. Just be neat and they'll love you forever.

Libra

The most romantic sign in the zodiac is Libra. People with this Sun sign are very desirous of companionship. They dislike doing things alone, and they want a buddy with them all the time. In short, you won't have to work too terribly hard to get them interested in you.

Of course, it will help if you dress nicely, have your hair neatly coifed, and make sure you smell good. Be sure to show all those good manners that your mama taught you: Libras dislike anything rough or unseemly. They want you to be ultra-polite and charming, and they like for others to admire their partners, so if you want to fit the bill, you know what to do.

Since Libras like classical music and other uptown endeavors, start out with tickets to a concert or a play. They should be pretty easy to approach and of course they'd like to go someplace nice with you if you meet their idea of a partner. In turn, you will find Libras clean up very well and are conscientious about their dress—and you can bet they will smell very nice indeed.

Never leave your Libra love sitting alone if you can help it—Libras just can't stand to be alone, and it's your job to see that that doesn't happen. Trust me when I tell you that all this effort will be worth it!

Scorpio

Scorpios are very powerful and strong. Unfortunately, they're not quite as strong as they'd have you think. Lurking under that mysterious façade is a very sensitive person—but they'd go to any extreme possible to keep you from knowing about it. They fear if you know their weaknesses you'll take advantage of them, so you're going to have play along with these folks if you want to get anywhere.

You probably know that Scorpios are very sensual and sexual—in fact, they ooze with sex appeal. These are the people with whom you may want to be a little "hard to get." Also, try to be as mysterious as you can, because they're determined to get to the bottom of people they don't quite understand. They're drawn to mystery and secrets, so grab some tickets to a very mysterious play, or a whodunit movie. Invite them out and they're sure to go.

By the way, you can trust them with any little secret you have. They'll never reveal it to anyone else. However, you need to make sure that if they confide in you that you, in turn, keep their confidences: they'll never forgive you if you reveal things to others.

Sagittarius

Be ready for a lot of action and fun with these guys. They love telling jokes and they're usually considered the salesmen of the zodiac. They almost always have a good sense of humor, which can be a blessing with anyone. And hopefully, you enjoy traveling and racing around everywhere. In fact, it won't be surprising if you meet your Sagittarius friend when one or both of you are out of town.

Sagittarians love challenges. If things get too boring, however, they'll check out in a heartbeat, so you'll need to keep things lively when you're together. These signs are always looking for new friends and situations. Don't be offended if you go to a party with one of them and he or she starts flirting with others—it just goes with the territory.

There are many of this sign who are drawn to the law. There are a lot of lawyers, judges, and even policemen in this sign, so you might want to keep your nose clean around them. Don't start bragging about how clever you were when you cheated on your math test or other similar experiences.

Sagittarians also love the outdoors—and that includes outdoor sports—so be prepared to do a little hunting or fishing, or join them at some of their favorite games. They love to applaud their favorite teams, and they'll expect you to do the same.

Capricorn

Most people are surprised to find out that Capricorns are excellent lovers. They prefer to be alone with you in some dark room, however—you'll seldom see them being affectionate to others in public. In their minds, it just isn't fitting!

It's also true that Capricorns are almost always successful at whatever they do. They're very determined, and if they've set their minds on something, then they'll hang in there until it gets done. This includes you: if they've decided they want you for a partner, they'll hang in there forever until you finally give in and agree.

You've probably already heard about the famous Capricorn frugality. Well, it's very true: they will indeed squeeze a penny or nickel to death. So if you want to get along with these folks, don't look for expensive presents, or for them to take you to some pricey place to visit. In fact, if you can figure out a cheap place to go to, they'll appreciate it forever. Just make sure it's in good taste.

Because Capricorns are almost always successful, you'll need to show that you're pretty successful yourself. They don't want to drag some seedy looking partner around, so make sure you fix yourself up well, and by all means make sure you look expensive in your dress.

Aquarius

Hopefully you like unusual, because that's exactly what you'll get with an Aquarian. You can pretty much do what you want with them, but you must at all times make them think that it's their idea, not yours. Be sure you don't even remotely sound like you're trying to run things: they'll disappear quicker than you can click your heels if you do.

Aquarians bore easily, and they tire of the same routines all the time. That said, it is also true that they can get into a rut, and it's necessary to change that rut without them knowing that's what you did. Aquarians are interested in absolutely everything, and they really like something new and unusual. Find a new rock and tell them all about it. They'll be fascinated.

Most Aquarians are also above-average in intelligence, so don't be surprised if they start talking over your head. That's where they feel safe—telling others about all the strange things that they see and hear.

Never hold an Aquarian too tightly: they can't stand to be hemmed in. If you start getting possessive, you'll find that they'll start backing off. Let them be detached—that's where they'll be happy.

The best way to get them to notice you is to wear unusual clothing or jewelry. Be joyful. Laugh at their jokes. You'll be surprised at just how interested they can get.

Pisces

Now we come to the most sensitive sign of the zodiac. You really need to be careful what you say and how you say it around these folks. Generally, they can read you pretty well, so it's pointless to lie to them. They tend to be more psychic than most of the other signs.

Pisceans often daydream about things they want and cherish. You may hear others telling them to tune in and get their heads out of the clouds. Sometimes they're so "out there" that they don't even notice you're out there too, so you may have your work cut out for you.

Pisces signs are attracted to the unusual and strange, and that may work to your advantage if you happen to be either of those. Pisceans are affectionate and loving and very kind. They love to wait on others and they often find themselves in trouble because they let others take advantage of them. If you are attracted to a Pisces, be sure you treat this sign carefully, and don't wind up trying make him or her your latest doormat!

For Further Reading

Pond, David. *Astrology & Relationships*. St. Paul: Llewellyn, 2001.

Rakela, Christine. *The Love Relationship Formula: Predicting Romantic Success with Astrology*. St. Paul: Llewellyn, 2004.

Townley, John. *Composite Charts: The Astrology of Relationships*. St. Paul: Llewellyn, 2001.

Feng Shui Astrology

by Alice DeVille

Knowledge of feng shui (the art of placement) and astrology (the study of the planets) can help you better connect with the forces of energy that constantly move through the universe. In this article, you'll see how astrology influences the timing and detail of your purchase, while feng shui addresses the quality, style, location, and floor plan of your home choices.

Both the Fourth House of home and real property and the Tenth House of career and business matters relate to this sector. Your Second House of income and personal resources relates to discretionary spending, and people affiliated with this house include bankers and investors competing for your business. The conditions under which you place your mortgage loan, whether you have help from a partner in securing this debt, and how long you take to pay back your obligation correspond to matters of the Eighth House of lenders, insurers, and funding dollars.

The Real-Estate Market Basket

Never has the real-estate market been so hot as during the last few years, when record low-interest rates enticed new and move-up buyers into purchasing homes. Mortgage bankers, brokers, and lenders could not keep up with the number of customers seeking loans. The increase in business in most companies was 50 to 150 percent higher than at any previous time, and staff was either overworked or in short supply. These lenders had to hire mortgage processors, settlement clerks, loan officers, and underwriters. Since all property has to be appraised before a loan is granted, real-estate appraisal and home inspection enterprises experienced the same surge of activity. Real estate firms accelerated the hiring of new agents, and some brokers opened satellite offices. Homebuilders grabbed up available land and built new communities in every imaginable price range. Construction workers could write their own tickets, as builders competed for their specialized skills and coped with hard-to-meet home delivery deadlines. Real-estate schools churned out thousands of new agents, brokers, real-estate appraisers, home inspectors, and loan officers.

Individuals who were solidly enjoying their foothold in the rental market (with not necessarily the most renter-friendly leases) suddenly saw the advantages that tax incentives gave to homeowners, and recognized home buying as an affordable way to put more spending dollars in their pockets. To retain their renters, landlords subsequently became eager to renew multiyear leases with attractive privileges, but the lure of a cherished "home sweet home" was too much to resist for excited house seekers.

Buyers purchased homes with 0 to 5 percent down payments—in contrast to the 10 to 20 percent investment that had traditionally been the norm. The federal government added incentives for first-time buyers. Many home purchasers benefited from energy initiatives that gave them greater buying power if they purchased homes with easy access to public transportation and actually used the buses, trains, and vanpools to ride to work and save gasoline.

Planets and Their Influence

Followers of astrology know that Mercury relates to the signing of contracts of all types. When it is retrograde (in apparent backward motion for three weeks at a time, three times a year) the astrologer looks carefully at the chart of the homebuyer before selecting a signing date. If at all possible, the astrologer recommends postponing the settlement date until the retrograde period passes. The main reason is to avoid mix-ups, unnecessary delays or contractual mistakes in the amount needed for settlement, a misquoted interest rate, or an unrecorded deed of trust.

The Moon, Saturn, and Jupiter influence the public attitudes, attraction, and buying power in real-estate investment. Jupiter moved into Cancer, the sign of house, home, residence, and foundations. The planet stimulated the frenzy of interest that sent the public on a buying spree in search of houses, retirement homes, buildable land, investment rental properties and vacation time-shares. Next, Uranus, the planet of sudden surprises, played a role in generating unusual economic conditions that affected not only the stock market but also the supply and demand of real-estate inventory and the number of buyers and sellers competing for loans. When Saturn trined Uranus, as it did from mid-2001 to mid-2003, interest rates on home mortgages and home equity loans plunged to record low numbers.

Millions of homebuyers accelerated their home purchases and raced to mortgage bankers to lock in rates that hovered at about 5¼ percent for a thirty-year fixed, tax deductible note. Not since the mortgage industry began keeping records forty years ago had interest rates been that attractive to the pool of renters who quickly converted themselves into serious buyers.

Saturn advanced through contract-oriented Gemini and made positive aspects to "show me the mansion" Jupiter in Leo during late 2002 and through mid-2003, when the *really* low rates rattled the housing market with even greater excitement. The lower the rates fell, the higher the selling price rose on the desirable properties. The population who weren't buying a new residence were refinancing their existing homes two, three, or four times in a year! The objective was to keep pocketing the savings going into their bank accounts from a new and lower mortgage payment, and to use the growing equity in their value-enhanced homes to remodel and upgrade the features of the property.

Preferred Housing Amenities

What do people look for when searching for a home in a hot market? Just ask your favorite realtor. Location is the prime factor. The closer a house is to the hub of activity and the commercial zone, the higher the demand and the more you will pay. Traffic patterns intensify far faster than new roads are built, and in high-density urban areas with considerable suburban sprawl, a typical commute to work may take an hour or more. Homeowners want attractive, affordable housing within a reasonable distance to work. The trend is to look for a residence with easy access to transportation, shopping, churches, and recreation. Buyers with children look for proximity to schools.

Most major design trends start in the high-end market (check out *Architectural Digest* for visual nirvana) and filter their way down the housing food chain to the homes everyone can afford. Each year the list of "must-have" features grows, adding excitement to the quest for the perfect home. The idea is to create a high-end look without breaking the bank. Dozens of inexpensive steps borrowed from savvy custom builders turn even the most mundane property into a breathtaking showstopper that is heads above the run-of-the mill, cookie-cutter floor plan from which it sprang. Interior decorators (a combination of Fourth and Seventh House energies) create images for model homes or sale properties that inspired buyers want to duplicate in their cherished residences. When a home goes on the market, some real-estate agents hire "stagers" to give the home a facelift and make it presentable for a quick sale. They know all too well that interested buyers have a "wish list" and they want their hot property to be the best competition in town.

What's on the "must have" list in the current market? **Aries** investors check out options for code-adjustable electronic garage door openers, fire alarms, and sophisticated security systems. They want homes outfitted with doorbells that ring on every floor, room monitors, intercoms, and (if the checkbook permits) the ultimate smart house, where automated appliances and lighting make chores a breeze for this "action-oriented" homeowner.

Taurus opts for curb appeal and puts a little color or brickwork into concrete walks. Members of this sign like a dark and distinguished color on the front door to give a more expensive, elegant look to the home. Their love for distinctive hardware shows up in ornate doorknockers, lampposts, and cabinet knobs and handles. Topiaries and statues frequently grace their walkways and gardens, lending an air of material success—one of Taurus's prerequisites for emotional security.

Colored plumbing fixtures aren't a budget buster for **Geminis**. They like building a room around at least two colors and can be quite artistic when they choose a theme. Double shelves and poles in all the closets and fluorescent lighting behind wall mirrors show up in the homes of the zodiac's twins. They fall right in line with feng shui principles: the Gemini usually wants two of everything— mirrors, magazine racks, or dishwashers.

Designer kitchens with multiple sinks and garbage disposals, stainless-steel dishwashers, dual fuel ranges, and granite countertops are popular with **Cancers**, and wallpaper accents and borders appeal to Cancer's decorating scheme.

Regal touches appeal to **Leos**—Ionic or Corinthian columns to mark entrances to dining and living rooms, two-story foyers with dramatic chandeliers and imported marble floors, and sweeping staircases at just the right angle from the front door to help them make dramatic entrances when they meet their guests. So they can stay fit running up and down the stairs of their several-storied homes, Leos want an exercise room outfitted with equipment like treadmills, exercise bikes, and home gyms.

Virgos like a garden wall integrated into the home's façade, with room for gorgeous vines and showy flowers. If that is not possible in the exterior plan of the residence, Virgo may install garden windows, plant morning glory along a deck, or use trellises abundantly in the garden. This sign, also known for efficiency and cleanliness, desires fully functional laundry rooms with sensory technology and superior engineering in the washer and dryer.

Sunrooms with a cheerful decorating scheme and space for the piano, or house extensions that include a covered, screened deck to expand entertainment space appeal to **Libra**, the ultimate party host. For companion-conscious Libra, there is never too much leisure space in the home—a loft converts to a playroom for the kiddies; a recreation or game room in the finished basement gives the teen crowd privacy. Trend-conscious Libra's "must have" upgrade is the media room with theater-style seating to house state-of-the-art plasma TVs, DVDs, and CD players—and collections of movies and home videos. Just in case company pops in, a well-stocked refrigerator and snack bar, complete with popcorn machine, entice guests to settle down for the evening and enjoy the entertainment.

Luxury baths with shower seats and two showerheads, whirlpool tubs, and a separate dressing room are high on the list of preferences for **Scorpios**. Scorpio also resonates to use of bead board and wainscoting to define characteristics of the boudoir walls and other personal rooms.

Sagittarius's pet projects revolve around the family room, recreation room, or den. The look of customized imported cabinets as built-ins around the fireplace or as a base for a wet bar may have its origins in one of their pleasure trips. They are known for having antique- or estate-sale finds shipped home and integrated into the decorating scheme.

Never far from their work, **Capricorn** buyers (though hardly the only sign doing so these days) look for housing options that include space for the home office. They won't want to use a spare bedroom, and are likely to claim the study or library for their own, outfitting it with built-in bookcases, a computer workstation, glassed-in étageres for their crystal collections, and privacy doors so family members know they mean business. When space permits, Capricorns often build custom office suites in their basements, complete with a private entrance and bathroom for clients.

Aquarius signs find a way to afford wood floors in as many rooms as possible. In keeping with emerging trends, the water bearer discovers that laying wood in a diagonal pattern to draw the eye through the space creates an illusion of more square footage than is actually there. To satisfy their spatial requirements, many Aquarians use striking visual treatments. For example, instead of flat header areas above doors to rooms on the main living level, Aquarius goes for arches—and may even carry them across multiple areas. They also like to include windows to make the space feel larger.

Pisces signs want to splurge on the master-bedroom arrangements with at least two walk-in closets—complete with storage drawers, built-in shelves, and shoe cubbies for their usually ample collection of footwear. The adjoining bath in the Pisces suite has separate his and hers vanities (as opposed to one long countertop with two sinks), and a separate room for the toilet and accompanying bidet.

Discriminating homebuyers have a myriad of options for making purchasing power go a long way toward satisfying their astrological lifestyles. With the additional help of feng shui, they can live harmoniously ever after.

The Feng Shui Factor

Location means a great deal to feng shui experts. They advocate arrangements that help you prosper in your new home and create the flow of positive energy and balance. When you are house hunting, look at the location of the lot. If it is a corner lot with traffic patterns in two directions, it may be a more expensive house than others in the neighborhood. Corner lots are usually priced higher, yet distractions to the residence's energy are considerable. The school bus stops on the corner, pet walkers flock to the corner of the street, visiting cars park on the side or front curb of the house, and shars (negative chi created by sharp angles from nearby structures) may come from homes situated at angles aimed toward the front, side, or back of the house.

Although a cul-de-sac is often touted as a privacy benefit, if the home you are looking for is at the center of the circle, every vehicle that drives down the street is going to send a shar directly to your front door. To the feng shui practitioner, the front door represents the property owner's wealth, and the constant flow of these shars dissipates prosperity and energy. Today, intelligent homebuyers hire feng shui practitioners to assess the compatibility of their planned home purchase or to give advice on remodeling projects. The following section refers to amenities the Sun signs prefer that were described in the previous section. Use these feng shui tips to put pleasure in your house hunting and designing plans. This advice is useful for every sign.

Aries: You love gadgets and built-ins, but keep electromagnetic energy from TVs, VCRs, and computers out of the bedroom. These vibes are detrimental to the quality of your rest.

Taurus: Choose a solid front door instead of an all-glass entrance. A decorative touch with beveled glass is fine, but clear glass offers little protection to your home and allows prosperity to leak out. Be sure the door is in proportion to your home—not too large and not too small. Mirrored or shiny doorknockers deflect shars from the street.

Gemini: Do use soft greens (health and prosperity) or blues (harmony and serenity) in the bathroom. Use scented candles in the closets or bath to purify the space, help you relax, and sleep restfully. Accent ceilings with borders or crown molding.

Cancer: Put something tasty in your stainless-steel ovens, but please don't install your range underneath the plumbing fixtures of a second-floor bathroom. A wall behind the stove provides solid support for your family in lieu of placing burners on a middle-of-the-room island. Kitchens represent the family's wealth.

Leo: Be sure the dramatic staircase you desire is one that curves rather than spirals, or else there'll be too much confusing chi. Look for stairs that angle away from the front door rather than fall directly in front of the entrance. When you enter your front door, make sure you don't face a mirror, which only sends your prosperity vibes back into the street.

Virgo: Balance yin and yang, light and dark in the various plants and materials in your landscaping. Incorporate curving paths in your garden to attract positive energy. Use statues, gazing balls, benches, and water treatments for flow. Be sure trees do not block the clear view from your front door.

Libra: Put round or curved tables in the family room or sun room to encourage harmony, conversation, participation, or family equality. Guests feel more at ease when no hard angles from sharp table corners cut into their bodies.

Scorpio: If your heart is set on a sumptuous master bath, be sure it is not located near or above your front door. Energy (and waste in the pipes) flows out of the house and blocks positive energy from entering your home. Avoid placing your bed on a wall adjacent to your bathroom. Keep seat covers and doors to bathrooms closed at all times, especially if the toilet faces the bedroom.

Sagittarius: Apply the "luxury for less" principle by knocking out confining walls and adding columns or railings to highlight your family room. Fire and water elements don't mix, so keep decorative mirrors off the wall that houses your fireplace.

Capricorn: Use a combination of closed and open bookshelves in your libraries to reduce piercing shars. Arrange your home office workspace so that you don't look out into a corridor or face stairs, closets, or storage areas.

Aquarius: Warm up your favorite rooms with dramatic area rugs to break up the lines of your expensive all-wood floors. Choose a home with a large "gathering room," and arrange furniture in cozy groups conducive to conversation and your eclectic mix of friends.

Pisces: Create a harmonious relaxation spot to recharge your body and spirit. Accent with bold colors, but make sure the main color scheme is elegantly restful. Placing your bed under a ceiling fan or beam interferes with healthful vibrations—and so does sleeping under the crease of an arched ceiling.

For Further Reading

Hale, Gill. *The Practical Encyclopedia of Feng Shui*. London: Lorenz, 1999.

Webster, Richard. *Feng Shui for Beginners*. St. Paul: Llewellyn, 2003.

Grassroots and Groundswells
World Predictions for 2005

by Leeda Alleyn Pacotti

Since Neptune entered Aquarius in 1998, it has closely chased Pluto in Sagittarius with a comforting astrological aspect. Pluto, the planet of hidden agendas, and Neptune, the ruler of oil, have gradually revealed the depth of the economic stranglehold held by oil trusts and cartels on the struggling peoples of the world. This peepshow of disclosure continues into 2008, as the hidden continues to come to light. Uranus casts the vouchsafed light, as it transits through Neptune's sign, Pisces. This mutual exchange of signs lasts through spring 2011, building into a powerful three-year crescendo of astrological energies, while these two giants remain companionably separated by no more than thirty-two degrees.

Although Uranus resides in quiet, indolent Pisces, its essential nature of reformation predominates the astrological landscape, affecting humanity at large. The influence of Uranus is disruptive and cataclysmic, which would lead most to think its methods are readily or easily observable. However, Uranian focus can be very diffuse, deflecting observers with peculiarities of the moment as it subtly works its changes. Then, suddenly, we become aware things have changed—irrevocably.

In its transits since 1990, most conjecture about Uranus in Capricorn suggested a toppling of old business structures; instead, Uranus brought the entirety of humanity into global trade through recognized corporate giants—and later wrestled their strangleholds away. As the gas giant moved through its own sign of Aquarius, we suspected changes in communications linking us throughout the world, and we were treated to the Internet, mobile communications, the Y2K scare, and long-distance calling wars. Just as easily, Uranus toppled these new paradigms with hackers, computer viruses, and costly corporate collapses and shareholder losses.

Now, with Uranus in Pisces, we must prepare for the idiosyncratic events this eccentric planet can deliver.

In the House of Hidden Enemies

As the higher vibration of Mercury, which rules the individual mind, the principal effect of Uranus is on the aggregate mind, or the mind of cumulative humanity. The body politic and the legislature of a nation is often attributed to Uranus and Aquarius. The body politic reflects the accepted and promoted national mores, which a legislative body intends through enactment of laws.

This body politic, like Uranus, can be both exciting and calamitous. Within it are the totality of hopes, fears, dreams, wishes, and goals of the population. Given this broad accumulation of concepts and partialities, the national mind is often paradoxical and contradictory with current law, as some ideas become more prevalent than others. The body politic exists, even when it appears to have been dictated by one person, and can lead to overthrown governments, coups, and revolutions—times when ideas burst beyond the seams and limits of standing legalities. In the United States and other free-expression countries, the body politic often changes focus and proprieties as population segments demand acknowledgment.

Although the body politic seems like an abstract speculation, it is a living mass mind. The acceptance and investigation of this mind was well developed in Aristotle's *Nicomachean Ethics*, in which the noted philosopher explained how the ethics of individuals, in accumulation, establish the politics of a state or nation.

The things each of us considers important, as a hope or fear, develops and alters this national mind. Understanding that helps us realize that we are not so much influenced by it as it is influenced by us. However, when we believe we are tossed on the turbulent currents of legalized ideas that don't coincide with our own thinking, we can fall victim to a private paranoia, looking everywhere for the opponents or enemies that seek to alter our minds.

The trek of Uranus through Pisces, which brings forth influences for good or ill—sometimes referred to as "hidden enemies"—forces us to confront inner issues that prevent our acceptance of new ideas (the influence for good) or that reinforce our stance for outmoded values (the influence for ill). At the end of this relentless excursion of Neptune and Uranus in each other's signs, we will be prepared for the full force of the sea god Neptune in its own sign (Pisces) of murky depths and psychological deep waters. Our reflection on that internal Uranian reformation will be best and quietly summed up by the statement, "I have seen the enemy, and he is me."

The House of Self-Undoing

In the houses of the horoscope, Pisces bears affinity to the Twelfth House—also termed the "house of self-undoing." Persons with the Sun, Moon, or several planets in Pisces or the Twelfth House often go through situations that resemble breakdowns, whether they are physical, emotional, mental, or spiritual. Only when internal attitudes are unyielding and crystallized will the circumstances of breakdowns be severe. Otherwise, situations arise that force an individual to reassess values, knowledge, and preferences that no longer suit the evolving soul. Sometimes the coddled baby is thrown out with the bath water. Other times portions of current thinking are salvaged, becoming the foundation for an entirely new direction of thought.

While all this internal activity is happening to individual people, it is also molding and reshaping the mass minds of individual nations—and subsequently the entire body politic of the global mind. Although we may not have been cognizant of the brilliance of this principle, which describes the potency of singular human thought, we have seen this demonstrated in our lifetimes by individuals who heeded the call to change. Woodrow Wilson laid the foundations for the United Nations. Franklin D. Roosevelt turned the horrific tide of global economic depression in the 1930s. Martin Luther King, Jr., and Nelson Mandela proved unequivocally that minorities and majorities of every type are parts of the whole of a nation. Helen Gurley Brown and Gloria Steinem provoked and demanded recognition of the feminine psyche.

Uranus is no respecter of mechanisms; whatever causes the reformation of thought and social structure is acceptable from Uranus's indifferent viewpoint. This need to reform causes us to fight wars, set up blockades, and create trade embargoes. When a time for change has come, the global mass mind isolates obstinate components, such as unyielding national minds, and forces those nations to buckle under their outmoded ideas and methods—a global form of peer pressure.

First, and foremost, Uranus begins its work within the individual human mind by bringing us into situations where we confront the realities and outcomes of our hopes and fears. All this may sound terrifying, but we must remember that the undoings are for good or ill. What, really, is terrifying about undoing prejudice, hatred, character assassination, deceit, or slander? Would we be better off without racism, class distinction, and blood-letting? Would it be so wrenching to feel cordiality, concern, or helpfulness toward every other human being on the planet—without even a thought to color, creed, gender, or ethnicity? Is it worth the pain of undoing something hideous or dark within ourselves to be able to live the highest precepts of our beliefs?

Now and for the next six years, we have many opportunities to make friends with our true humanity. Otherwise, when Neptune enters Pisces, we may find ourselves embroiled in confusions as we are forced into change. Tragically, though, many of us will probably choose to believe that someone out there is trying to destroy our lives.

Behold! The Jihad

In 1990, the West scoffed at the pompous braggadocio of the fateful remark of Saddam Hussein at the beginning of the Gulf War: "This is the mother of all wars." Some Americans had expected an unimaginable assault that would rally national pride. Others saw the real atrocities of the conflict as irreparably torn alliances held in place by the merest gossamer threads of diplomacy and essential trade. On all sides, the vitriol of blame produced an abundance of angry bile.

In the Middle East, standing rancor against Britain's presumptuous involvement in fashioning sheikdoms into kingdoms and nations, with everything bartered against commodity oil, ripped at the social fabric of civilization's cradle. The Muslim nations of the Middle East and Africa believed themselves precariously balanced over a chasm of annihilation. Disrespected by the West for their social mores, differing religion, and scant distributions of economic wealth, these countries saw lashing out as their only salvation from destruction.

But Saddam's prediction may have been more broadly foretelling than even he had suspected. In 2005, the Muslim nations of northeastern and northern Africa lie in the path of total eclipse. While not all changes necessarily occur this year, history's finger will point at this breathtaking moment, when the true jihad from within burst upon these beleaguered Muslim nations so desperately in need of change. Their hope lies in regaining trust in the beautiful mandates of their guiding faith.

Nations in Focus

This year, two total eclipses in April and October command the astrological center stage. As mentioned, northern Africa takes the brunt, as does Spain in western Europe, while earlier in the year the turbulent northern countries of South America and the islands of New Zealand lie in the path of totality.

Algeria: The October eclipse covers northern Algeria and cuts directly into its capital, Algiers. The second largest country in Africa, Algeria suffers domestic unrest from the native Berbers and relies heavily on its oil reserves for export. The border to Morocco is closed and the one with Libya is disputed—in keeping with the nebulous astrological patterns at the country's inception. If it can withstand pressure from other Muslim countries, Algeria stands to benefit handsomely from oil exports to the U.S. and Western Europe. The need to train and stabilize its military, solidify the domestic economy, and build capital reserves demand that Algeria extend itself independently, as Tunisia has. Late in the year, poor harvests show signs of approaching famine in the western provinces. With more foreign investment in its banks and active trade alliances, Algeria's legislature looks toward health programs and preservation programs for art and literature.

Colombia: This violently ravaged country is coming to a reckoning of its nefarious foreign trade in cocaine, heroin, and marijuana. Colombian financial houses have long eyed the off-shore banking in Panama, and covet dominance of fertile Venezuela. Bogotá is in the April eclipse path of totality, suggesting a sudden change in the presidency prior to the 2006 elections. The president has attempted legislation to heal domestic finances, but illicit foreign partners stand ready to promote any coup to prevent the bleeding off of even a petty part of their profits. At mid-year, the president is at cross purposes with domestic bankers and the military, and is distanced from the legislature. Widows and orphans have become an emotional drain on the fighting men. In 1991, this country's natal chart showed that the drug lords hold all the financial and power cards. At this point, only foreign intervention in off-shore money-laundering breaks their stranglehold.

Kenya: Possibly the home of King Solomon's mines, Kenya is wealthy in gold, rubies, garnets, and extraordinarily abundant agriculture. Rich in natural wonders and wildlife preserves, this international favorite enters an Aquarian phase. An accepted financial center for eastern Africa, Kenya enjoys this reputation throughout the year, until troubles begin in December. Having run on an anticorruption platform, the president finds himself embroiled in scandals over money-laundering and narcotics activities. He does, however, retain the faith of the population. Border control along Sudan is amicable, but charged, and must be settled in 2006 to avoid future disputes. Northeastern Kenya is blanketed by the October eclipse.

Libya: Libya is the fourth country in the October eclipse path. Tripoli, its capital, suffers. This desert country simply cannot provide the food to support its population. All wealth comes from oil exports, utilized by revolutionary leader Qaddafi to impress his mixture of socialism and Islam throughout Africa's Muslim countries. The colonel may lose a beloved woman within the next two years. This year, daring souls question Qaddafi's dedication to the philosophies that organized the country. These people are aided by respected civil servants, the military, and women in the universities. The leader is in the spotlight, but he is hiding wealth amassed from subversive and terrorist groups, who pay well for forged documents and refuge. Foreign trade recipients have a vested interest in Libya's sizeable oil export and are covertly striking deals with those willing to oppose the leader, who may lose military control in 2006.

New Zealand: The path of the April eclipse ends over the north island of New Zealand. This British territory retains the appearance of a sleepy hamlet. Throughout the first nine months of 2005, the governor general enjoys strong public support, as exports remain in demand. The islands' summer suggests parched conditions and reduced harvests. In the latter part of the year the government secures additional trade alliances, but at the cost of land leases for foreign military training. Although incidents are kept quiet, some domestic terrorism is directed toward land use, to delay the inevitable progress of New Zealand as secret base of operations. The government needs to address the extent of commitments to foreign allies and show its citizenry that the national integrity is safe and sound.

Panama: This entire country falls in the April total eclipse path. The president is under domestic threat, and his removal from office, even forcibly, is seen as an act of healing for the nation. The president needs to tighten foreign alliances rather than relying on illicit financial maneuvers within the banking system. Panama is strategic, with the canal as an major benefit in East-West shipping. However, the smallness of the country—and its revenues—shows how easily that strategic benefit can be used as leverage in the global landscape. Toward the end of the year the president is in a slightly better situation, although drug-lord allegiances within the civil service are deeply entrenched. Security forces and special police units are champing at the bit to alter the domestic situation, gathering support all year from the populace.

Somalia: Stripped of its national identity in 1991, this country on Africa's eastern coast is now split into three regions. Of those three, southern Somalia, home of warlords, remains without governmental direction. Here is where the October eclipse has its greatest effect, encompassing the old capital, Mogadishu. The transitional government may be toppled by August, creating panic for the nation's youthful population—of which 45 percent are under fifteen years of age. Kenya is unlikely to accept more refugees, and land-locked Ethiopia may advance for a land-grab and control of oceanic ports. After August, astrological influences demand a renewed national character, permanent borders, and a wealth of foreign investment. The populace is exalted, marked for assistance with health, family security, and food shipments. Unfortunately, as though Romans had salted the ground, it may be several years before agricultural harvests resume.

Spain: Like Algeria, Spain and its capital, Madrid, are bisected with the October eclipse path. The king is probably not lost. Although aging, his health is generally good, except for precursor indications of brain deterioration. A major alliance overseas is in jeopardy; the prime minister is threatened. This year, the prime minister seeks to solidify nebulous trade pacts. However, he must be careful with military agreements, which carry empty promises of technology. Trade partners want land in strategic Spain. Spain's unemployment problems appear to be healing, with programs of reeducation for the populace and an upturn in domestic investment.

Sudan: Torn by civil for all but ten of the last forty-nine years, Sudan, the largest geographical nation in Africa, and its capital, Khartoum, are covered by the October eclipse. Another nation with 44 percent of its population under fifteen years, Sudan attempted a constitution in 1998, which was partially suspended eighteen months later. Only those in the Islamic government and the military have reason to hold the status quo. Through June, the president is weakened. Most threats on the national integrity are insurgencies from neighboring countries. Egypt and Kenya have tired of ongoing mediation and are willing to annex the land they administrate in the absence of strong government. After June, the astrological patterns show overthrow. Sudan is bankrupt—drained by a high birth rate, a young populace, and failed harvests. Wealthy countries are withholding investments and delaying international loans for recovery.

Tunisia: The October total eclipse tracks directly through Tunisia and its capital, Tunis. Like a Switzerland of Africa, Tunisia remains nonaligned, influenced by French civil law. Offshore drilling increases its already diverse economy and exports to middle and western Europe. Tunisia started under stable astrological configurations in

1959, which secure public support of the president. Through May, health matters and land disputes require legislative address. Tunisians who speculated abroad need to fold and withdraw their resources. Foreign investors, however, find low prices after drops in tourism, and a president eager to bolster the domestic economy. After May the nation tries a more stable footing, although it may close some of its borders to refugees. Tunisia resists pressure from Muslim countries to repress its more open society. Those with terrorist ties—particularly educators entering the universities—are uncovered and expelled. This small country retains its own social identity.

United States: Progressed Mars suggests outright war this year—an influence that lasts for the next fifteen years. The American public stands practical and stalwart. As the year begins, the public is bolstered by the successful presidential election; the leadership has military support and the experience to use it well. In early March, the bloom, as usual in American politics, is already off the rose for the president. The press takes the role of critical taskmaster as squabbles in foreign countries over wealthy enterprises usurp the president's energies. Hidden agendas of global conglomerates and their wealthy investors from the U.S. produce an economic stalemate, subverting domestic recovery. This is precarious moment in U.S. history, as the financially drained public sees annihilative efforts abroad as a trade for their unrequested sacrifices.

Venezuela: The path of the April eclipse starts in Venezuela, blanketing its capital, Caracas. If the six-year-old government survives the first national election, the country may be able to rout drug lord insurgents from Columbia—only to find them controlling domestic banking in five years. This year, the president and government focus on establishing a national character, but the population has lost its identity, believing the drug cartels hold all the power. Foreign financial interests have held off helping Venezuela. There is hope within the National Assembly to pass banking laws that induce foreign investment. However, military enforcement against drug lords is questionable, because regulars are inexperienced and see money-laundering as security for their families.

(This article was written in September 2003.)

Mundane Natalogy

People's Democratic Republic of Algeria
November 22, 1976, 00:00:00 am UT, Algiers

Republic of Colombia
July 5, 1991, 00:00:00 am EST, Bogotá

Republic of Kenya
December 12, 1963, 00:00:00 am BAT, Nairobi

Great Socialist People's Libyan Arab Jamahiriya
December 11, 1969, 00:00:00 am EET, Tripoli

New Zealand
September 26, 2007, 00:00:00 am NZ, Wellington

Republic of Panama
October 11, 1972, 00:00:00 am EST, Panama City

Somalia
August 26, 2000, 00:00:00 am BAT, Mogadishu

Kingdom of Spain
December 29, 1978, 12:00:00 pm, Madrid

Republic of the Sudan
June 30, 1998, 00:00:00 am EET, Khartoum

Tunisian Republic
June 1, 1959, 00:00:00 am CET, Tunis

United States of America
March 4, 1789, 12:13:12 am LMT, New York City

Bolivarian Republic of Venezuela
December 30, 1999, 00:00:00 am AST, Caracas

About the Authors

Nina Lee Braden is a Scorpio. She is the daughter of a Cancer and a Virgo, the sister of a Pisces, the wife of a Libra, and the mother of a Sagittarius and a Capricorn. She is the author of *Tarot for Self Discovery*.

Stephanie Clement, Ph.D. has been practicing astrology for over thirty years. A board member of the AFA and member of NCGR, she has served on the faculty of Kepler College and has been a speaker at many conferences. Stephanie has published numerous articles and has written several books, including *Charting Your Spiritual Path with Astrology*, *Power of the Midheaven*, *Mapping Your Birthchart*, and *Mapping Your Family Relationships*.

Alice DeVille is an internationally known astrologer, writer, and metaphysical consultant. She specializes in relationships, real estate, government affairs, career and change management, and spiritual development. She has developed and presented more than 130 workshops and seminars related to astrological, feng shui, metaphysical, motivational, and business themes.

Sasha Fenton is probably the most prolific author of books on astrology and the psychic sciences, as she now has 120 books to her credit, and she is still writing! Her knowledge is based on years of work as a consultant and teacher, but she says that she is still an enthusiastic student, as there is still so much for her to learn.

Leeda Alleyn Pacotti practices as a naturopathic physician, nutritional counselor, and master herbalist, specializing in dream language, health astrology, and mind-body communication. A former legal analyst in anti-trust and international law, with judicial and executive governmental experience, she enjoys poking a finger in political machinations of all sorts.

Bruce Scofield, C.A. NCGR, is a professional astrological consultant who works with clients in the United States and abroad. His special interest is the astrology of ancient civilizations, especially those of the Maya and Aztecs. He is the author of thirteen books and numerous articles, and is on the faculty of Kepler College.

Rowena Wall has been a professional astrologer since 1984. Relationship charts are one of the major parts of her practice.

The Most Popular Astrological Calendar in the World

A must for everyone who wants to plan 2005 wisely, with an amazing amount of astrological data laid out on forty pages. Colorful, contemporary art by Ciro Marchetti kicks off each month, and monthly horoscopes by Carole Schwalm include the most rewarding and challenging dates for each sign. You'll find major daily aspects, planetary sign changes, and the Moon's sign, phase, and void-of-course times. The calendar also includes a table of retrograde periods and ephemerides for each month.

LLEWELLYN'S ASTROLOGICAL CALENDAR 2005
40 pp. • 13 x 9 ½ • 12 full-color paintings
0-7387-0135-1 • U.S. $12.95, Can. $17.50
To order call 1-877-NEW-WRLD

A Planetary Perspective of Our Times

What are the planets saying about our world? Find out in Llewellyn's new *Starview Almanac*. Renowned astrologers provide reliable insight into politics, entertainment, health, and fashion. Forecasts and trends relating to current events and issues, such as homeland security and America's obesity problem, are discussed without astrological terminology. Also included are financial and weather forecasts for 2005, profiles of famous people, facts about living with Mercury-retrograde periods, and a weekly calendar with fun forecasts by Sally Cragin.

LLEWELLYN'S 2005 STARVIEW ALMANAC
288 pp. • 5¼ x 8
0-7387-0539-X • U.S. $8.95 Can $10.50
To order call 1-877-NEW-WRLD

Best-selling Guide to Successful Living Since 1905!

No other book on the market tops the *Moon Sign Book* in supplying tips for daily success, weather forecasts for eight U.S. zones year round, economic forecasts, tips on planting, best hunting and fishing dates, and timing tips for personal and financial decisions. Plus, there are special articles on topics that affect us all. This year's features include "Night Gardening" by Janice Sharkey, "Kitchen Concoctions for Pest Control" by Louise Riotte, "Cross-cultural Perspectives" by Robin Antepara, and "Adaptive Gardening for Seniors" by Maggie Anderson.

**LLEWELLYN'S 2005
MOON SIGN BOOK**
384 pp. • 5¼" x 8"
0-7387-0136-X • $7.95 U.S. $10.95 Can.
To order call 1-877-NEW-WRLD

The Most Complete Astrology Datebook on the Market

M ore than a datebook, the *Daily Planetary Guide* is a powerhouse of planetary insight. It has all the day-to-day astrological information anyone could want between two covers. Knowing when to schedule a long-awaited vacation or ask for that much-deserved raise is made a whole lot easier when you tap into the powerful energies that affect you every day.

- Spiral binding
- Ephemeride tables
- Moon sign, phase, and void-of-course
- Planetary hours chart with instructions
- Planet and Moon ingress times
- Sunrise and sunset tables

**LLEWELLYN'S 2005
DAILY PLANETARY GUIDE**
208 pp. • 5¼ x 8
0-7387-0143-2 • U.S. $9.95 Can. $13.50
To order call 1-877-NEW-WRLD

Read your Future in the Cards

T arot enthusiasts rejoice! Look for an array of news, advice, and in-depth discussions on everything tarot in Llewellyn's new *Tarot Reader*.

Renowned authors and tarot specialists deliver deck reviews and articles concerning card interpretation, spreads, magic, tarot history, and professional tarot reading. Each year's almanac will also feature a calendar with pertinent astrological information, such as Moon signs and times. This year's *Tarot Reader* includes articles by Ruth Ann and Wald Amberstone, Joan Cole, Mary K. Greer, and James Wells.

**LLEWELLYN'S 2005
TAROT READER**
288 pp. • 5¼ x 8
0-7387-0538-1 • U.S. $8.95 Can. $11.95
To order call 1-877-NEW-WRLD

Be Your Own Astrologer

Mapping Your Birthchart removes the mystery from astrology so you can look at any chart and get a basic understanding of the person behind it. Learn the importance of the planets, the different signs of the zodiac, and how they relate to your everyday life. Stephanie Jean Clement introduces the basics of the astrology chart, devotes a chapter to each planet—with information about signs, houses, and aspects—provides simple explanations of astrological and psychological factors, and includes examples from the charts of well-known people including Tiger Woods, Celine Dion, and George W. Bush. The free CD-ROM included with this book allows you to calculate and interpret your birthchart, and print out astrological reports and charts for yourself, your family, and friends.

MAPPING YOUR BIRTHCHART:
UNDERSTANDING YOUR NEEDS & POTENTIAL
Stephanie Jean Clement, Ph.D.
240 pp.• 7½ x 9⅛ • Includes CD-ROM
0-7387-0202-1 • $U.S. $19.95 Can. $30.95
To order call 1-877-NEW-WRLD

Let the Stars be Your Guide

Take your relationships to a deeper level. There is a hunger for intimacy in the modern world. *Astrology & Relationships* is a guidebook on how to use astrology to improve all your relationships. This is not fortunetelling astrology, predicting which signs you will be most compatible with; instead, it uses astrology as a model to help you experience greater fulfillment and joy in relating to others. You can also look up your planets, and those of others, to discover specific relationship needs and talents.

This book goes beyond descriptive astrology to suggest methods and techniques for actualizing the stages of a relationship that each planet represents. Many of the exercises are designed to awaken individual skills and heighten self-understanding, leading you to first identify a particular quality within yourself, and then to relate to it in others.

ASTROLOGY & RELATIONSHIPS
David Pond
416 pp. • 7½ x 9⅛
0-7387-0046-0 • U.S. $17.95 Can. $29.95
To order call 1-877-NEW-WRLD

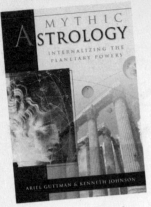

Walk With the Gods

Enter a new dimension of spiritual self-discovery when you probe the mythic archetypes represented in your astrological birth chart. Myth has always been closely linked with astrology. Experience these myths and gain a deeper perspective on your eternal self.

Learn how the characteristics of the gods developed into the meanings associated with particular planets and signs. Look deeply into your own personal myths, and enjoy a living connection to the world of the deities within you. When you finally stand in the presence of an important archetype (through the techniques of dreamwork, symbolic amplification, or active imagination described in the book), you will have the opportunity to receive a message from the god or goddess.

MYTHIC ASTROLOGY
Internalizing the Planetary Powers
Ariel Guttman & Kenneth Johnson
400 pp. • 7 x 10
0-87542-248-9 • U.S. $24.95 Can. $38.50
To order call 1-877-NEW-WRLD

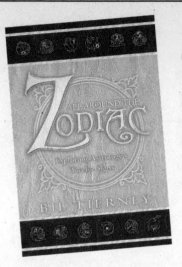

Take a Tour of the Zodiac

This book provides a revealing new look at the astrological signs, from Aries to Pisces. Gain a deeper understanding of how each sign motivates you to grow and evolve in consciousness. How does Aries work with Pisces? What does Gemini share in common with Scorpio? *All Around the Zodiac* is the only book on the market to explore these sign combinations to such a degree.

Not your typical Sun sign guide, this book is broken into three parts. Part 1 defines the signs, part 2 analyzes the expression of sixty-six pairs of signs, and part 3 designates the expression of the planets and houses in the signs.

ALL AROUND THE ZODIAC
Exploring Astrology's Twelve Signs
Bil Tierney
480 pp. • 6 x 9
0-7387-0111-4 • U.S. $19.95 Can. $29.95
To order call 1-877-NEW-WRLD

You get the best of the old and the new in this updated best seller!

A textbook . . . encyclopedia . . . self-study course . . . and extensive astrological dictionary all in one! More American astrologers have learned their craft from The *New A to Z Horoscope and Delineator* than any other astrology book. First published in 1910, it is in every sense a complete course in astrology, giving beginners all the basic techniques and concepts they need to get off on the right foot. Plus it offers the more advanced astrologer an excellent dictionary and reference work for calculating and analyzing transits, progression, rectifications, and creating locality charts. This new edition has been revised to meet the needs of the modern audience.

**THE NEW A TO Z
HOROSCOPE MAKER & DELINEATOR**
Llewellyn George
480 pp. • 7½ x 9⅛
0-7387-0332-2 • U.S. $19.95 Can. $30.95
To order call 1-877-NEW-WRLD